UNIONS IN POLITICS

UNIONS IN POLITICS

Britain, Germany, and the United States

in the Nineteenth and Early

Twentieth Centuries

GARY MARKS

PRINCETON UNIVERSITY PRESS

PRINCETON, NEW JERSEY

Published by Princeton University Press, 41 William Street,
Princeton, New Jersey 08540
In the United Kingdom: Princeton University Press, Guildford, Surrey

This book has been composed in Linotron Baskerville

Clothbound editions of Princeton University Press books
are printed on acid-free paper, and binding materials are
chosen for strength and durability. Paperbacks, although satisfactory
for personal collections, are not usually suitable for library rebinding

Printed in the United States of America by Princeton University Press,
Princeton, New Jersey

Library of Congress Cataloging-in-Publication Data

Marks, Gary Wolfe.
Unions in politics : Britain, Germany, and the United States in the nineteenth
and early twentieth centuries / Gary Marks. p.   cm.   Bibliography:
p.   Includes index.
ISBN 0-691-07801-7 ISBN 0-691-02304-2 (pbk.)
1. Trade-unions—Great Britain—Political activity—History. 2. Trade-unions—
Germany—Political activity—History. 3. Trade-unions—United States—
Political activity—History. I. Title.
HD6667.M37 1989   322'.2'09—dc19   88-25054

To my parents, Eileen and Bobby Marks

CONTENTS

LIST OF TABLES

LIST OF FIGURES

PREFACE

Since the Industrial Revolution individual trade unions have been the chief organizational means for those towards the bottom of society to express their economic and political demands. No one who has studied the subject can help but be struck by the remarkable variety of institutional forms, strategies, and goals of trade unions across Western societies. As organizations rooted in particular occupations and industries, unions have been shaped by the particular characteristics of their members and their work experiences as well as by national forces. Although we often speak of national union movements, in most countries unionism is really characterized by a complex mosaic of diverse, often overlapping, organizations with a variety of political orientations.

Is it possible to generalize about unions and their political orientations—to create a comparative politics of union political activity—while acknowledging the remarkable diversity of unionism within and across Western societies? This is the fundamental objective of my book and it motivates the questions raised in successive chapters. Why did some unions focus their activities in the labor market while others tried to gain political regulation of employment conditions? How did state repression or tolerance affect the political orientations of unions? Why have unions in all Western societies come to participate in national politics on a routinized basis? Are there patterns of union political activity within individual countries, and, if so, do those patterns travel across Western societies?

In coming to grips with these questions I have focussed my attention on the experience of unions in Britain, Germany, and the United States in the nineteenth and early twentieth centuries. These societies provided divergent political contexts for unionism and saw the establishment of contrasting national union federations, as the shorthand descriptions of British laborism, German socialism, and American business unionism suggest. If, indeed, there are patterns of individual union political orientation to be discovered, these societies provide a strong test for their generalizability. But these societies are not just natural laboratories for testing hypotheses. The experience of unionism in each society is important and interesting on its own terms, and I have endeavored to explain some of the particularities of each case.

While the comparison of union movements across societies has proved a fruitful line of inquiry, such an approach cannot account for the wide variations that are found within societies. In this book I begin at a more elemental level of analysis by focussing on the individual unions that make up national union movements. This brings the analysis of union political orientation one step closer to the experiences of people who joined labor organizations. Over the course of this project I came to realize that their working conditions and the occupational communities they formed were vital influences on the political orientations of their unions. Fortunately my interest in the working lives of those who belonged to unions coincided with a renaissance in the historical study of the everyday conditions of working people. A supposition of this book is that the established study of labor institutions and the new social history are potentially inclusive, rather than exclusive, endeavors. By comparing individual unions and the role of working conditions and occupational community in shaping their political orientations I have tried to make the systematic connections between these fields explicit.

In understanding social causality the researcher is frequently compelled to follow a path that crosses the boundaries between the social science disciplines. In no field of study is this more true than that of union political activity. Unions are social and economic as well as political institutions, and none of these facets of unionism can be understood in isolation from the others. The political strategies adopted by unions are intimately linked to the social resources of workers in their occupational communities and their bargaining power in the labor market, and in analyzing these causal relationships I have pursued a self-consciously eclectic approach, drawing on the work of sociologists, economists, and historians, alongside that of political scientists.

The first three chapters of the book set out a theoretical framework for explaining union political orientation, beginning with labor market influences and working upwards to the national political context. Chapter One focusses on the social relations of groups of workers in their occupation, tracing the effects of the varying capacity of groups of workers to sustain unions through their occupational communities and pursue strategies to defend their niche in the division of labor.

The following chapter shifts the emphasis to national politics, analyzing the effects of variations in the legal environment on union political orientation. Unions have always been extremely sensitive to the legal context of industrial relations and have frequently been impelled into politics to gain basic freedoms even when their preferred strategy has been to bargain in the labor market. This chapter explores the way in which differing degrees of state repression or tolerance shaped union/party relations, relations among unions, and union reformism or radicalism.

Chapter Three examines the transformation of industrial relations and union political orientation that took place in the most economically advanced societies from the decades around the turn of the twentieth century. In these years the development of unionism was part of an immense expansion in the organization of economic, social, and political life—conceptualized here in terms of the Organizational Revolution—that blurred the institutional boundaries of the economy and polity and in so doing created the context for the highly politicized unionism of today.

Chapter Four and Chapter Five are case studies of individual unions—printing unions and coalmining unions—compared cross-nationally. These chapters explore the scope of variation within countries and the extent to which similiar unions shared common orientations in different national contexts. Printing unions generally focussed their activity in the labor market rather than in politics. When they did turn to politics this was usually out of necessity, not choice, in an attempt to assure themselves of the legal space to go freely about their business in the labor market. Within their respective union movements printing unions were leading advocates of pragmatism and political moderation. But printing unions were not at all "soft." While they were relentless in defending their niche in the division of labor, they rarely saw political activity as the way to achieve this. Coalmining unions, in contrast, tended to look to politics to gain improvements in the welfare and employment conditions of their members. These unions were in the vanguard among their respective union movements in pressing for working-class political representation and using their legislative influence to gain political regulation of working conditions on a permanent and universal basis.

The final chapter of the book examines some of the linkages between sectoral and national levels of analysis, asking what our understanding of the sources of individual union political orientation adds to cross-national comparisons. It takes up a venerable question of national comparison, that of American Exceptionalism, and sets

out the thesis that the absence of a labor party in the United States
was linked to the unique character of American unionism.

This book grew out of a dissertation that I completed, put down
for three years, and then returned to. By the time I reread the original manuscript I was still convinced that the questions it raised
were important ones that were not systematically dealt with in the
literatures on union political activity, but I was not satisfied with the
substantive analysis. The resulting work thus reanalyzes some basic
issues in the comparative development of union political activity
that were originally raised in my dissertation.

Much of the writing of this book was done with the support of
summer grants and a Sesquicentennial Associateship from the University of Virginia and a grant from the Institute for the Study of
World Politics. As a National Fellow at the Hoover Institution in
1986/1987 I was free to finish my book and begin a new project
with no external duties or pressures.

Over the course of this project I have been fortunate to receive
careful criticism from scholars who daily prove the existence of an
overarching community of political scientists, sociologists, and historians. In particular, I would like to thank Christopher Allen, Ronald Aminzade, Craig Calhoun, Samuel Cohn, James Cronin, Leon
Fink, Gerald Friedman, Miriam Golden, Jeffrey Haydu, Joel Krie-
ger, Peter Lange, Robert Liebman, Barrington Moore, Jr., Steven
Rhoads, Wolfgang Schmidt, Philippe Schmitter, and Charles Tilly.
James Ceaser and Steven Genco have been generous in giving advice on a number of questions relating to the project. Sandy
Thatcher of Princeton University Press has expertly guided the
manuscript along and Cathy Thatcher has removed numerous in-
consistencies in the text. My research assistants, Paul Holland, Pam
Messerschmidt, Cathy Crawford, and Sharon Sylvester have helped
considerably at the various stages of writing and preparation.

Since the book reflects many of my intellectual concerns as they
developed over several years, I think it appropriate to acknowledge
some of the major debts I have accumulated. I have an enduring
obligation to Gabriel Almond for his guidance in framing my project and for instilling in so many of his students, myself included, a
vision of the breadth and challenge of comparative politics. From
Alexander George, the most sophisticated exponent of qualitative
methodologies in the social sciences, I learned to appreciate the
case study as a systematic tool for testing and refining generaliza-

tions. My greatest debt is to Seymour Martin Lipset who has revealed more than anyone else the richness of interdisciplinary social science and in so doing has shaped the study of the social bases of politics. Without his encouragement and ongoing work in the field this book would be immeasurably poorer.

Finally, my wife Emma and son Joshua have been an inexhaustible source of affection and support. It is only fair that they have agreed to share responsibility for what is in reality a family project.

UNIONS IN POLITICS

A COMPARATIVE APPROACH TO
UNION POLITICAL ACTIVITY

Understanding the development of union political activity in the nineteenth and early twentieth centuries has been the preserve of labor historians, industrial relations specialists, and sociologists. This book is written in the belief that the subject deserves the attention of scholars of comparative politics and is guided by the hope that a comparative approach may yield a convincing, yet detached, way of coming to grips with some fundamental questions about how and why unions acted in politics.

Looking back over the development of labor movements in the nineteenth and twentieth centuries it is evident that trade unions have been at least as important as working-class political parties in providing an avenue for workers to express their interests in society. Of course, the political party has generally been the principal instrument of labor in the national political arena, but even in this sphere unions have played a vital and independent role.

This is most evident in the Anglo-American societies, where unions preceded the formation of labor parties, encompassed a far greater proportion of the work force, and were instrumental in shaping the character of working-class political parties when they eventually developed. In Britain, unions themselves helped establish the Labour party, and they soon came to dominate it. In the rough and very pointed words of Ernest Bevin, "the Labour Party has grown out of the bowels of the TUC [Trades Union Congress]."[1]

The American Federation of Labor kept its distance from national politics until the last years of the nineteenth century, but some of its largest and most powerful affiliates, the United Mine Workers chief among them, were actively involved in politics at the state and local levels. The strength of business unionism in the United States forced socialists to make a difficult choice, either to try to transform established unions by joining them and boring from within, or attempt to create a new union movement alto-

[1] Quoted in Samuel H. Beer, *Modern British Politics* (New York: Norton, 1982), p. 113.

gether. In the United States, as in Britain, political parties had to recruit members, devise platforms, and pursue strategies against a background of unions already entrenched among the most skilled and educated sections of labor.

In Germany the relationship was the other way around. Although a few unions existed before the rise of socialist parties in the 1860s, most unions were created by political parties for expressly political purposes, and their orientation mirrored that of their party-political founders. But party domination was challenged as soon as unionists came to realize that they could stand on their own feet. From the 1890s, when the relaxation of state repression gave the socialist Free Unions a little breathing room, they established their own national organization, emphasized their political independence from the Social Democratic party, and rapidly increased their membership. The German socialist party was the largest and most influential working-class political party in the world before the First World War, but it found itself being dwarfed by its union wing. By 1906, the first year for which we have national data on the membership of the Socialist party, the Free Unions had about four times as many members: one and a half million to less than four hundred thousand party members.[2] As the unions grew in size and strength, they became more confident of their ability to fight their own battles and more aware of potential conflicts between their own interests and those of the party. From the mid-1890s they claimed the right to pursue their own policies in politics as in the labor market, and this brought them to the center of the political stage.

UNIONS AND UNION MOVEMENTS

In all Western societies unions have formed national organizations that mediate their interests directly in national politics. Thus the AFL-CIO, the British Trades Union Congress, and the West German Union Federation (Deutscher Gewerkschaftsbund) represent contemporary unions on broad questions of national policy. But such federations are only one channel of union political activity. In each of these countries, as in other Western societies, individual unions themselves pursue policies on a variety of political issues from worker participation and industrial relations legislation to

[2] Dieter Fricke, *Die deutsche Arbeiterbewegung, 1869–1914* (Berlin: Dietz, 1976), pp. 245, 720.

questions of incomes policy, unemployment, and industrial policy. To the extent that we restrict our view of union political activity to union federations, we ignore a vital and fascinating source of diversity: that among individual unions themselves.

This concern is all the more important because union federations have rarely been able to compromise the self-determination of their individual union constituents. The American Federation of Labor and the Trades Union Congress were successful precisely because they offered unions the opportunity to join with others to pursue limited but common goals in a way that left their autonomy substantially intact. The first national association of socialist unions in Germany, the Generalkommission, was weakly centralized and had to tread warily in order to avoid committing constituent unions to policies that some of them opposed.

In this respect unions are very different from political parties. The latter attempt to participate in government, contest elections, and otherwise aggregate the political interests of their supporters, and this has led them to create broad-based, usually national, organizations. Their organizational structure is determined largely by the political system in which they operate. Union organization, in contrast, reflects the structure of labor markets, because it is the labor market that defines the potential membership of a union and provides it with the most direct channel to improve its members' welfare and job control. The existence of numerous segmented labor markets has fostered an extraordinary degree of diversity and sectionalism in union movements. Whereas party-political representation has tended to be national, that in unions has been sectoral, composed of numerous organizations encompassing workers in specific industries or occupations.

When political scientists have analyzed union political activity they have treated unions as a kind of parallel to political parties, and this has led them to aggregate union political activity to the national level as a basis for making comparisons across societies.[3] In

---

[3] Outstanding analyses in this genre are Seymour Martin Lipset, "Radicalism or Reformism: The Sources of Working-Class Politics," *American Political Science Review* 77, no. 1 (March 1983), and Adolph Sturmthal and James G. Scoville, *The International Labor Movement in Transition: Essays on Asia, Europe, and South America* (Urbana, Ill.: University of Illinois Press, 1973). A recent suggestive analysis sensitive to variations within union movements is Ira Katznelson and Aristide R. Zolberg, eds., *Working-Class Formation: Nineteenth-Century Patterns in Western Europe and the United States* (Princeton, N.J.: Princeton University Press, 1986).

other words, they have carried the methodological baggage of party-political analysis over to the study of unions. The problem with this approach is that it ignores the decentralized structure of most union movements, the fact that union movements were made up of a variety of more or less autonomous organizations having a variety of political orientations. The real locus of decision making within union movements has not been at the national level but on the level of the individual union.

When we examine the experience of union political activity in the United States, Britain, and Germany, we find a considerable diversity within each society. It is no exaggeration to say that this internal diversity is as impressive as the difference in the general tenor of union orientation from country to country. In the United States there was, for example, a sharp difference between the antipolitical business unionism of many unions affiliated to the American Federation of Labor and the radical political orientation of unions linked to the Knights of Labor. Later, unions in the AFL were locked in an intense ideological conflict with the revolutionary syndicalism of the Industrial Workers of the World. The AFL itself was far from homogeneous. The doctrine of voluntarism, which was supported by a majority of craft unions, was continually subject to attack by socialists entrenched in some of the largest affiliates of the AFL, including the International Association of Machinists, the International Ladies Garment Workers' Union, and the United Mine Workers of America.[4] On several occasions in the first two decades of the twentieth century the UMWA pressed for the socialization of the coalmines by the state and the creation of a labor party backed by unions to represent American workers.

In Germany one source of diversity lay in the establishment of competing union movements representing rival political parties. But there were also significant differences within the union movements. Among the socialist Free Unions, the printers and cigarworkers pursued a far more moderate political strategy than the metalworkers or laborers.[5] From the 1890s national congresses of the Free Union movement saw frequent heated debates in which

[4] See John Laslett, *Labor and the Left* (New York: Basic Books, 1970).

[5] See, for example, Ulrich Engelhardt, *"Nur Vereinigt sind wir stark": Die Anfänge der deutschen Gewerkschaftsbewegung 1862/3 bis 1869/70* (Stuttgart: Klett-Cotta, 1977), and Dick Geary, *European Labour Protest, 1848–1939* (London: Croom Helm, 1981), chap. 2.

unions lined up for and against the principles of collective bargaining and political neutrality from the SPD.[6]

In Britain the picture is essentially no different, although socialism was a much weaker and later development than in Germany. In the early nineteenth century we can find some unions, notably those formed by textile workers, demanding fundamental political change and extensive legislation of employment conditions, alongside numerous unions that were generally content to focus their strategy in the labor market.[7] The range of goals narrows as we move into the twentieth century, but our notions of British unionism must still encompass the radicalism—some have called it potential revolutionism—of the syndicalist movement in the years leading up to the First World War.[8]

These contrasts do not invalidate conventional countrywide characterizations of the development of business unionism in the United States, laborism in Britain, and socialism in Germany. But they do serve to open up the field and pose some basic questions that cannot be answered at the national level. To the extent that we are left with a picture of national differences, it is one interlaced with a remarkable diversity within each society. At some point, cross-national comparison of trade union movements at the macro level must confront union political activity at the level of the individual union, for we cannot reduce the comparative study of union political activity to the comparison of union movements.

GUIDING SUPPOSITIONS

The approach taken in this book is based on two convictions, and it would be well to make them explicit at the beginning. The first is

[6] Most especially at the 1905 Congress (*Protokoll über die Verhandlungen vom funften Kongress Freien Vereinigung deutscher Gewerkschaften*, May 1905, Köln).

[7] The clearest statement of such contrasts is A. E. Musson, *British Trade Unions, 1800–1875* (London: Macmillan, 1972). See also Iowerth Prothero, *Artisans and Politics in Nineteenth-Century London* (London: Methuen, 1979), pp. 68–69, 300–301, and 332–338, and I. Prothero, "London Chartism and the Trades," *Economic History Review*, 2d series, vol. 24 (1971). Notwithstanding his thesis regarding the creation of a working class in England in the decades before the first Reform Act, such contrasts are also observed by E. P. Thompson in his monumental work *The Making of the English Working Class* (London: Penguin, 1968).

[8] See, for example, Robert J. Holton, *British Syndicalism, 1900–1914* (London: Pluto Press, 1976), and James Hinton, *The First Shop Stewards' Movement* (London: Allen & Unwin, 1973).

that our comparative understanding of union political activity should be multilevel, encompassing the sources of union orientation in work groups, occupations, and labor markets as well as those at the level of national politics. Neither can be deduced from the other, and we should operate at both levels of analysis to explain patterns of union political activity across and within societies.

The second conviction that underlies my approach is that our comparative understanding of union political activity should be interdisciplinary. No single discipline can claim sovereignty over the questions raised in this book. In the study of political parties, legislatures, or governments, the realm of politics appears all-encompassing, and political analysts have claimed these subjects as the institutional core of their discipline. These institutions are more or less monopolized by their political functions. But no study of unions can afford to make that assumption, for politics is only one means by which a union may pursue its goals. Unions are rooted in particular labor markets, and the labor market itself presents a union with a direct opportunity to influence the welfare and job control of its members. Industrial, or economic, activity has been as important a strategy for unions as political activity, and to understand the one, I believe we must pay attention to the other.

Unions have been conceptualized from a variety of perspectives, and no one social science can encompass them all. We may view unions as close-knit communities providing economic security and dignity for their members,[9] businesslike organizations attempting to monopolize the supply of labor to better bargain with employers,[10] and/or political movements seeking diverse goals, from legislation of wages and hours to the revolutionary overthrow of the system of capitalist wage labor.[11] While the focus of this book is union political activity, not union social bases or economic bargaining, my supposition is that each of these perspectives may provide useful insights into the others. In the course of the discussion, I argue that the social resources of workers in their occupational

[9] Frank Tannenbaum, *A Philosophy of Labor* (New York: Knopf, 1951).

[10] This perspective infused the American Federation of Labor and particularly its first leader, Samuel Gompers. A clear, if overly psychologistic, statement of this view is put forward by Selig Perlman in his classic *A Theory of the Labor Movement* (New York: Augustus M. Kelley, 1928).

[11] Unions feature strongly in recent social movement literature. The best overview remains that of Charles Tilly, *From Mobilization to Revolution* (New York: Addison-Wesley, 1978).

communities and their bargaining power in the labor market are intimately linked to the political strategies that unions have pursued.

There is a more practical reason for an interdisciplinary approach, and it echoes this theoretical concern. The field of union political activity has been plowed from many directions, and much of what has been written is relevant to the task at hand. Historians, sociologists, economists, and political scientists have all had much to say about the questions that animate the following pages, and my own arguments would be the poorer without their scholarship.[12] The study of unions and industrial relations is an intellectually cosmopolitan discipline, and this is nowhere more apparent than in the field of union political activity. An interdisciplinary approach was not a choice but a necessity given the nature of the questions I am asking.

THEMES

Patterns of Variation

My first substantive theme is that variations in the political orientation of individual unions seem to be patterned in a way that is generalizable across societies. Similar influences are associated with similar political orientations across a range of Western societies. The most important of these influences is the strength of union organization, the capacity of groups of workers to create and sustain unions. Nothing is more fundamental to political activity than organization. In this connection, organization provided workers with the most basic precondition of gaining some control over their working lives—a capacity for strategy. It gave them the ability to pursue their interests over the long haul in a concerted fashion. Organization opened up the prospect of transforming sheer numbers into a resource of economic and political power.

Union organization was one of the great innovations of modern times. Before the rise of capitalist relations of production and the

[12] In particular see Lipset, "Radicalism or Reformism"; Barrington Moore, Jr., *Injustice: The Social Bases of Obedience and Revolt* (New York: M. E. Sharpe, 1978); Geary, *European Labour Protest, 1848–1939*; Tilly, *From Mobilization to Revolution*; Craig Calhoun, *The Question of Class Struggle* (Chicago: University of Chicago Press, 1982); and H. A. Turner, *Trade Union Growth, Structure and Policy* (London: Allen & Unwin, 1962).

emergence of competitive labor markets, artisans felt themselves to be a part of an immutable order of production, based on the guild, in which the apprentice had the prospect of becoming a journeyman and the journeyman a master. To the extent that interests were defined antagonistically, it was in vertical terms, by trade, rather than horizontally, by class. Unions emerged in response to the breakdown of this traditional order. For many journeymen, capitalism and economic competition dashed their hopes of eventual respectability as independent masters, intensified their vulnerability to labor-saving innovation, and created new and potent sources of wage competition from unapprenticed laborers.[13]

Alongside this there is another, more subtle, source of organization that has to do with a growing awareness that social relations were not natural phenomena but were the result of human purpose and conscious manipulation.[14] The world was changing, and more acutely than ever before those on the lower rungs of society could see that change was purposeful, that it was carried out by people for their own ends. Although workers were informed by classical political economists that their attempts to organize to influence wages and working hours were doomed to failure, experience told them that by combining their individual efforts they could indeed gain a measure of control over their working lives. Unions were a response both to new conceptions of the possibility of organization and intensified perceptions of the need for it.

Yet it is abundantly clear that these were not sufficient causes of unionization. Those workers who had the greatest need for organization—the poorest and least-skilled workers—were least able to provide themselves with it. In fact, workers who formed unions

[13] See, for example, Ulrich Engelhardt, "Gewerkschaftliches Organisationsverhalten in der ersten Industrialisierungsphase," in Werner Conze and Ulrich Engelhardt, eds., *Arbeiter im Industrialisierungsprozess: Herkunft, Lage und Verhalten* (Stuttgart: Klett-Cotta, 1979); J. Bergman, *Das Berliner Handwerk in den Frühphasen der Industrialisierung* (Berlin: Colloquium Verlag, 1973); and Sidney and Beatrice Webb, *The History of Trade Unionism*, 2d ed. (London: Longmans, Green, 1920). On developments in America, see Herbert Gutman, "Work Culture, and Society in Industrializing America, 1815–1919," in Herbert Gutman, *Work, Culture, and Society in Industrializing America* (New York: Vintage Books, 1977); David Montgomery, *Workers' Control in America* (Cambridge: Cambridge University Press, 1979), chap. 1; and Susan E. Hirsch, *Roots of the American Working Class: Industrialization of Crafts in Newark, 1800–1860* (Philadelphia: University of Pennsylvania Press, 1978).

[14] This theme is explored by Barrington Moore, Jr., *Injustice: The Social Bases of Obedience and Revolt.*

were a small minority in every Western society in the nineteenth century. In Britain, which had the most unionized labor force in the world, only one worker in eight belonged to a union in 1900. In the United States and Germany the proportion was one in twenty, and in most other Western societies, it was lower still.[15] Even today the majority of unskilled workers in virtually every Western society remain unorganized.[16]

Union organization was an innovation, yet it seems to have been based on social continuity and tradition rather than change. Where union organization flourished, it had its roots in more elemental forms of solidarity that made people willing to organize even at great personal cost.[17] Unions tended to be strongest among workers who were part of cohesive occupational communities, who formed close-knit groups in the workplace, who remained in their occupation long enough to set down deep roots, who shared deep-seated cultural norms and expectations, who, in one way or another, were bound together by a shared sense of tradition and community consciousness.

There is ample evidence that groups of workers who lacked occupational community and organization tended to be politically apathetic about their working lives. This is a response that is acutely analyzed by Barrington Moore in terms of what he calls "a sense of inevitability."[18] Because unorganized workers had no collective power over their working lives, they saw their conditions as being beyond purposeful control and accepted them accordingly, as part of the natural order of things.

But this does not appear to be the only response that we find among the unorganized. The other face of impotence was a violent potential for protest or revolt, for short, sharp bursts of political activity. Without organization based in community it was difficult, if not impossible, to sustain political opposition over an extended

[15] George Sayers Bain and Robert Price, *Profiles of Union Growth* (Oxford: Basil Blackwell, 1980).

[16] The only clear exceptions are Israel and Sweden with overall levels of unionization exceeding 80 percent and rates of over 60 percent for unskilled workers. Data on Swedish union membership is provided in ibid. For data on Israeli union membership see A. P. Coldrick and Philip Jones, *The International Directory of the Trade Union Movement* (New York: Facts on File, 1979).

[17] See Craig Calhoun, *The Question of Class Struggle*, and Michael P. Hanagan and Charles Stephenson, "The Skilled Worker and Working-Class Protest," *Social Science History* 4, no. 1 (February 1980).

[18] Barrington Moore, Jr., *Injustice: The Social Bases of Obedience and Revolt*.

period of time. But under certain conditions unorganized workers could provide volatile support for radical political movements, often with an emphasis on immediate grievances and political violence.

To explain the political orientations of groups of workers who were able to form stable unions we need to come to grips with a second set of factors concerning the uses to which organization could be put and, in particular, the extent to which the union could operate effectively in the labor market. Here my guiding hypothesis is that unions able to adapt to the challenges of their economic environment tended to pursue an economistic strategy. They were content to bargain directly with employers in the labor market rather than try to change the terms of employment, or do away with wage labor altogether, through political activity.

Where economic conditions were unfavorable to a strategy of piecemeal bargaining in the labor market, unions were led to political activity as a means of improving wages, hours, and working conditions. At the extreme, a union, no matter how strongly entrenched in a cohesive community, could be overwhelmed by economic change, perhaps because the market for its members' product shrank as new and better substitutes came along or because their skills were simply displaced by new technology. These were groups that were condemned in the sense that there was little they could do to stop the rot. They had strong unions that could express their collective grievances, but given dramatic changes in the division of labor there was not much they could do directly in the labor market. Their position can be summed up in terms of a frustrating combination of strength and weakness, of the capacity to create organization but an inability to use it to defend their niche in the division of labor. They came, I think quite rationally, to believe that their communities, and their traditional way of life in general, were doomed by economic changes beyond their control and that their only hope lay in some form of political regulation of the labor market.

Repression, Unions, and Politics

The second substantive theme of this book is based on an attempt to generalize about the effects of state repression or toleration for union political activity. As the analysis moves from the level of occupational community and individual labor markets to national politics, secondary sources become noticeably sparser. Many labor historians have come to focus their attention on questions having to do with the everyday lives of workers and have paid much less attention to the effects of the legal context of industrial relations on trade unions. With the exception of the pathbreaking work of Seymour Martin Lipset on the political orientations of labor organizations and the suggestive analyses of some students of social movements, social analysts have rarely sought out historical generalizations concerning the effects of state repression or tolerance on unions.[19]

The topic is an important one because unions in Western societies have developed under sharply contrasting legal climates, and unions have always been extraordinarily sensitive to laws regarding strikes and other methods by which they can press their members' interests. As organizations representing workers with little power or prestige against employers having both, unions everywhere had to struggle to gain legal acceptance. But the severity of repression and its duration varied immensely, from the relatively tolerant legal climates of Britain and the United States to the far harsher ones of Germany or Russia.

Despite repeated attempts to encompass all workers, regardless of occupation or industry, into a single union, the configuration of union organization in every Western society has more nearly resembled a patchwork of segmented pieces than a unitary bloc. This is one of the most fundamental characteristics of Western trade unions, and it underlies the theme of patterns of variation developed here. But unions in a particular society share a similar fate in an important and overtly political respect. All unions in a given society are subject to the same laws; their ability to organize, strike, and picket is determined beyond the labor market by the state. Every union, no matter how economistic it is, is concerned to gain the legal breathing room to go about its business in the labor market. The legal regulation of industrial relations is thus an essential link between the labor market activities of a union and its political activities. However clearly we may distinguish between them conceptually, in practice they can never be entirely divorced. Political and economic activity, state and labor market, are inherently linked

[19] Lipset, "Radicalism or Reformism." See also Robert Liebman, "Repressive Strategies and Working-Class Protest," *Social Science History* 4, no. 1 (February 1980); Robert J. Goldstein, *Political Repression in Nineteenth-Century Europe* (London: Croom Helm, 1983); Geary, *European Labour Protest, 1848–1939*, pp. 58–65.

because the state is itself the authoritative source of the rules under which economic activity is pursued.

State repression of the right of workers to combine in the labor market appears to have had three related consequences for unions. First, and most obviously, repression politicized unions because it compelled them to try to change the rules of the game even if their preferred strategy was to bargain improvements in their members' conditions of employment in the labor market. In Germany stiff legal constraints on unions during the nineteenth century made it very difficult for unions to pursue the kind of business strategy typical of many unions in the United States or Britain. As organizations that were considered to be subversive, most German unions were thrust into politics whether they liked it or not.

In the United States and Britain the intensity of state repression was milder. But legal constraints frequently precipitated union political activity. All unions stood to gain if their legal rights were extended, and this was a powerful justification for national federation. The gradual development of AFL involvement in politics from the end of the nineteenth century, the establishment and growth of the British TUC, and, later, the Labour party itself, were profoundly influenced by the desire to create the collective good of a favorable legal climate.

A second consequence of repression is that, if sufficiently severe, it could reduce differences among workers originating in their contrasting capacities to form effective unions. In this respect state repression was a leveler, creating a sense of cohesion under enforced political and economic exclusion. In practice, the worst effects of state repression might be avoided by workers in particularly small and closely knit occupational communities, for such workers could exercise some control over their working lives without relying on formal organization and highly visible strikes. But the perception of shared victimization could create a powerful sense of working-class unity. Repression in an authoritarian political system was profoundly radicalizing. Where the law could not be changed by union efforts, unions logically sought to change those who made the law, and where this also was impossible, the only activist alternative was to try to change the regime itself. It is no coincidence that the "heroic years" of German Social Democracy coincided with the worst period of repression under the Anti-Socialist Laws (1878–1890). This was a time when unity and revolutionism were virtually imposed upon the socialist movement by heavy-handed state suppression.[20]

Finally, I argue that repression politicized unions in an additional, and more subtle way, by giving the initiative within the labor movement to political parties, which were created specifically to act in politics and which could best develop the ideological basis of resistance to unjust authority. The existence of a repressive state apparatus shaped the priorities of labor away from short-term amelioration in the labor market towards larger party-political tasks of gaining the basic rights of political and economic citizenship.[21]

The attempt to generalize about the effects of state repression on union political activity suggests some fundamental contrasts with the effects of variations in occupational community and the labor market. All workers had to sell their labor power, and in this respect they were in a common position. But their communitarian resources and the effectiveness of their unions differed decisively, and this led to a variety of political orientations. In explaining unity among unions, as expressed in shared political allegiance and union federation, I believe we must focus on the national legal context of unions rather than on their situation in the labor market. The legal context of industrial relations appears to be a vital source of common political purpose, whereas the labor market was a source of differentiation and sectionalism.[22]

The Organizational Revolution

The comparative politics of union political activity has been concerned mainly with contemporary unions and their participation in public policy making.[23] When we look back from the present to the

---

[20] See Hans Mommsen, "The Free Trade Unions and Social Democracy in Imperial Germany," in Wolfgang J. Mommsen and Hans-Gerhard Husung, eds., *The Development of Trade Unionism in Great Britain and Germany, 1880–1914* (London: George Allen & Unwin, 1985), especially p. 374. Alfred Förster, *Die Gewerkschaftspolitik der deutschen Sozialdemokratie während des Sozialistengesetzes* (Berlin/DDR: Verlag Tribune, 1971).

[21] This point was made incisively by Lenin in *What Is To Be Done?* (Peking: Foreign Languages Press, 1973), p. 139.

[22] This is, of course, to take issue with Karl Marx, as discussed in Chapter Two.

[23] There is now a considerable literature on contemporary union political activity. See, for example, Gary Marks, "Neocorporatism and Incomes Policy in Western Europe and North America, 1950–1980," *Comparative Politics* 17 (April 1986), and Phi-

nineteenth century, it is clear that unions today are oriented to politics in a way undreamt of in the years of their early growth. National union federations exist in every Western society, and these organizations, along with individual unions, are deeply embedded in the practice of public policy. They participate in numerous government agencies, commissions, etc., concerned with employees' welfare. Beyond this, they attempt to influence public policy decisions that impinge on their organizations and their members' interests, broadly defined, and this involves them in virtually the whole compass of economic policy, labor policy, and social policy. Variations in the way unions influence public policy in contemporary Western societies are well known and much researched; the development of their intense involvement in politics has received much less attention.[24]

My third theme concerns this shared and fundamental development: why, when, and how did unions become politicized on a routinized basis? To answer this I believe we have to examine some fundamental developments that occurred in the period prior to the First World War. The roots of this distinctly modern political orientation are to be found neither in the experience of the Second World War, nor in the post-Second World War extension of state responsibility for social welfare and economic performance, but in the decades around the turn of the twentieth century. In these years a set of developments, with consequences arguably as profound as those of the Industrial Revolution, transformed the most advanced industrial societies of the time, the United States, Britain, and Germany.

At the heart of the process was an immense expansion in the organization of economic, social, and political life. This had multiple causes. These decades saw a rapid concentration of finance and production into ever larger units under the influence of innova-

---

lippe Schmitter and Gerhard Lehmbruch, eds., *Trends toward Corporatist Intermediation* (Beverly Hills, Calif.: Sage, 1979).

[24] Schmitter makes some interesting comments on this development in the book cited above. See also Rudolf Hilferding, *Das Finanzkapital* (1910; reprint ed., Berlin: Dietz, 1955), pp. 548–549, and Karl Born, "Der soziale und wirtschaftliche Strukturwandel am Ende des 19. Jahrhunderts," *Vierteljahrschrift für Sozial- und Wirtschaftsgeschichte* 50 (1963). For a comparative overview of the growth of union organization in Britain, Germany, and France in this period, see James E. Cronin, "Strikes and the Struggle for Union Organization: Britain and Europe," in Wolfgang J. Mommsen and Hans-Gerhard Husung, eds., *The Development of Trade Unionism in Great Britain and Germany, 1880–1914* (London: George Allen & Unwin, 1985).

tions in communication, power generation, and mass production. The demand for political organization grew with the rise of mass democracy. And as competition among groups intensified, organization became self-generating. These changes appear to have been mutually reinforcing. They form what a psychologist would call "a syndrome" and as such deserve some kind of designation: borrowing a term from Kenneth Boulding, I have called this development the "Organizational Revolution."[25]

The Organizational Revolution had profound consequences for unions and industrial relations. The growth in the scale of organization in the labor market transformed industrial conflict. Strikes were no longer a local matter but could bring entire industries to a standstill with national, and therefore political, consequences.[26] The largest strikes precipitated intensive state intervention in the labor market to suppress union resistance or find some grounds for conciliation. At the same time the role of the state expanded as governments became more willing, and more pressured, to exert their own influence on market conditions, particularly in aid of those who were sick, aged, or unemployed. As the state took on these new responsibilities, unions demanded, and received, a privileged position in their administration in exchange for their public consent and expertise.

The struggle between unions and employers increasingly spilled over into the political arena. Industrial conflict, once a matter of hundreds or thousands of workers opposing small groups of employers in particular localities or regions, now became a clash of organizational titans. Individual unions, numbering up to hundreds of thousands of members, and union federations, which encompassed millions, were pitched against employers and employer associations having hundreds of millions, or even billions, of dollars in capital. Such resources could be used to obvious effect in politics, and unions and employers were induced to try to outflank each other in the labor market by gaining party-political leverage and legislative influence.

These developments share a common denominator: each implied the interpenetration of labor market institutions and the state, of economics and politics. The Organizational Revolution saw a quan-

[25] Kenneth Boulding, *The Organizational Revolution* (New York: Harper, 1962).
[26] Chris Wrigley, "The Government and Industrial Relations," in Wrigley, ed., *A History of British Industrial Relations, 1875–1914* (Amherst: University of Massachusetts Press, 1982).

tum leap in the attempt to exercise human will over social, economic, and political life. The autonomy of economics and politics as two entirely separate spheres of activity was maintained in neoclassical economics (and in departmental boundaries in universities), but in practice it had disappeared.

It would be misleading to see the Organizational Revolution as leading to convergence in union political activity. National differences were as pronounced as ever, as I emphasize in the final chapter. Most importantly, the distinctive relationships between unions and parties that had been forged in the United States, Britain, and Germany in the last decades of the nineteenth century were a determining influence on union political activity in the twentieth century. But despite these differences, unions in each of these countries now participated in politics as a routinized means of pursuing a wide range of policy goals. From this standpoint the Organizational Revolution created a context for union political activity that, for the first time, was recognizably modern.

CHAPTER 1

VARIATIONS IN
UNION POLITICAL ACTIVITY

Our comparative understanding of working-class political activity in the nineteenth and twentieth centuries is highly skewed to comparison at the national level. Variations in the mass support, strategies, and political orientation of working-class political parties across societies have been explained in terms of equally macro variables, including the timing and character of industrialization, social structure, the openness of the political system, and the duration and intensity of state repression of working-class economic and political rights. But insofar as we widen our view of working-class political activity beyond the political party to include trade unions, a complementary set of questions come sharply into view having to do with variations within, as well as between, societies.

In the first place it is useful to recognize just how great such variations in union political activity within societies were. In the United States we must contend with the revolutionary syndicalist Industrial Workers of the World alongside the business unionism of most unions affiliated to the American Federation of Labor. In Britain our understanding of union political orientation must encompass the desperation of the handloom weavers' organizations alongside the gradualist strategies of established unions formed by craft workers, while in Germany we must acknowledge that, despite the strength of socialist influence within the union movement, some unions, such as those formed by printers and cigarworkers, were more oriented to business unionism than revolutionary socialism.

Numerous factors may plausibly be regarded as influencing such variations. Among them are the social background, status, cultural traditions, and expectations of workers; the organization of work, methods of payment, and relations in the workplace; political variables, including the openness of the political system, the timing of working-class economic and political rights, the role of the state in the labor market, and relations between unions and political parties; economic variables, including the relevant supply and demand for labor; and organizational variables, particularly the degree of institutionalization of collective bargaining, union market power, and the degree of competitiveness among unions.

The task of building a convincing theory that encompasses the variety of influences on union political orientation has hardly begun.[1] In this chapter I propose to discuss two fundamental sources of variation in union political strategy. The first is the organizational strength of the union, indicated most tellingly by the extent to which the union encompasses its potential membership. Groups of workers who could form stable unions had an organizational lever for pressing a variety of demands on employers, political parties, the state, and the public. In short, organization provided workers with the most basic precondition of gaining some control over their working lives—a capacity for strategy. Unorganized workers, by contrast, were forced back on uninstitutionalized collective protest, from spontaneous strikes to political riots, or had to seek their own individual remedies, from absenteeism to self-improvement. But most common of all was apathy, perhaps grounded in the quite rational belief that working conditions, in their broadest sense, were largely beyond their means of control.

Union organization opened up new channels for workers to defend or improve their working conditions. But even a strong organization could not guarantee the effective defense of its members' working conditions in the labor market if it had to cope with decisive changes in the division of labor or particularly powerful and intransigent employers. The second set of factors that I shall ex-

---

[1] The most ambitious and clearly conceptualized efforts in this direction have been undertaken by theorists of social mobilization, particularly Charles Tilly, *From Mobilization to Revolution* (Reading, Mass.: Addison-Wesley, 1978); Sidney Tarrow, *Struggling to Reform: Social Movements and Policy Change during Cycles of Protest* (Ithaca, N.Y.: Center for European Studies, n.d.); and Ronald Aminzade, "Capitalist Industrialization and Patterns of Industrial Protest: A Comparative Urban Study of Nineteenth-Century France," *American Sociological Review* 49 (August 1984). Peter Lange, George Ross, and Maurizio Vannicelli, *Unions, Change and Crisis* (London: George Allen & Unwin, 1982), is a suggestive analysis of contemporary union movements. In the field of labor history there have been very few attempts to compare the political orientations of individual unions, an outstanding exception being John Laslett's comparison of six American unions in *Labor and the Left* (New York: Basic Books, 1970). Eric J. Hobsbawm and Joan W. Scott, "Political Shoemakers," in E. J. Hobsbawm, *Worlds of Labour* (London: Weidenfeld and Nicolson, 1984), is a cross-national comparison of experiences within an occupation. Dick Geary, *European Labour Protest, 1848–1939* (London: Croom Helm, 1981), provides a useful overview of working-class political activity in Western Europe that includes comparisons of unions.

amine in this chapter thus has to do with the economic and political context of union organization in the labor market.

Some fortunate groups of workers could adapt their organizations to the challenge of economic change and employer opposition if these were not too severe. But others were faced with the prospect of industrial reorganization and the wholesale introduction of labor-saving innovations, which threatened to devalue their skills, to multiply the potential supply of labor in their occupation, and eventually to undermine their organization. Such a situation was politically combustible. Organization gave such workers the capacity for collective resistance, but economic changes beyond their control could condemn all their efforts to defend themselves in the labor market. Here I hypothesize that one important source of radical political activity on the part of workers lies in this combination of power and impotence, in the collective ability to act and the inability to act effectively in the labor market. Figure 1.1 sets out a typology of political response derived by dichotomizing union organization and union market power.

The form such political activity took depended on the local and national political context, particularly the character of union/party relations, the extent of state repression or toleration of workers' economic and political rights, the status system, and the political channels available to workers to express their grievances.[2] The sup-

MARKET POWER

		high	low
	high	ADAPTIVE	CONDEMNED
ORGANIZATION			
	low	SURGENT	VOICELESS

Figure 1.1 Typology of Union Political Orientation

[2] The influence of the local political context has been explored in Herbert Gutman's writings, especially "Class, Status, and Community Power in Nineteenth-Century Industrial Cities," reprinted in his book, *Work, Culture, and Society in Industrializing America* (New York: Vintage Books, 1977), and by Leon Fink, *Workingmen's Democracy* (Urbana: University of Illinois Press, 1983). The influence of workers' economic and political rights and the character of the status system is analyzed by Seymour Martin Lipset, "Radicalism or Reformism: The Sources of Working-Class Politics," *American Political Science Review* 77, no. 1 (March 1983).

position of this chapter is that if these factors are held constant for unions within a society, variations in union political orientation will reflect the constraints on union strategy in the labor market.

In the following pages I analyze the requisites of union organization and market power and examine their consequences for working-class political orientation. My illustrations are drawn from the experiences of groups of industrial workers and artisans in the United States, Great Britain, and Germany, societies that provide diverse political contexts in which to gauge the influence of organizational and market constraints on working-class political activity.

THE REQUISITES OF UNIONISM

A particularly striking observation of unions in Western societies in the nineteenth century is that, relatively speaking, so few workers joined them. Reliable data on membership until the last decade of the nineteenth century is hard to come by, but we can be quite certain that even in the best of times unions encompassed no more than about 12 percent of the nonagricultural work force in any society of Western Europe or North America. This figure was reached in Britain near the turn of the century.[3] In the United States and Germany the level of unionization was considerably lower. Even when we exclude the vast number of agricultural laborers from the calculation of potential union membership, the level of unionization in the United States and Germany at the turn of the century was little more than 5 percent.[4]

At various times these figures were temporarily inflated by the inrush of unskilled workers into broad union movements. In Britain the Grand National Consolidated Trades' Union, formed by Robert Owen in the early 1830s, had a membership that might have reached 100,000; while in the United States the membership of the Knights of Labor peaked at about 700,000 in 1886 and propelled the proportion of unionized workers to almost 10 percent. But such movements were extremely unstable; the Grand National collapsed only two years after it was formed, and the membership of the

---

[3] In 1899 the level of union density in Great Britain reached 12.1 percent. George Sayers Bain and Robert Price, *Profiles of Union Growth* (Oxford: Basil Blackwell, 1980), p. 37.

[4] Ibid., pp. 87 and 133.

Knights of Labor fell by more than half by 1888 and virtually disappeared by 1891.[5]

When we take into account the immense difficulty of creating viable union organizations, perhaps the remarkable thing is that they were established at all. The act of joining a union had clear and present costs: membership fees would have to be paid; in many occupations there was the possibility of being fired by an intransigent employer; and in some countries there was the likelihood of attracting the attention of the police as a potential subversive. According to the theory of collective goods, moreover, many of the benefits secured by the union are appropriated by nonmembers as well as members. If the union succeeds in restricting the entry of labor into the occupation, bargaining higher wages, or improving some other aspect of working conditions, all workers in the occupation are likely to gain, irrespective of whether they are union members or not. From this standpoint then the rational worker has no material incentive to join the union. He or she may "free ride," that is, gain the economic advantages secured by the union without paying the costs of membership.

This fundamental insight about the difficulty of providing collective goods, developed by Mancur Olson and elaborated in the literature on collective mobilization, provides an elegant explanation of the paradox that many workers who were in greatest need of organized defense in the labor market were unable to provide themselves with it.[6] At the same time this approach alerts us to the ways in which union organization can be sustained. The challenge of inducing potential members to join can be met in two ways, both of which were pursued by unions. First, a union may offer selective incentives to its members, that is, it may provide private benefits that are available only to those who pay the costs of membership.

[5] On the Grand National Consolidated Trades Union see G.D.H. Cole, *Attempts at General Union, 1818–1834* (London: Allen & Unwin, 1953); W. H. Oliver, "The Consolidated Trades' Union of 1834," *Economic History Review*, 2d series, vol. 19 (1964/ 1965). On the membership of the Knights of Labor see Leo Wolman, *The Growth of the American Trade Unions, 1880–1923* (New York: National Bureau of Economic Research, 1924), p. 32.

[6] Mancur Olson, Jr., *The Logic of Collective Action* (Cambridge, Mass.: Harvard University Press, 1965). Aspects of Olson's work have been applied to early unionism by Robert Max Jackson, *The Formation of Craft Labor Markets* (Orlando: Academic Press, 1984), pp. 45–46, and Norbert Eickhof, *Eine Theorie der Gewerkschaftsentwicklung* (Tübingen: J.C.B. Mohr, 1973). For an overview of the literature on collective mobilization see Tilly, *From Mobilization to Revolution*.

Second, a union may create and sustain the bond of membership on noneconomic grounds because potential members feel themselves committed, or compelled, to join. The study of union political activity necessarily focusses on those atypical groups of workers who could effectively adopt these methods of organization. Let us analyze them in turn.

The selective incentives that unions have offered their members are diverse. They include seniority rights, procedures for handling individual grievances, opportunities for companionship and social recreation, and, most important of all, individual economic benefits ranging from sickness, old-age, accident, and funeral benefits to traveling and various forms of out-of-work benefits. Many unions began by emphasizing these benefits to the virtual exclusion of collective bargaining with employers. The role of such private economic benefits was so large that some unions continued to refer to themselves as a "friendly society," "mutual association," or "protection society" in Britain, "benevolent society" in the United States, or "*Unterstützungsverein*" in Germany.[7]

Although it makes sense to distinguish the task of creating stable organization from that of formulating the union's strategy in the labor market, in practice the two were often closely intertwined. Many of the earliest unions based their function of improving working conditions on what Sidney and Beatrice Webb called the method of "Mutual Insurance."[8] If the union was not able to come to an agreement with employers, it would try to "turn out" the workers from all the shops and support them with benefits for the duration of the dispute. Some unions went further and attempted to regulate working conditions unilaterally. Rather than bargain directly with employers, the union itself set a "just price" for labor

    [7] There are numerous examples of unions adopting such names. In Britain among the most prominent were the Friendly Society of Ironfounders, the Operative Stonemason's Friendly Society, the Flint Glass Makers' Friendly Society, the Northumberland Miners' Mutual Confident Association, the Glass Bottle Makers of Yorkshire United Trade Protection Society, and, most explicit of all, the United Operative Bricklayers' Trade, Accident, Sick, and Burial Society. In the United States a variety of unions used the term "benevolent" in their names, including the Workingmen's Benevolent Association of the anthracite coalminers. In Germany several combinations, including those of coopers, coppersmiths, cigarworkers, hatters, potters, and printers, designated themselves *Unterstützungsverein*, a term that reflected their benefit functions while providing a legal front for broader union activities.

    [8] Sidney and Beatrice Webb, *Industrial Democracy*, 2d ed., 2 vols. (London: Longmans, Green, 1920), esp. vol. 1, chap. 1.

and provided union members who were working at substandard rates with out-of-work or traveling benefits so that they could find better employment.[9] As a result, employers who persisted in paying a substandard rate were denied a steady supply of labor. Under the method of Mutual Insurance, union benefits played a double role, sustaining the organization while underpinning its market power.

In addition to such noncollective economic incentives, union strength and stability have always depended on some mixture of loyalty, social norms, and compulsion that transcend economic considerations. Such pressures were particularly strong in stabilizing unions when there were close social ties among workers in the occupation or industry. The simplest and, at the same time, perhaps the most profound answer to the question of why workers joined unions is that the alternative was never much considered, least of all from the perspective of the rational economic actor. When we read what literate artisans and workers themselves had to say, we often hear that they joined unions because their fellows did so, because this was regarded as the right and socially accepted thing to do.[10] Not to join would have flouted norms of behavior that were shared by friends and workmates, by the very people with whom they spent their working hours and, in most cases, much of their leisure time.

The ability of groups of workers to enforce unionism through social norms varied through time as changes in the division of labor and industrial structure facilitated worker solidarity in some labor markets and undermined it in others. Such norms were potentially strongest where workers had job stability, regular employment, and were hived off from others by distinctive skills, work habits, or industrial location.[11] Social norms conducive to unionism also re-

---

[9] Unilateral regulation was especially well developed among English craft unions. An employer who did not adhere to the standards set by the union would be denied a steady supply of labor and would thus be pressured towards compliance. Occasionally the union might try to withdraw all workers from employers in a particular locality, but such strikes were limited in scope and were viewed as a secondary tactic. The testimony of William Allen, a leading New Model unionist, to the Royal Commission on Trade Unions in 1867 describes this strategy and is reported by Sidney and Beatrice Webb in *Industrial Democracy*, 1: 167.

[10] See, for example, Thomas Burt, *An Autobiography* (London: Fisher Unwin, 1924), and Thomas Wright, *The Great Unwashed* (London: Frank Cass, 1868).

[11] See James E. Cronin, "Strikes and the Struggle for Union Organization: Britain and Europe," in Wolfgang J. Mommsen and Hans-Gerhard Husung, eds., *The Devel-*

sulted form the efforts of workers themselves in their conflicts with employers or the state. Industrial conflict could provide a valuable learning experience in the benefits of labor solidarity and could instill among previously isolated workers a notion of the occupation as a community with its own history and myths.

Occasionally such norms were buttressed by violence, or the threat of violence, against those who did not join the union. But we miss the character of early trade unionism if we attempt to draw a sharp line between consent and compulsion here, for the distinction between the exercise of strong group norms and the subtle use of coercion against nonconformists is blurred where group solidarity is so crucial to welfare. However, brute violence was less common. Because the use of force is only effective for very short periods of time unless it is institutionalized, it has been much more important in conflicts between workers and employers—for example, in deterring strikebreakers or strikers—than in meeting the longer-term problem of organizational stability.[12]

Groups of workers who were unable to provide themselves with selective incentives and lacked the ability to enforce the norm of membership through ties of loyalty generally had to wait for organization to be brought to them from the outside, by radical activists who could mobilize workers through their own example and exhortation or by the efforts of already entrenched unions and their financial muscle and organizational experience.[13] The difficulty of these means of consciously introducing organization are amply illustrated by the fact that most unskilled workers in all but a very small handful of Western societies remain nonunionized to this day. External aid was particularly useful when the initial organizational impetus could be translated into stability through the closed or union shop. When these were unavailable, the difference between creating and sustaining union organization could be enormous.

---

opment of Trade Unionism in Great Britain and Germany, 1880–1914 (London: George Allen & Unwin, 1985), pp. 60–61.

[12] A further, and very effective, form of compulsion is the closed or union shop enforced legally or by agreement with employers, for it guarantees a high level of organization with the minimal amount of continuous effort on the part of the union. But such an arrangement assumes considerable prior organization, for it needs to be enforced in the first place. Thus the closed or union shop may stabilize a union that is already strong, but it is less relevant during the period in which the union is established. This point is made by Olson, *The Logic of Collective Action*, p. 69, and James Q. Wilson, *Political Organizations* (New York: Basic Books, 1973), p. 120.

[13] Wilson, *Political Organization*, pp. 130–131.

Thus where external union creation has been effective, it has usually had the benefit of legislation favorable to the union or closed shop, or of employers who were prepared to acquiesce to them. Under these circumstances the goal of a union drive from the outside is simply to mobilize workers to vote for the union or pressure employers to recognize it. Once that has been accomplished the union can coast on its enforced monopoly in the workplace.

But external aid and ideology are likely to be weak as a substitute for selective incentives or incentives exercised through social norms and subtle compulsion. This can be seen very clearly by comparing a union with a political party. Political parties may succeed in gaining a mass membership if they mobilize only a fraction of the total population by emphasizing their ideological distinctiveness. But if a union is to be effective it must try to organize all workers within a particular labor market or markets. Few independent unions have followed workers' political parties in retaining as members just that minority of their constituencies who are likely to be most receptive to ideological appeals. Unions cannot afford to "choose" their members, and this has usually led them to appeal to the lowest common denominator of their target memberships. Thus unions wishing to encompass all workers in a particular industry or occupation have tended to emphasize the virtue of union solidarity as an end in itself, even though this may not be so compelling as the more incisive, but potentially more divisive, ideology of a workers' political party.

UNIONISM AND OCCUPATIONAL COMMUNITY

The previous paragraphs have sketched the chief means by which unions were able to establish themselves as stable organizations. Is it possible to generalize about the social conditions of unionization in the nineteenth and early twentieth centuries? When we examine the historical experience of union formation we find some strikingly similar patterns among Western societies. The earliest unions were formed by journeymen in traditional occupations. Alongside printers, who were the first, or among the first, to unionize in several societies and who are discussed in detail in Chapter Four, we find shoemakers, carpenters, tailors, and a catalogue of artisans working in much the same way as they did in guild times.

The priority of these groups is open to several interpretations, including those that emphasize the personal characteristics of craft workers, their higher level of worldly experience, education, in- come, and so forth. But soon after these craftsmen, workers with less distinguished qualities began to organize. Unions in textiles and coalmining go back to the nineteenth century and, in some cases, the eighteenth century. The very diversity of workers who could form unions—from artisans to domestic handloom weavers and coalminers—suggests that personal characteristics cannot explain the ability to organize. Let us turn from the historical experience back to our discussion of the means available to provide the collec- tive good of unionization. What, then, are the social requisites of the noncollective and noneconomic incentives sketched above?

The provision of extensive benefits rested on rather narrow con- ditions. In the first place it required that potential members earned enough money to be able to put by a surplus for hard times. The maintenance of out-of-work benefits had to be set at a high enough level not just to provide minimum subsistence but to reduce the incentive of taking "illegal" employment. This kind of benefit gen- erally cost between three and six times more than a simple strike benefit, and the subscription it demanded was not an inconsider- able part of many workers' incomes in the nineteenth century.[14]

In addition, sickness, accident, old-age, and unemployment ben- efits required that potential members planned to remain in the union long enough to gain a satisfactory return on their "invest- ment." This condition was all the more important because unions were compelled to scale their benefits with respect to length of membership in order to dissuade workers from joining only when they saw the immediate prospect of unemployment or incapacita- tion. In other words, workers who were occupationally mobile could rarely be induced to join unions that offered benefits provid- ing long-term economic security. The provision of benefits was most effective for workers who, when they looked to the future, saw themselves remaining in the same occupation.

A similar, and in some respects even more unusual, set of social conditions was required by groups of workers if they were to en-

---

[14] If anything, this range is estimated too conservatively. In 1878 the German print- ers' union, which at that time was the most expensive union to join, had a weekly subscription of 40pf., while those unions that maintained just strike benefits de- manded between 20pf. and 40pf. per month. The subscription rate of the London Society of Compositors began at 1s. a week in 1848 and rose to 2s. by 1920. Members of unions without an extensive benefit system, such as the Workers' Union, contrib- uted just a few pence a week.

force union membership as a social norm. As sociological studies have shown, stable, relatively closed groups or communities provide a favorable context for powerful social norms governing individual beliefs and actions, especially where those norms involve individual sacrifice.[15] Close-knit communities engender a sense of belonging that, as Craig Calhoun has observed, may "even mobilize people for collective action over long periods of time, in pursuit of highly uncertain goals and at high personal costs."[16]

The degree to which workers or artisans are members of a community is influenced by several factors. Among the most important of these are the collective experience of independence and cooperation in the workplace, cultural homogeneity, and geographical or social isolation.

The first of these, the mutually reinforcing combination of cooperation among workers and independence from employer supervision, was particularly strong among artisans whose traditional methods of production were least disrupted by specialization and compartmentalization. The skills of the journeyman in traditional industry, unwritten and closely guarded against employer intervention, were a source of pride for the occupation as a whole. Contemporary artisans spoke quite frequently of their sense of honor (or *Ehre*) in belonging to a manly, skilled, and independent class of artisans, by which they were referring specifically to those in their occupation.[17]

Compositors, whose craft was to set up matter for printing, are an archetypal example of an occupational group that formed a strong community in the workplace. The institutional expression of their community was the Chapel, a fascinating preindustrial organization of printers in the workplace that combined economic, so-

[15] R. T. Golembiewski, "Small Groups and Large Organizations," in James G. March, ed., *Handbook of Organizations* (Chicago: University of Chicago Press, 1965), reports research in this area.

[16] Craig Calhoun, *The Question of Class Struggle* (Chicago: University of Chicago Press, 1982), p. 180. See also Calhoun, "Community: Toward a Variable Conceptualization for Comparative Research," *Social History* 5, no. 1 (1980), and "The Radicalism of Tradition: Community Strength or Venerable Disguise and Borrowed Language," *American Journal of Sociology* 88, no. 5 (March 1983).

[17] See George Sturt, *The Wheelwright's Shop* (Cambridge: Cambridge University Press, 1923); E. P. Thompson, *The Making of the English Working Class* (London: Penguin Books, 1968), chap. 8; Iowerth Prothero, *Artisans and Politics in Nineteenth-Century London* (London: Methuen, 1979), chap. 2; David Montgomery, *Workers' Control in America* (Cambridge: Cambridge University Press, 1979), chap. 1.

cial, and political functions touching on virtually every aspect of the printer's working life. It operated in an age-old and seemingly mysterious way, an amalgam of ancient rites, masoniclike secrecy, and primitive democracy, but the implicit principles that lay behind its operation were those of maintaining the autonomy of the printers' craft from employer supervision, while opposing any possible threat to the printers' occupational solidarity.[18] For the printers, autonomy and solidarity were closely meshed. The printers' influence over the division of labor restricted the freedom of employers to compartmentalize and divide the work force, their insistence on maintaining strict apprenticeship regulations limited the ability of employers to introduce less skilled workers into the composing room, and long-standing customs concerning the acceptable pace of work made it difficult for employers to reward the most efficient workers through piece rates.

The sense of occupational community that made such efforts possible was expressed in social norms concerning the division of labor, dealings with employers, and relations among printers themselves. As for many other tightly knit communities, the printers' collective experiences shaped even everyday language and created, over time, distinctive expressions shared by those who belonged that were inaccessible to those who did not. In Britain printers still speak of "a 'ship" (a companionship of men working together permanently), "getting him out" (playing a prank on somebody), a "Wayzgoose" (outing), a "bang-out" (celebration when a printer leaves the composing room), and a "gobbler" (someone over-willing to work overtime).[19] Descriptions of printers' Chapels spanning the

[18] J. Moxon, *Mechanick Exercises*, vol. 2 (London, 1683), especially p. 356; F. C. Avis, *The Early Printers' Chapel in England* (London: Avis, 1971); E. Howe and H. E. Waite, *The London Society of Compositors* (London: Cassell, 1948), pp. 30–41; W. Krahl, *Der Verband der Deutschen Buchdrucker* (Berlin, 1916), pp. 81–98; G. A. Stephens, *New York Typographical Union No. 6* (New York: New York State Department of Labor, 1912), pp. 114–130. For an insightful discussion of the chapel see Charles F. Sabel, *Work and Politics* (Cambridge: Cambridge University Press, 1982).

[19] See I. C. Cannon, "Ideology and Occupational Community: A Study of Compositors," *Sociology* 1, no. 2 (1967). Also relevant are Seymour Martin Lipset, Martin A. Trow, and James S. Coleman, *Union Democracy: The Internal Politics of the International Typographical Union* (New York: Anchor Books, 1956), esp. sec. 2; A.J.M. Sykes, "Trade-Union Workshop Organization in the Printing Industry—The Chapel," *Human Relations* 13, no. 1 (1960); Sykes, "Unity and Restrictive Practices in the British Printing Industry," *The Sociological Review*, n.s., vol. 8, no. 2 (1968); and "The Cohesion of a Trade Union Workshop Organization," *Sociology* 1, no. 2 (1967).

entire period of industrial society over the last two centuries are astonishingly similar, a testament to the way the printers' strong community allowed them to adapt to evolving technology in their industry.

Although traditions of autonomy and solidarity in the workplace were most frequently found among artisans, they were not confined to them. Coalminers and various groups of domestic workers shared self-reliance, freedom from managerial control, and acute mutual dependence that fostered intense group loyalty.[20]

A second important influence on the strength of occupational community is the degree to which a group of workers is culturally homogeneous. This was not an issue for artisans whose occupations were effectively guarded by apprenticeship regulations against the influx of unskilled labor. Although journeymen were highly geographically mobile, especially in their *Wanderjahren* (young tramping days), once they had invested their early working years in an apprenticeship they were loath to change occupations. The labor force in such occupations also tended to be ingrown, for apprentices were often recruited from among the families of the artisans themselves. But in many of the newer, rapidly expanding, and less-skilled occupations the work force was culturally fragmented, either through the influx of peasants drawn to the towns or forced off the land, or through the immigration of foreign workers—Poles in Germany; Irish, Welsh, and Scots in England; English in Wales; and the successive waves of immigrants in the United States. The process can be seen most acutely in many mining industries that combined rapid growth with highly labor-intensive methods of production. In such cases occupational solidarity had to overcome the intense competition and mutual jealousies of ethnic groups who brought different cultural traditions and expectations to the workplace.[21]

[20] See Klaus Tenfelde, *Sozialgeschichte der Bergarbeiterschaft an der Ruhr im 19.Jahrhundert* (Bonn-Bad Godesberg: Neue Gesellschaft, 1978), pp. 219–229. The relationship between forms of technology, work, and group relations in coalmining are analyzed in E. L. Trist et al., *Organizational Choice: Capabilities of Groups at the Coal Face under Changing Technologies* (London: Tavistock Publications, 1963). Sections 2 and 3 are particularly relevant to this discussion. On domestic handloom weavers see Duncan Bythell, *The Handloom Weavers* (Cambridge: Cambridge University Press, 1969), chap. 8; H. A. Turner, *Trade Union Growth, Structure and Policy* (London: Allen & Unwin, 1962), pp. 81–85; Thompson, *The Making of the English Working Class* chap. 9.

[21] A particularly vivid description of cultural heterogeneity in coalmining is that of

A further decisive influence on the strength of occupational community is the extent to which those who work in the occupation are socially isolated. Although geographical isolation is the most obvious form of social isolation, it can have more subtle forms arising in, for example, a shared perception of social inferiority or unusual working hours that isolate a group of workers from those outside their occupation. Perhaps the most extreme example of social isolation was found among coalminers, whose work made them distinctive in appearance, demanded unusual hours of work, and often enforced crowding and geographical isolation on them. The influence of geographical isolation also appears to be important in the solidarity of English handloom weavers, who often formed close-knit communities, although they did not benefit from the kind of solidary relations in the workplace characteristic of many groups of artisans and miners. They were domestic workers, weaving in their homes, and isolated from other workers, save those in their own families. But many of the localities where handloom weaving was carried out were small, homogeneous villages or towns.[22]

The common feature of these influences on the degree to which groups of workers or artisans formed a community is that each is conducive to the creation of dense networks of bonds among individuals. Thus we must look to the shared experiences of a group and the lessons it draws from them, as well as to the determinants of the labor force and work situations. Such a context can provide the social cohesion and moral authority in which group norms, such as union membership, are most easily enforced.

But if one were to try to reduce community to its objective features, our analysis would be a pinched one, for the relative strength of community rests not only on the number and intensity of the bonds that tie together a given group but on consciousness of kind, on what the sociologist Joseph Gusfield has called "a sense of participating in the same history."[23] This subjective dimension alerts us to the prospect that a community may be actively created as well as passively formed. While at any one point in time a community may appear as a given set of objective relations among individuals, from

Rowland T. Berthoff, "The Social Order of the Anthracite Region, 1825–1902," *Pennsylvania Magazine of History and Biography* 89 (July, 1965). See also Robert Asher, "Union Nativism and Immigrant Response," *Labor History* 23, no. 3 (1982).

[22] Bythell, *The Handloom Weavers*, pp. 48–49.

[23] Joseph Gusfield, *Community: A Critical Response* (New York: Harper, 1975), p. 35.

a longer historical perspective the coherence of an occupational community is influenced by the individual and collective choices and perceptions of those who participate in it.

The strength of occupational community for many groups of workers and artisans has been profoundly influenced by the conflicts that they have had with employers or the state. This was particularly evident in the creation of community among the diverse ethnic groups of coalminers in the United States and Germany. The major strikes that took place in the last decades of the nineteenth century provided an opportunity for workers with very different cultural backgrounds to communicate their shared grievances not just to employers or the state but also to each other. Contemporary reports reveal that it was in such strikes that traditional stereotypes of immigrant workers as stupid peasants accustomed to poor working conditions and authoritarian management began to break down.[24]

POLITICAL RESPONSES

The Unorganized

The strength of occupational community distinguishes those groups who had the resources to create for themselves the collective good of organized self-defense from those who did not. This book is concerned specifically with the former groups of workers. But first, let us turn to those who were less fortunate and ask how they defended themselves in the absence of an institutionalized presence in the labor market.

The most frequent answer to this question is that they did virtually nothing. Having no collective voice or organized defense, such workers were often resigned to their fate, suffering their conditions as if they were inevitable. Two contrasting examples, drawn from Barrington Moore's book *Injustice: The Social Bases of Obedience and Revolt*, illustrate this very clearly.[25] Moore compares the expe-

[24] See Stephen Hickey, "The Shaping of the German Labour Movement: Miners in the Ruhr," in Richard J. Evans, ed., *Society and Politics in Wilhelmine Germany* (London: Croom Helm, 1978), pp. 233–234.

[25] Barrington Moore, Jr., *Injustice: The Social Bases of Obedience and Revolt* (New York: M. E. Sharpe, 1978), chap. 7. Here I have also relied on David Crew's comparison of miners and metalworkers in *Town in the Ruhr: A Social History of Bochum, 1860–1914* (New York: Columbia University Press, 1979). Crew argues persuasively that

riences of two groups of workers, coalminers and iron and steelworkers, in the German Ruhr during the late nineteenth and early
twentieth centuries. The coalminers, a group I discuss in more detail in Chapter Five, were able to create a reasonably effective organizational presence that could express their sense of injustice as
the traditional defenses of the coalmining artisan were beaten down
in the last decades of the nineteenth century. As state regulations
on working relations and coal production were removed and coalminers found themselves subject to the arbitrary authority of employers and the labor market, they expressed a range of concrete
grievances for decent treatment and more humane working conditions in the largest strikes that had been seen up to that time in
Germany.

This is a course of action that iron and steelworkers had every
reason to take, for they were about as economically insecure and
exploited as coalminers. But in the final decades of the nineteenth
century and the first decade of the twentieth century we hear virtually nothing from this part of the work force. Moore tells us that
a detailed account of strike activity put together by the Metalworkers Union "passes over the Ruhr in silence."[26] In part this appears
to be a reflection of traditional attitudes of submissiveness before
figures of authority, attitudes that were never challenged by the experience of unionism. But the reluctance to express grievances was
also perhaps the outcome of a rational fear of the consequences in
a situation where employers and their foremen held all the aces,
from fining insubordinate workers to firing them at a moment's notice.

Moore explains the stark contrast between these groups of workers in terms of the extent to which they could draw on their past
experience and their work situations to develop standards of injustice with which they could judge the present. Although he does not
analyze the bases of organization in the labor force, the conditions

---

"misery, uprooting, and change can all create grievances experienced individually by
workers, but there is no guarantee that these grievances will be expressed collectively
if they are all that binds the group together. Indeed it is not difficult to see how some
of these conditions of working class life, rather than building solidarity, isolated workers from each other" (pp. 186–187). For a comparison of coalminers' activities in Germany and Britain see Gaston Rimlinger, "The Legitimation of Protest: A Comparative
Study in Labor History," *Comparative Studies in Society and History* 2, no. 3 (April 1960).
   [26] Moore, *Injustice*, p. 260.

that he views as crucial for sustaining standards of injustice are remarkably similar to those underlying organization.

Coalminers had rich traditions of collective organization to draw on. The Knappschaften, which provided miners with benefits and economic security on the lines of a closed and privileged craft guild; the Gedinge, a form of collective bargaining predating unions that expressed the solidarity of face-to-face work groups; the Berggesetz, the framework of legislation that ordered productive relations in mining: each of these expressed and, at the same time, buttressed the sense of collective identity among coalminers and provided them with concrete standards against which they could judge their fate. The influence of these traditions was all the greater because the miners' situation in the workplace did not change greatly in the tremendous expansion of coal production in these years. The absence of dramatic technological innovation protected the coalminers' strong occupational community. Their traditional skills, shared sense of danger, and enforced mutual dependence continued as the scale of production grew.

Iron and steelworkers were in a vastly different position. They were almost wholly bereft of collective traditions, and those that they did have were obliterated with the introduction of mass production in new plants from the 1880s. The resulting labor force was closely supervised, split, and isolated in different parts of the plant and fragmented by a wide range of skills, pay scales, and prospects for promotion, all of which, according to Moore, "must have rendered very difficult any sense of common fate as the basis for collective action."[27]

The social isolation and rootlessness of groups such as iron and steelworkers has been regarded as a recipe for political radicalism by scholars writing in the tradition of Emile Durkheim.[28] According to Durkheim, the advancing division of labor strains traditional social institutions and shared social consciousness, creating anomie, antisocial forms of behavior, and extensive conflict.[29] In the words of one much-quoted study that develops this theme:

---

[27] Ibid., p. 273.

[28] Chalmers Johnson, *Revolutionary Change* (Boston: Little, Brown, 1966); Clark Kerr, John Dunlop, Frederick Harbison, and Charles Myers, *Industrialism and Industrial Man* (Cambridge, Mass.: Harvard University Press, 1960); William Kornhauser, *The Politics of Mass Society* (New York: Free Press, 1959).

[29] Emile Durkheim, *The Division of Labor in Society* (New York: Macmillan, 1933), bk. 3, and *Suicide: A Study in Sociology* (Glencoe, Ill.: Free Press, 1951), p. 253.

The wrenching from the old and the groping for the new in the industrializing communities create a variety of frustrations, fears, uncertainties, resentments, aggressions, pressures, new threats and risks, new problems, demands and expectations upon workers-in-process, their families and work groups. . . . The surface may be quiet by virtue of strong controls, dedication to a national dream or an ideology, a sense of futility or resignation, or on account of hopes spurred by small tangible evidences of improvements. But beneath the exterior is always latent protest, seething and simmering, to erupt in violence or to overflow in indolence in times of crisis or tension.[30]

In recent years this view of working-class radicalism has born the brunt of substantial criticism from political scientists, sociologists, and social historians. A variety of studies have revealed that it was not the isolated and uprooted proletarian who was the archetypal radical but rather the artisan or handworker, rooted in a close-knit community, who desperately sought to defend himself against the threat of being reduced to the proletarian.[31]

This conception of the sources of radicalism has carried the day too completely. There can be little doubt that the depressed artisan and handworker provided a core of political protest, particularly in the early stages of industrialization. But there is much evidence that workers who lacked communitarian roots were also present in revolts against established authority. An open-textured approach to working-class political activity must try to find room for both types of radical orientation.

Workers who lacked the capacity to organize were unlikely to be able to mount sustained political opposition over an extended period, but they provided volatile support for a variety of radical political movements. Although political apathy is the most common expression of lack of collective identity and powerlessness, it is far from the only one. The other face of impotence is revolt, the sudden explosion of deep-seated grievances that cannot be expressed through less violent channels. There is always an element of unpredictability in such revolt, but it seems most likely in times of social and political dislocation when old inevitabilities, constraints, and threats suddenly disappear.[32] Thus, the previously silent Ruhr iron

[30] Kerr et al., *Industrialism and Industrial Man*, pp. 205–206.
[31] Calhoun, *The Question of Class Struggle*; Tilly, *From Mobilization to Revolution*; and Crew, *Town in the Ruhr*, take up this issue directly.
[32] See, for example, Tilly, *From Mobilization to Revolution*, pp. 202–204.

and steelworkers erupted in support of the extreme Left and the movement for plant councils as the old order crumbled in the final stages of the First World War.[33]

Under exceptionally favorable circumstances, unorganized workers have sometimes been able to exert leverage in the market and engage in successful strikes for better wages and working conditions. This is a transitory condition, usually arising during an economic boom when the balance of market power is most favorable to workers. Unless they are able to utilize their surgent economic power to build organization, the leverage of such workers lasts only as long as the economic boom. Lacking stable defenses in the labor market, unorganized workers are swept forward and backward by changing economic conditions.

The participation of unorganized and weakly organized workers provides a key to explaining radical and revolutionary episodes in Western societies. The two most revolutionary movements in the societies discussed here, the Works Council movement in Germany from 1916 and the Industrial Workers of the World in the United States from 1906, were movements encompassing previously unorganized workers who fought against established unions and institutionalized channels of bargaining.

The iron and steelworkers were typical of several groups of workers who participated in the revolutionary discontent in Germany after the First World War. In these years the radical Left had great success in mobilizing railroad workers, shop clerks, state employees, and workers in the chemical and textile industries.[34] These workers were driven by diverse concrete grievances, but they appear to have had in common the experience of social isolation and division in the workplace and what Peter von Örtzen, in his study of plant councils, observes was "the first condition for penetration of council ideas . . . the absence of trade union organization and the protection that it provided."[35]

---

[33] Moore, *Injustice*, pp. 318–320.

[34] Peter von Örtzen, *Betriebsräte in der Novemberrevolution* (Berlin: J.H.W. Dietz, 1976), chap. 12. A study of the social backgrounds of those killed during the revolution in Berlin reveals that active participants tended to be young (60 percent were less than thirty-one years old) and geographically mobile (63 percent were born outside Berlin), findings that are congruent with the hypothesis that revolutionary activity was most common among those least integrated into a community setting.

[35] Ibid., p. 279. A similar social basis of revolt can be observed in other societies during these years. James Cronin has pointed out that "the prewar socialist and labor parties had their social roots among the skilled and the organized not just in France but in England, Germany, Italy, and Austria. The emergent factory proletariat, on

In the United States the revolutionary syndicalist Industrial Workers of the World had their strongest support among workers who were unable to create effective unions to press employers for decent working conditions. The most militant and loyal of the IWW's following worked in the lumber, sawmill, and construction camps, and in the metal ore mines and agricultural regions of the West. These were migratory workers without fixed social roots, shifting from place to place in search of work. The unions they formed were fiercely opposed by employers, particularly the national corporations that came to dominate the mining industry from the 1890s. The individualistic resistance to arbitrary authority that had long been a characteristic of such workers was intensified in the decades around the turn of the twentieth century under conditions of rapid economic growth, extreme social dislocation, and the widening gulf between worker and employer. In the East the IWW found support mainly among new immigrants and blacks. There, as in the West, the union stood up for those excluded from the mainstream of American society and who, for one reason or another, were unable to create stable organizations to defend themselves in the labor market.[36]

The Condemned

Groups of artisans and workers who formed close-knit occupational communities were strongly placed to express their demands

the other hand, had remained largely unorganized and unrepresented. When the wartime labor shortage gave these workers some additional social leverage, they organized massively and became the core, of not always the articulate leadership, of the post war insurgency." See James E. Cronin, "Labor Insurgency and Class Formation: Comparative Perspectives on the Crisis of 1917–1920 in Europe," in James E. Cronin and Carmen Siriani, eds., *Work, Community, and Power: The Experience of Labor in Europe and America, 1900–1925* (Philadelphia: Temple University Press, 1983), p. 35.

[36] See Melvyn Dubofsky, *We Shall Be All: A History of the Industrial Workers of the World* (Chicago: Quadrangle Books, 1969), pp. 7–9, and Larry Peterson, "One Big Union in International Perspective: Revolutionary Industrial Unionism, 1900–1925," in James E. Cronin and Carmen Sirianni, eds., *Work, Community, and Power: The Experience of Labor in Europe and America, 1900–1925* (Philadelphia: Temple University Press, 1983). As Mark Wyman in his book *Hard Rock Epic: Western Miners and the Industrial Revolution, 1860–1910* (Berkeley: University of California Press, 1979) has observed: "Radicalism, viewed in the context of the long-term experiences of hard-rock miners across the West, stemmed most immediately from a mounting sense of desperation among workmen who felt that they were suddenly losing their capacity to protect themselves in a world dominated by trusts and corporations that could count on government allies. Sensing this, they clutched at alternatives" (p. 227).

through unions. But that is not to say they could do so effectively. Organization provides the capacity for strategy, but the success of that strategy depends upon a variety of conditions, including the power and determination of employers, conditions in the labor market, and the orientation of the state. The heart of the matter is that the organizational strength of a union is a necessary condition for its effectiveness in the labor market, but it is not a sufficient condition. Sweeping innovations in the division of labor may render carefully guarded skill and apprenticeship regulations useless; rapidly changing tastes or new products may suddenly shrink the demand for certain skills; the nationalization, or internationalization, of competition may increase the militancy of employers, even to the point that they refuse to deal with unions, or the supply of labor in an occupation may be hopelessly flooded by immigrants or those displaced from other occupations.

The combination of union organization and weakness in the labor market appears important in explaining divergencies from economistic unionism and political reformism in Britain and the United States. Chartism, which was the largest radical working-class movement in nineteenth-century Britain and which departed significantly from the later development of reformist unionism, was supported predominantly by unions that were beaten down in the labor market. In the United States the principal opposition among unions to voluntarism before the First World War—the Knights of Labor and support for a third-party strategy within the AFL—was rooted among unions that faced particularly stiff opposition from employers or were subject to decisive changes in the division of labor.

In Britain, handloom weavers, whose conditions deteriorated drastically in the first half of the nineteenth century, provided the core of a series of radical movements from Luddism to Chartism. Their activity was essentially defensive; we do not hear much from them in intervals of relative prosperity.[37] But in recurring depressions they were spurred into action by cutthroat competition that screwed down their wages and forced them to add further to the labor surplus by working longer hours. Their response was typical of threatened handworkers and artisans; they tried to secure the legal enforcement of customary conditions of employment, first at the local level and later by petitioning Parliament. When these ef-

[37] H. A. Turner, *Trade Union Growth, Structure and Policy* (London: Allen & Unwin, 1962), pp. 75–78.

forts proved useless, they were forced back on their own resources, to large-scale strikes, demonstrations, and selective machine breaking. Finally, after they had learned the futility of resistance in the labor market, they turned, in sheer desperation, to political radicalism. From the 1830s, after the Reform Act had further shifted the political balance away from workers by enfranchising their employers and when the fate of handloom weavers in the emerging industrial order was sealed, weavers flocked to Chartism and to those of its leaders who advocated the use of physical rather than moral force.[38]

Chartism gained significant support from artisans who had the capacity to organize yet could not defend their jobs, wages, and working conditions. The advantages of sectional unionism were generally unavailable to the "lower" trades, such as tailors, shoemakers, and carpenters, whose occupations were invaded by "dishonorable" (i.e., unapprenticed) workers employed by subcontractors, garret masters, and sweaters to produce cheap goods. Once they realized that they could neither look to Parliament for protection nor defend themselves adequately in the labor market, they sought remedies through general unionism and a variety of radical political causes, including Chartism. Their unions were in the forefront of attempts to expand organization to all workers in their respective occupations, whether apprenticed or not, and to build federations encompassing several trades for mutual support.[39] These schemes were generally avoided by artisans in the "upper" trades, such as printing and engineering, where sectional unions were reasonably effective. Unions composed of artisans in these trades distanced themselves from Chartism.[40]

---

[38] Turner, *Trade Union Growth, Structure and Policy*, p. 103. See also Thompson, *The Making of the English Working Class*, chap. 9; Bythell, *The Handloom Weavers*, chap. 9; and Dorothy Thompson, *The Chartists* (New York: Pantheon Books, 1984), pp. 112–115.

[39] The mobilizing role of threatened artisans is stressed in the context of French class formation by Michael P. Hanagan, *The Logic of Solidarity: Artisans and Industrial Workers in Three French Towns, 1871–1914* (Urbana: University of Illinois Press, 1980), pp. 211–212.

[40] See A. E. Musson, *British Trade Unions, 1800–1875* (London: Macmillan, 1972), pp. 33, 46; Prothero, *Artisans and Politics in Nineteenth-Century London*, pp. 68–69, 300–301, and 332–338; Iowerth Prothero, "London Chartism and the Trades," *Economic History Review*, 2d series, vol. 24 (1971); Robert Sykes, "Early Chartism and Trade Unionism in South-East Lancashire," in James Epstein and Dorothy Thompson, eds.,

In the United States the Knights of Labor, which was the most impressive attempt to create a labor movement encompassing individual trades in any Western society in the nineteenth century, drew its support mainly from those unions that were under pressure in the labor market. As Leon Fink observes in his study of the Knights:

> The spreading confrontations with national corporate power, beginning in the 1870s, indicated just how much erosion had occurred in the position of those who relied on custom, skill, and moral censure as ultimate weapons. Industrial dilution of craft skills and a direct economic and political attack on union practices provided decisive proof to these culturally conservative workingmen of both the illegitimacy and ruthlessness of the growing power of capital. It was they, according to every recent study of late nineteenth-century laboring communities, who formed the backbone of local labor movements. The Knights were, therefore, first of all a coalition of reactivating, or already organized, trade unions.[41]

The hypothesis linking union market power to political activity is confirmed by John Laslett's analysis of the strength of socialism in six American unions from 1890 to 1918. He argues that the experience of threatening technological change, originating either in the labor market or product market, was a vital and common ingredient in the strength of the Left across his cases. The shoe industry and machine industry were transformed by the introduction of labor-saving machinery; the garment industry saw the growth of the sweating system as the market for ready-made clothes rapidly expanded; and both the coalmining and metal mining industries were subject to greater competitive pressures and the consequent determination on the part of employers and local governments to repress unions. Conversely, Laslett argues that the most decisive influence on the turn of unions in these industries away from political radicalism was the eventual establishment of collective bargaining relationships that gave workers the prospect of greater security of

---

The Chartist Experience: Studies in Working-Class Radicalism and Culture, 1830–1860 (London: Macmillan, 1982).

  [41] Fink, *Workingmen's Democracy*, p. 14. See also Alan Dawley, *Class and Community* (Cambridge, Mass.: Harvard University Press, 1976), especially pp. 228–229, which discuss shoemakers.

employment and amelioration of their conditions of employment through union activity in the labor market.[42]

The contrast between the ability to organize and weakness in the labor market was particularly acute in the early stages of industrialization, when settled modes of economic and social life were overturned by new methods of capitalist production and exchange. The corresponding political tensions were expressed in the desperate attempts of affected occupational communities to protect their skills and independence, their traditions and culture—in short, their way of life—against economic forces over which they had no control. For some communities that effort was intensified by the most elemental struggle of all, the struggle to avoid starvation.

It is not difficult to understand why groups that were condemned by the changing division of labor were radical. They had to try to recast the society in which they lived because immediate palliatives through labor market activity appeared to be hopeless. In many cases depressed handworkers dreamed of panaceas for their ills that appeared, even to many of their contemporaries, to be utopian, but the lack of viable alternatives allows us to see in their radical political activity an essential element of rationality. No complex line of reasoning or political sophistication was necessary to justify radical political activity for such groups. Their political concerns were squarely based on their concrete grievances and acute sense of injustice. In this vein George Rudé observes that Chartism was viewed by many of its adherents as a "knife and fork" question.[43] In the words of a radical journalist writing in 1838, Chartism was the means by which workers could "furnish their houses, clothe their backs, and educate their children."[44]

Because depressed artisans and outworkers lacked the possibility of defense as an isolated group, they provided the core support for broad social movements that appealed beyond sectional trade unionism to all those condemned by capitalism. E. P. Thompson writes of the handloom weavers that:

> As their way of life, in the better years, had been shared by the community, so their sufferings were those of the whole com-

[42] Laslett, *Labor and the Left*, pp. 300–301.

[43] George Rudé, *The Crowd in History, 1730–1848* (New York: John Wiley, 1964), p. 180.

[44] Quoted in R. Church, *Economic and Social Change in a Midland Town* (London: A. M. Kelly, 1966), p. 128.

munity; and they were reduced so low that there was no class of unskilled or casual laborers below them against which they had erected economic or social protective walls. This gave a particular moral resonance to their protest, whether voiced in Owenite or Biblical language; they appealed to essential rights and elementary notions of human fellowship and conduct rather than to sectional interests.[45]

Such analyses of the sources of radical discontent in England and elsewhere have led a number of scholars to argue that the decline of revolutionism in mature industrial societies was due to the eradication of traditional communities.[46] Although skilled workers in the new factories might be threatened by continuing economic development, they rarely faced the obliteration of their whole way of life. Unlike the handworker and the artisan, the factory worker, according to this view, did not find himself defending a traditional way of life against inexorable economic change. The factory worker attempted to improve his condition within the industrial order rather than by overthrowing it, and he could do this gradually through the exchange relationship in the labor market.

If it is not pressed too far this argument contains an important insight. Those who could adapt themselves and their organized defenses to the changing division of labor were generally content, as I argue below, to pursue improvements within the system of wage labor. But it is quite another thing to argue that backward-looking radicalism is unique to early industrialization. Strongly organized occupational communities with a vested interest in traditional industries are a feature of contemporary as well as preindustrial society. Coalminers, steelworkers, and shipbuilders are the most prominent examples of workers who have built particularly strong unions based in communities that were established as industrial societies matured. Although workers in contemporary Western societies are cushioned to some extent by state unemployment and welfare provisions, the restructuring of contemporary economies away from heavy industries is a process that appears to have some striking parallels to the upheavals of the Industrial Revolution. Contemporary industrial workers locked in stable and close-knit occupational communities, with correspondingly entrenched unions, have fought rearguard battles against economic change almost as intense

---

[45] Thompson, *The Making of the English Working Class*, p. 326.
[46] Calhoun, *The Question of Class Struggle*; Moore, *Injustice*, pp. 477–479.

as those fought by artisans and domestic workers more than a century ago.

The Adaptive

So far I have discussed groups of workers and artisans who had little collective control over their working lives, either because they lacked the ability to organize or because the forces they had to contend with swept away their defenses. But what of those groups who could adapt to the changing division of labor and project their influence over working conditions into the future through stable and effective unionism? Such groups formed an even smaller proportion of the work force than is indicated by the aggregate figures for union membership noted above, for they formed just one stream of unionism in the nineteenth century. But their historical importance is far greater than their numerical weight suggests, because in their struggle to defend and improve their working conditions while adapting to capitalism they were in the vanguard of the labor movement in Western Europe and North America.

Where gradual improvement in the labor market was possible, unions were generally content to pursue a sectional strategy of business unionism. Radical political involvement was the refuge of those who had few opportunities to defend their wages, working conditions, and self-respect in the labor market. As E. P. Thompson has argued:

> Each advance within the framework of capitalism simultaneously involved the working class far more deeply in the status quo. As they improved their position by organization, so they became more reluctant to engage in quixotic outbreaks which might jeopardize gains accumulated at such cost. Each assertion of working-class influence within the bourgeois-democratic state machine, simultaneously involved them as partners (even if antagonistic partners) in the running of the machine.[47]

Classical political economists argued that unions were anachronistic because they were unable to secure higher wages for their members in the long run, but workers themselves learned from experience that they could use their capacity for effective organiza-

[47] E. P. Thompson, "The Peculiarities of the English," in R. Miliband and J. Saville, eds., *The Socialist Register, 1965* (London: Merlin, 1965), pp. 343–344.

tion to press for higher wages, shorter hours, healthier working conditions, a measure of respect from employers, and greater control over their working lives. In short, they were drawn into the struggle to improve their conditions under capitalism instead of trying to abolish the system of wage labor. If we wish to find the first sources of reformism among workers in Western societies we need look no further than their earliest successes in creating viable and effective unions in the early nineteenth century and in some cases the eighteenth century.

A strong bargaining capacity in the labor market was a vital ingredient in the ability of workers to advance within the framework of capitalism. But it rested on broader conditions, the most important of which were the basic rights of economic and political citizenship. Where workers were denied the freedom to combine in the labor market, and to use their combinations to press their claims against employers and the state, the moderating influence of a strong bargaining position was negated. Under these conditions, analyzed in the next chapter, unions had to try to change the rules of the game, and this led them away from sectional market strategies to support broad political movements.[48]

Extending the work of theorists of industrial relations, it is possible to indicate one important source of political differentiation among adaptive unions that reflects the basic distinction between craft unionism and industrial unionism.[49]

The differences between craft unions and industrial unions are rooted in their patterns of membership, their orientation to nonmembers, and, above all, in the distinctive strategies they pursued in the labor market. In each of these respects craft unions can aptly be described as closed. They restricted membership to workers in a particular occupation, leaving those outside to their own resources. These unions were composed of the aristocrats of labor, relatively skilled workers who tended to be the most educated and have the highest status jobs. The strategy of craft unions was closed in the sense that they attempted to improve conditions of employment by restricting the supply of labor available to employers by making it difficult for them to hire workers who did not belong to the craft. These unions were not simply bargaining agents for workers con-

[48] Lipset, "Radicalism or Reformism," pp. 6–12; Geary, *European Labour Protest, 1848–1939*, pp. 58–63.

[49] This distinction is developed most carefully in Turner, *Trade Union Growth, Structure and Policy.*

cerning wages and employment conditions but were, in addition, intimately concerned with the organization of production on the shop floor. Their strategy emphasized the boundaries between their craft and other types of labor, and this led them to battle employers over a wide range of control issues including apprenticeship regulations and traditions of craft autonomy.

Rather than bargain with employers collectively in formal negotiations, craft unions usually preferred to estalish minimum standards of employment unilaterally and support those of its members who could not find work meeting those standards. Most of these unions maintained an extensive benefit system to provide their members with the means to refuse substandard wages or working conditions. Traveling benefits allowed artisans ("journeymen") to find work where it was available and thus avoid competing with fellow members of the occupation where the supply of labor exceeded the demand. The provision of an extensive system of benefits expressed the sense of mutual obligation within the occupational community while it provided private incentives for joining the union.

The closed character of craft unions led them to the paradoxical position of battling employers so as to remain above the unskilled proletariat. On the one hand, craft unions were brought into direct conflict with employers in the struggle to control production and the supply of labor; on the other hand, they were determined to exclude unskilled workers from their job territory. Although workers in closed unions were often conscious of their status as labor aristocrats, they did not avoid conflict if their vital interests were affected. Closed unions could be extremely militant, and they have been associated with some of the most bitter strikes in American and Western European labor history. But the struggle of workers in these unions was to remain above the common laborer, to preserve their niche in the division of labor. Their motivating fear was that of losing their craft, and, as a result, being driven down into the lumpen proletariat.[50] Many socialists viewed this strategy as irrational because it combined militance and sectionalism, yet these ambiguities were a response to the opportunities and constraints that faced craft unions in the labor market.[51]

---

[50] Andrew Dawson, "The Parameters of Craft Consciousness: The Social Outlook of the Skilled Worker, 1890–1920," in Dirk Hoerder, ed., *American Labor and Immigrant History, 1877–1920* (Urbana, Ill.: University of Illinois Press, 1983).

[51] Charles Sabel makes this point from the perspective of the individual worker's psychology in *Work and Politics*, p. 176.

Workers who were less able to control the supply of labor into their occupation, either because they lacked traditional barriers to occupational mobility or because they were simply less skilled, could not pursue a strategy of closed unionism. If they were to defend or improve their working conditions, they had to put pressure on employers directly, and this induced them to try to organize all those workers hired by their employers, regardless of occupation. This strategy is aptly termed open unionism for it is marked by expansionism on the part of the union, an effort to make up for its lack of control of entry into the occupation through strength of numbers.

Because open unions could not influence the labor market from the inside by controlling the supply of labor, they focussed on enforcing changes externally, through legislation and by threatening employers with the consequences of a complete shutdown of their enterprises. What they could not achieve through the subtle exclusive tactics adopted by closed craft unions, they had to make up for by organizing all the workers in a particular industry and using their broad-based solidarity and force of numbers to put maximum pressure on employers.[52] Both closed and open unions politicize the labor market by introducing power relations in place of the impersonal logic of market competition. But open unions have had to introduce political considerations in a more explicit way, by force of numbers rather than by controlling the supply of labor, and this has led them to support extensive political regulation of the labor market.

The contrasting labor market strategies of closed and open unions created differences in political resources that reinforced these orientations. The means by which open unions compensated for their inability to control the supply of labor gave them sources of political pressure denied to most closed unions. Open unions were the political heavyweights of labor; their inclusive strategy led them to encompass much larger constituencies and have greater financial resources than closed unions. Moreover, many open unions could take political advantage of the fact that they were based on industry rather than occupation. The geographical distribution of the membership of an industry-based union mirrors that of the industry in question, and where the industry is concentrated, as is generally the case in coalmining and textiles, the union may find

[52] See Turner, *Trade Union Growth, Structure and Policy*, pt. 5, chap. 1.

that the extension of manhood suffrage presents it with direct access to the legislature.

Both closed and open unions were brought into conflict with employers, but their strategies led them to face other workers very differently. The strategy of closed unionism was based on the defense of a niche in the division of labor, and this brought it into conflict not only with employers wishing to standardize labor but also with other less privileged workers who might break into a particular job territory. Open unions, on the other hand, had no preferential job territory to defend; they had to try to exercise overt pressure against employers through strength of numbers and organization. This strategy implied a greater sensitivity to the benefits of inclusiveness, of working-class solidarity in pressing for standards that apply to all workers equally.

CONCLUSION

While there have been sustained efforts to generalize about the political orientations of labor movements across Western societies, the comparative analysis of individual unions has received much less attention. The former line of analysis presupposes far greater homogeneity of working-class political orientation than has actually been the case. National characterizations of union orientation are really aggregations of the diverse activities of individual unions and groups of workers. National tendencies can be observed and legitimately contrasted, but we should not forget that individual unions have been a more important locus of decision making than the union movements they have formed at the national level. In this respect the study of political parties cannot provide a model for that of unions. Political parties tend to be centered in national politics in a way that few unions have been. To the extent that the comparative politics of unions has borrowed the methodological presuppositions of party-political analysis it has ignored a vital source of diversity at the level of individual unions.

This chapter advances the claim that it is possible to generalize about the political orientations of individual unions and that these generalizations hold up across Britain, Germany, and the United States. In coming to grips with variations within Western societies in the nineteenth and early twentieth centuries I have conceptualized the structure of constraints and opportunities facing groups of workers in terms of their capacity to organize and control their working lives. The line of argument developed here links the political orientations of workers to their occupational communities, their situation in the labor market, and their resources in the workplace. What appears to be crucial in the logic of working-class political activity is the interaction between the ability of workers to act collectively and their ability to do so effectively in the labor market.

From workers who lacked ties of occupational community and were unable to create or sustain unions we hear very little. Their response tended either to be one of political apathy or, if they managed to act in concert, it tended to be in sharp, but short-lived, bursts of political opposition and violence. They could be mobilized in times of crisis to fill the streets but lacked the social glue to sustain political opposition on a day-to-day basis. By contrast, those workers who formed close-knit occupational communities and could adapt their collective capacity to the challenge of controlling their fate in the labor market were in the vanguard of business unionism and labor reformism. Finally, sustained political radicalism was strongest where the impotence of the unorganized and the organized strength of the adaptive were combined. Workers who formed strong occupational communities but who were overwhelmed by economic change had the capacity to act, yet were denied the ability to defend their jobs and conditions of work directly in the labor market. Their ability to organize rested on the stability of their social relations, yet the ongoing division of labor against which they attempted to defend themselves undermined their traditional communities. They were, in other words, caught in the tension between tradition and change in modern society.

This chapter has analyzed the social and economic situation of groups of workers as a basic influence on their political orientations without reference to national political factors and the broader context of political freedom or repression within particular countries. Yet no analysis of working-class political activity can afford to ignore the structure of political alternatives at the national level. Sectoral and national factors both need to be given weight if we wish to understand union political activity. The labor market strategies discussed in this chapter are inconceivable without basic political freedoms, including the right to combine and strike. In the following chapter I analyze the influence of varying national legal contexts on unions, their relations with each other, and their relations with political parties.

CHAPTER 2

UNIONS, REPRESSION, AND POLITICS

No matter how much a government attempts to leave the regulation of wages and working conditions to the market, it is inevitably involved in relations between employers and unions. As the source of authoritative legislation in a society, even the minimal state cannot avoid the crucial role of regulating the legal rights and status of labor market organizations. The consequences of this for union political orientation are intensified because unions are extraordinarily sensitive to their legal environment. The rights of workers to combine in the labor market and defend their interests by striking are a *sine qua non* of trade unionism. Moreover, further legal rights and immunities are necessary if a union is to effectively act on behalf of its members in the labor market. The right to picket and to boycott; the right to maintain the union or closed shop; legal immunity from prosecution for economic damages resulting from its lawful activities: these basic freedoms constitute the minimum legal framework for effective trade unionism.

In this chapter I will examine the consequences of variations in the legal context of industrial relations in the nineteenth and early twentieth centuries. The basic supposition is that such variations are vital to an understanding of three key aspects of union political activity: (1) relations among unions, and particularly the willingness of unions to come together to form and strengthen their national federations; (2) the orientation of unions to the state and its legitimacy; and (3) the type of links between unions and political parties.[1]

---

[1] This analysis can draw on several sources, although there is no detailed overview of the subject. The most comprehensive is Seymour Martin Lipset, "Radicalism or Reformism: The Sources of Working-Class Politics," *American Political Science Review* 77, no. 1 (March 1983). Robert J. Goldstein, *Political Repression in Nineteenth-Century Europe* (London: Croom Helm, 1983), provides a useful summary of repressive measures that were taken against unions. See also Gerald Friedman, "Politics and Unions" (Ph.D. diss., Harvard University, 1986); Robert Liebman, "Repression Strategies and Working-Class Protest," *Social Science History* 4, no. 1 (February 1980); and Dick Geary, *European Labour Protest, 1848–1939* (London: Croom Helm, 1981), pp. 58–65.

The history of national union federation has been profoundly influenced by the common experience of threats to the legal status of unions. Laws concerning the rights of unions are comprehensive in coverage, and regardless of differences in membership, structure, or market power, unions share the same formal legal context, in which to act. The need to change laws that restrict union activity is, therefore, likely to be shared by all unions in a given country, including those otherwise content to pursue their sectional interests in the labor market. This source of common purpose was crucial to the establishment of the Trades Union Congress and the American Federation of Labor. In Britain, as we shall see in the case studies below, the Trades Union Congress, and later the Labour party itself, were supported by unions in response to threats to their legal status. A similar dynamic can be seen in the growth and institutionalization of the AFL, with the constant concern of unions to preserve their legal breathing space so that they could go about their business undisturbed by government or the courts.

In Britain and the United States the legal context of industrial relations presented a challenge to unions that drew them into national federations despite their unwillingness to take an active role in party politics. Paradoxically, unions in these societies created national political agencies not because they wanted to press substantive demands on governments or fulfill political dreams but so that they could pursue sectional strategies without external hindrance. The role of the TUC and the AFL was circumscribed to defending unions in the political arena and settling their jurisdictional disputes. That which individual unions might do for themselves was denied to the national body. On questions concerning the day-to-day activities of their constituents, the TUC and the AFL had to lead from behind, always wary of stepping on the toes of individual unions.

Although the responsibilities and power of national union federations in Britain and the United States have grown in recent decades, their present strengths and weaknesses reveal the conditions under which they emerged. On legal issues they tend to be vigorous and assertive—as was the case, for example, in the TUC's reaction to the 1971 Industrial Relations Act—but on wage issues they are compelled to tread cautiously for fear of going beyond the lowest common denominator of their memberships. The defense of union legal rights remains a source of unity and common purpose; wage issues, by contrast, are still a source of heterogeneity and potential conflict among unions.

There are strong grounds for supposing that the legal position of unions influences their political orientation to the state in addition to their willingness to form national federations. As Seymour Martin Lipset sums up his broad-ranging analysis of the sources of working-class radicalism and reformism: "The greater the duration and intensity of state repression of working-class economic and political rights, the more likely workers were to respond favorably to revolutionary doctrines."[2] We may hypothesize that the denial of basic union rights engendered radicalism on the following grounds. First, the act of repression was itself likely to arouse in workers feelings of deprivation and resentment. Workers felt the injustice of their economic conditions all the more acutely under repression, for they were explicitly denied the chance to defend themselves through their own organizational efforts. The consequences of this would be all the more acute if, in addition, workers were excluded from political citizenship. Second, to the extent that legal repression weakened unions, so the most politically active and ambitious workers were denied a channel of upward mobility and prestige within the union movement. Third, the denial of basic union rights was likely to reduce both the pressure on employers to conciliate worker interests and the ability of workers to gain a share of economic power and responsibility in the society.[3]

The radicalizing effect of repression was noted by observers of unionism in the nineteenth century. Francis Place, the architect of the legislation repealing the repressive Combination Acts in 1824, observed that:

> The laws against combination were inimical to the working people in many respects. They induced them to break and disregard the laws. They made them suspect the intentions of every man who tendered his services. They made them hate their employers with a rancour which nothing else could have produced. And they made them hate those of their own class who refused to join them, to such an extent as cordially to seek to do them mischief.[4]

[2] Lipset, "Radicalism or Reformism," p. 6.
[3] See ibid., p. 2.
[4] Graham Wallas, *The Life of Francis Place* (London: Allen & Unwin, 1951), p. 239.

The more intensive and longer lasting state repression, the more drastic the consequences. Where the right to combine in the labor market was severely restricted, the decision to act in politics was forced on a trade union. Whether it liked it or not, the union became a political institution beyond the pale of legality; it had to change the rules of the political game before it could act in the market. Hence, repression narrowed the strategic choices available to unions, for it diminished the viability of business unionism. Under extreme repression the possibility of "pure and simple" unionism unencumbered by political involvement simply disappeared.

In practice, the effects of repression upon unions varied with their ability to hide their organizational activities from the watchful eye of authorities. Unions that were based in close-knit occupational communities were thus in a better position to defend their members under repressive legal conditions than were unions representing a large membership tied together only by formal organization itself. The more that unions were expressions of deeper social ties, the less they had to rely on membership lists, public meetings, union literature, and other manifestations of a formally structured organization that could be infiltrated and suppressed by police.[5] But such differences in the capacity to withstand repression were not generally great enough to drive a wedge among unions. Although the actual effects of state repression varied in intensity, all unions were disadvantaged to some degree, and none stood to lose under a freer legal climate.

In this respect the consequences of the legal climate for union political orientation were markedly different from the consequences of the labor market. As argued in the previous chapter, the labor market was a source of heterogeneity among unions. The ability of groups of workers to create organizations strong enough, and stable enough, to influence their wages and working conditions depended upon a variety of conditions that varied decisively from group to group. Some groups of workers were able to adapt their unions to the changing division of labor, others were condemned by economic developments outside of their control, while the majority remained unorganized. A repressive legal environment, on the other hand, appears to be a source of unity among unions.

[5] E. P. Thompson, *The Making of the English Working Class* (London: Penguin Books 1968), pp. 552–553, emphasizes the contrast between the degree of repression experienced by artisans, on the one hand, and that experienced by outworkers and factory workers, on the other.

Repression reduced the ability of privileged groups of workers to create effective sectional unions. At the extreme, all groups of workers were placed in a similarly disadvantaged position in the labor market. From this standpoint, then, repression tended to create the kind of commonality among workers that Marx believed to be the task of labor market homogenization and alienation. But the difference in the source of such commonality is important, for the trend in most Western societies over the period as a whole was towards greater legal toleration of unions. Instead of increased uniformity of powerlessness among workers, the late nineteenth and early twentieth centuries saw increased numbers of workers who were able to exercise some control over their jobs and conditions of employment through union organization.

Given sufficient market power and political space, unions tended to represent their members in the labor market in a sectional fashion, wary of both calls for strong national federation and the leadership of workers' political parties. As Dick Geary observes in his survey of working-class political activity in Europe: "To a large extent labor protest remained purely industrial where it could satisfy its needs through the application of industrial muscle. The absence of such muscle, however, or its thwarting by laws and the intransigence of employers, transformed attitudes and the arena of conflict."[6]

Finally, the legal context of industrial relations appears to have influenced the character of union/party relations. To the extent that unions suffered severe and continuous repression, they tended to rely on political parties for leadership. Conversely, the earlier that unions were tolerated by the state, the more likely they were to establish themselves independently of political parties and pursue autonomous policies. Under extreme repression the challenge facing unions was that of all working-class organizations, namely to change the law, or failing this, to change those who made the law, or if neither of these were possible, to change the way in which lawmakers were chosen. These were expressly political tasks involving organization and pressure at the national level. These tasks were more amenable to political parties than to unions themselves.

Although the goals of party and union tend to differ when both are tolerated by the state, under repression there is much less space for diversity. Extreme repression diminishes the difference be-

---

[6] Geary, *European Labour Protest, 1848–1939*, p. 69.

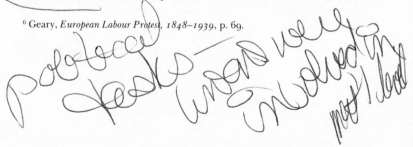

tween a trade union and a workers' political party. As Lenin observed in the context of Tsarist Russia: "The yoke of the autocracy appears ... to obliterate all distinctions between a Social-Democratic organization and trade unions, because *all* workers' associations and *all* circles are prohibited, and because the principle manifestation and weapon of the workers' economic struggle—the strike—is regarded as a criminal (and sometimes even as a political) offense."[7]

The intensity and duration of state repression have profoundly shaped the strategies adopted by unions. Where repression suppressed the growth of autonomous and effective unions, as it did in Germany before 1890, unions were dominated by political parties. Unions were led to radicalism both by the influence of party ideology and by the oppression they felt under an authoritarian political system that denied workers political and economic citizenship. Under such circumstances it seems sensible to consider revolutionary socialism not merely as an impractical flight of utopianism, or even an ideology imposed by party hegemony, but as a more or less rational response to constraints that straightjacketed the union's choice.

Where repression was shorter-lived and less intensive, as it was in the United States and Britain, the emergence of independent unions was hampered but not suppressed. Autonomous and sectional business unions had the legal room to grow and prosper, and when the need for national federations was eventually felt, they were based on the principle of individual union autonomy. Likewise, when political parties sought working-class support, they had to reckon with the already formed loyalties of organized workers to unions that were intent on guarding their independence.

In the remainder of this chapter I shall examine the effects of variations in the legal climate of industrial relations more closely by looking at the contrasting development of union movements in Germany, Britain, and the United States during the nineteenth and early twentieth centuries.

GERMANY: REPRESSION AND SOCIALIST UNIONISM

Until the very last decade of the nineteenth century German unions had to contend with almost continuous state repression.

---

[7] V. I. Lenin, *What Is To Be Done?* (Peking: Foreign Languages Press, 1973).

Only in the immediate wake of the 1848 Revolution and in the half dozen years after 1868 were unions able to organize and carry out their activities openly in the labor market without fear of legal dissolution.

Unions initially were subject to traditional absolutist controls applied to all political associations independent of the state. In Prussia these controls were systemized in the Prussian Civil Code of 1794 that, in reaction to the specter of the French Revolution, expressly prohibited all "secret assemblies."[8] With the first manifestation of economic conflict between masters and artisans in various industries in the early 1840s, the fledgling trade unions were singled out for novel and harsher treatment. In 1840 the Federal Congress of German States unified the policies of several principalities including Prussia against workers "who have committed offenses against the State Governments through participation in illicit combinations, journeymen's societies, and boycotts."[9] Strikes were specifically prohibited as "rebellious disturbances against the constituted authorities," and workers' organizations, including mutual benefit societies and educational associations that sometimes served as fronts for union activity, were placed under continuous supervision.[10] In 1845 articles 181 to 184 of the Industrial Code prohibited meetings of workers to obtain better working conditions and decreed that workers' combinations of any kind had to have police authorization.

After a brief respite from repression in 1848 and 1849 workers and their organizations bore the brunt of middle-class defeat and subsequent retreat from the political sphere. In the 1850s, under the "stamp of the victorious reaction" (as Hermann Wagener triumphantly called it), the old prohibitions were carried out with renewed vigor.[11] Official police activities of authorization and super-

<hr />

[8] Elisabeth Todt and Hans Radandt, *Zur Frühgeschichte der deutschen Gewerkschaftsbewegung, 1800–1849* (Berlin/DDR: Die Freie Gewerkschaft, 1950), pp. 46–48; Reinhard Bendix, *Nation Building and Citizenship* (Berkeley: University of California Press, 1969), pp. 98–99.

[9] Elisabeth Todt, *Die Gewerkschaftliche Betätigung in Deutschland von 1850 bis 1859* (Berlin/DDR: Die Freie Gewerkschaft, 1950), p. 30.

[10] Todt, *Die Gewerkschaftliche Betätigung in Deutschland von 1850 bis 1859*, pp. 31–32. These police activities were supplemented on occasion by military intervention. See Alf Lüdtke, "The Role of State Violence in the Period of Transition to Industrial Capitalism: The Example of Prussia from 1815 to 1848," *Social History* 4 (May 1979); and Charles Tilly, Louise Tilly, and Richard Tilly, *Rebellious Century* (Cambridge, Mass.: Harvard University Press, 1975), pp. 219–225.

[11] Hans-Ulrich Wehler, *Das deutsche Kaiserreich, 1871–1918* (Göttingen: Vandenhöck & Ruprecht, 1973), p. 30.

vision were supplemented in most of the German states by summary arrest and imprisonment or deportation, frequent searches of members' homes and association offices, and more thorough restriction of press freedom.[12]

Under these harsh circumstances unions able to regulate working conditions autonomously on the basis of small cohesive workplace organizations were best equipped to survive. But of this select subset of trade unions only the printing and cigarmaking unions had additional advantages in the labor market that allowed them to build effective organizations. Cabinet makers, leather-glove makers, ships-carpenters, cobblers, hatters, and certain other groups of artisans have left us evidence of intermittent strike activity, but they had to withstand the advance of technology within their trades as well as state repression.[13] From the remaining groups of less-skilled workers who, of course, constituted the overwhelming majority of the working classes, we hear almost nothing. For them, any form of organized defense in the labor market was out of the question.

The relaxation of the laws governing workers' associations in 1868 was followed by a groundswell of spontaneous trade union activity. But by this time the two German workers' parties, the Lassallean Allgemeiner Deutscher Arbeiterverein and the Marxist-leaning Sozialdemokratische Arbeiterpartei, were already established, and they wasted no time in forming constituent union organizations. In the same year they were followed by the middle-class Progressive party. Unions in Germany emerged under a constellation of political leadership that in each case viewed them as a mere appendage to a greater political cause.[14]

---

[12] Todt, *Die Gewerkschaftliche Betätigung in Deutschland von 1850 bis 1859*, pp. 43–47. Siegfried Nestriepke, *Die Gewerkschaftsbewegung* (Stuttgart: E. H. Moritz, 1922), 1: 168–175.

[13] In addition to the previously cited writings of Elisabeth Todt and Siegfried Nestriepke, see Jürgen Kuczynski, *Die Geschichte de Lage der Arbeiter unter dem Kapitalismus* (Berlin/DDR: Akademie-Verlag, 1961/1962), vols. 1 and 2; and H. Müller, *Geschichte der deutschen Gewerkschaften bis zum Jahre 1878* (Berlin: Verlag der Buchhandlung Vorwarts, P. Singer, 1918). There is a wealth of ideographical historical literature on individual trade unions and trade unions in individual localities in Germany, much of it written before 1914. There is much less on the unorganized, who have left us fewer sources of information about their working lives. But see W. Brepohl, *Industrievolk im Wandel von der agraren zur industriellen Daseinsform dargestellt am Ruhrgebiet* (Tübingen: Mohr, 1957); W. Fischer, "Innerbetrieblicher and sozialer Status der frühen Fabrikarbeiterschaft," in W. Fischer and G. Bajor, eds., *Die Soziale Frage* (Stuttgart: Köhler, 1967); Hieko Haumann, ed., *Arbeiteralltag in Stadt und Land: Neue Wege der Geschichtsschreibung* (Berlin: Argument Verlag, 1982).

[14] H. Langerhans, "Richtungsgewerkschaft and gewerkschaftliche Autonomie,

The climate of relative tolerance ended in the economic down-turn of 1873/1874 and the campaign led by Tessendorf, the Prussian minister of internal affairs, to increase the severity with which the existing laws against workers' economic combinations were applied. Four years later Bismarck succeeded in gaining legislative approval of his Anti-Socialist Law banning all "social democratic, socialist, or communist associations, meetings, and printed materials."[15] This law was intended to eradicate the Social Democratic party rather than the unions affiliated to it, but when it was put into practice it was the unions that suffered the most. Of the seventeen social democratic trade union organizations, with a total membership of about 50,000, all but one was suppressed in 1878.[16]

Many unions managed to reconstitute themselves after 1880 by changing their organizational form and statutes to eliminate their former political character. But their political neutrality was only formal; until 1890, when the Reichstag refused to extend the Anti-Socialist Law, the Social Democratic party and its unions were symbiotically fused in a strong and insular subculture of benefit associations, sport clubs, worker libraries, and pubs.[17] As Jürgen Kocka has argued, state repression strengthened the consciousness among groups of workers and journeymen that they constituted a distinctive and downtrodden class: "Government supervision and repression did not focus on specific occupations but on journeymen and workers in general. Probably this helped them to identify as workers instead of as members of particular crafts or special skill groups."[18]

1890–1914," *International Review of Social History* 2 (1957); Dieter Fricke, *Die deutsche Arbeiterbewegung, 1869–1914* (Berlin/DDR: Dietz Verlag, 1976), chap. 12; and Wolfgang Schröder, *Partie und Gewerkschaften* (Berlin/DDR: Verlag Tribune, 1975), chaps. 1 and 2.

[15] Karl Born, *Von der Reichsgründung bis zum Ersten Weltkrieg* (Stuttgart: Deutscher Taschenbuch Verlag, 1970), p. 129.

[16] Gerhard A. Ritter and Klaus Tenfelde, "Der Durchbruch der Freien Gewerkschaften Deutschlands zur Massenbewegung im letzten Viertel des 19.Jahrhunderts," in H. O. Vetter, ed., *Vom Sozialistengesetz zur Mitbestimmung* (Köln: Bund Verlag, 1975), p. 69; Vernon L. Lidtke, *The Outlawed Party: Social Democracy in Germany, 1878–1890* (Princeton, N.J.: Princeton University Press, 1966), pp. 80–81.

[17] Vernon L. Lidtke, *The Alternative Culture: Socialist Labor in Imperial Germany* (New York: Oxford University Press, 1985); Peter Lösche, "Stages in the Evolution of the German Labor Movement," in A. Sturmthal and J. G. Scoville, eds., *The International Labor Movement in Transition: Essays on Asia, Europe, and South America* (Urbana, Ill.: University of Illinois Press, 1973), p. 109; Wehler, *Das Deutsche Kaiserreich, 1871–1918*, pp. 88–89.

[18] Jürgen Kocka, "Problems of Working-Class Formation in Germany: The Early

During these years, there was an intense debate within the socialist movement on the future of the unions and the extent to which
they might turn away from revolutionary socialism to what reformists such as Heinrich Öhme called a "practical economic strategy"
once "the chains of political tutelage" were removed.[19] But under
repression the initiative lay with those who argued that there was
little alternative for unions but revolutionary resistance against the
state and subordination to the party. This was even recognized by
the Berlin Office of the President of the Prussian Police Force
which, in a series of remarkable reports, argued that "the apparent
ineffectuality of all other means available to improve [workers']
conditions has continually led new adherents to Socialism, and has
strengthened the conviction of previous adherents that in Socialism
alone lies salvation."[20] In a similar vein, but from a wider historical
perspective, Franz Mehring, the Marxist historian of the SPD, argued that union subordination to the party was a practical necessity:

> The German bourgeoisie renounced the struggle against ab-
> solutism and feudalism, so the working class had to throw their
> collective weight into this struggle to win the freedom of move-
> ment which they required in a modern civil society for their
> trade union organization. The most elementary instinct of self-
> preservation demanded of proletarian class conflict that politi-
> cal organization be placed over trade union organization.[21]

Years, 1800–1875," in Ira Katznelson and Aristide R. Zolberg, eds., *Working-Class Formation: Nineteenth-Century Patterns in Western Europe and the United States* (Princeton,
N.J.: Princeton University Press, 1986), p. 291.

[19] Alfred Förster, *Die Gewerkschaftspolitik der deutschen Sozialdemokratie während des Sozialistengesetzes* (Berlin/DDR: Verlag Tribune, 1971), p. 172.

[20] Quoted by Wolfgang Schröder, "Das Berliner Polizeipräsidium und die Gewerkschaftsbewegung 1878 bis 1886," in H. Bartel et al., eds., *Evolution and Revolution*
(Berlin/DDR: Akademie-Verlag, 1976), p. 569. On the influence of the Anti-Socialist
Laws on class formation see Mary Nolan, "Economic Crisis, State Policy, and Working-Class Formation in Germany, 1870–1900," in Ira Katznelson and Aristide R. Zolberg, eds., *Working-Class Formation: Nineteenth-Century Patterns in Western Europe and
the United States* (Princeton, N.J.: Princeton University Press, 1986).

[21] Franz Mehring, *Geschichte der deutschen Sozialdemokratie* (Berlin/DDR: Dietz Verlag, 1976), 2: 694. This position was taken by Karl Kautsky, the leading theoretician
in the SPD. In a letter he wrote to Eduard Bernstein in 1898, Kautsky argued that in
Germany repression was an ever-present possibility and that the proletariat must be
prepared to fight in place of the bourgeoisie to create the basic framework of political
democracy. See W. L. Guttman, *The German Social Democratic Party, 1875–1933* (London: Allen & Unwin, 1981), pp. 72–74.

With the nonrenewal of the Anti-Socialist Law in 1890, the socialist Free Unions wasted little time in placing their organization
on an independent footing. Although the General Commission of
German Trade Unions, established under the chairmanship of Carl
Legien, restricted its sphere of competence to nonpolitical questions of strike support, industrial agitation, and union organization,
the very existence of an independent and centralized trade union
body implied a differentiation of interest between unions and
party.[22] For this reason certain party leaders attacked even this hes-
itant act of self-assertion as a manifestation of "sinister schemes" on
the part of the union leadership.[23]

But, at least in the early 1890s, such a charge was unfounded.
Party hegemony was so deeply entrenched that it was taken for
granted. In 1893, August Bebel, the chairman of the party Central
Committee, could still speak of the unions in orthodox Marxist
terms as "recruiting schools for the political movement," "educational organizations of the party," "palliatives within middle-class
society," and "the best means of agitation for the political movement."[24]

However, by the mid-1890s many unions had strengthened their
organizations, stabilized their membership, and were rapidly gaining the ability to effectively regulate their members' working conditions in the labor market. This gave them a new realization that
their interests were not identical to those of the party and a growing
self-confidence to express this openly. In the first place, it was becoming increasingly obvious that although the voting power and
political representation of the SPD had grown enormously, the possibility of a revolution was receding; gains made by the SPD were
drawing the other parties into more willing cooperation against it,
and a socialist majority in the Reichstag was still not in sight.[25]

[22] See Gerhard A. Ritter, *Die Arbeiterbewegung im Wilhelminischen Reich* (Berlin-Dahlem: Colloquium Verlag, 1959), pp. 107–108.
[23] Langerhans, "Richtungsgewerkschaft und gewerkschaftliche Autonomie, 1890–
1914," p. 31. The term is Ignaz Auer's. In 1893 he wrote to Legien warning him that
"the German working class movement could never become a field in which the ideas
of Gompers and his fellows could flower" (ibid., p. 29).
[24] Quoted in Ritter, *Die Arbeiterbewegung im Wilhelminischen Reich*, pp. 126–127, and
Hans-Josef Steinberg, "Die Entwicklung des Verhältnisses von Gewerkschaften und
Sozialdemokratie bis zum Ausbruch des Ersten Weltkriegs," in Hans O. Vetter, *Vom
Sozialistengesetz zur Mitbestimmung* (Köln; Bund Verlag, 1975), p. 129.
[25] Selig Perlman, *A Theory of the Labor Movement* (New York: Augustus M. Kelley,
1949), p. 96.

Unions, therefore, began to view their role as defenders of the worker in the labor market in more permanent terms. At the same time it was evident that the party could do little to aid unions in this respect. Furthermore, the ratio of union membership to SPD voting power was beginning to shift in favor of the unions. In 1893 union membership was one-eighth of the SPD vote, in 1898 one-quarter, and in 1907 more than one-half.[26] If unions were no longer dependent on the guardianship of the party, why it was asked, should they be tied to party policy.

At the same time unions hoped to avoid provoking renewed state repression by emphasizing their autonomy from the radical political goals of the SPD. This question was intensively debated in the years after 1895 and reached its climax on the issue of the general strike. As far as Legien and the overwhelming majority of union leaders were concerned, any commitment to the general strike would provide a pretext for state repression, and this would hurt unions more severely than the party. In 1904, when it became plain that the subject could no longer be sidestepped, the unions, in defiance of the unwritten rule of party hegemony on political matters, preempted the forthcoming party convention and declared their absolute opposition to the general strike at their own congress. When the party convention went on to give its overwhelming support to a resolution, sponsored by Bebel, authorizing the general strike in defense of existing political rights, Legien's response was unwavering:

> The trade unions no longer feel under any obligation to accept the unrestrained attacks by the Party press in silence, but, from now on, they will express their own opinion without restraint, even at the risk of bringing on unpleasant discussions; the trade union press will freely use its right to criticize the actions of the Party in all cases where trade union principles are at stake; for the trade unions the resolution adopted at the Congress at Köln remains valid, not the one passed at the Party Convention.[27]

[26] Langerhans, "Richtungsgewerkschaft und gewerkschaftliche Autonomie, 1890–1914," p. 204.
[27] Quoted in Perlman, *A Theory of the Labor Movement*, p. 99. There is an almost endless literature on the debate between the unions and the party in these years, among the best of which is Carl Schorske, *German Social Democracy, 1905–1917: The Development of the Great Schism* (Cambridge, Mass.: Harvard University Press, 1955).

This rousing reply to the party leadership left little doubt that the unions were demanding not only a specific change in tactics but a formerly undreamt-of autonomy on questions of grand strategy. And the party had little alternative but to give way; after all, a general strike, or indeed any organized resistance in the labor market, was impossible without union support. The impasse was finally resolved in the Mannheim Agreement of 1906 in which the party formally agreed to relinquish its claim of supremacy within the labor movement.

The emergence of effective and autonomous unionism after 1895 saw a corresponding decline in revolutionary fervor. During the "heroic resistance" of 1874 to 1890, most Free Union leaders shared the party view that any gains the unions might achieve in the labor market would soon be overtaken by the socialist revolution. By the end of the century union sentiment had changed dramatically in favor of a more gradualist and more cautious approach. For the first time union leaders found themselves on the side of preserving the institutional gains of the past. As Carl Legien put it, "It is precisely we, the organized workers, who do not wish to see a so-called general uprising in which we would be forced to create new social institutions on the ruins of the old order, no matter whether they are better or worse than the present ones. We wish to maintain a state of tranquil development."[28]

The rejection of revolutionary socialism did not, however, imply a turn to the business unionism of Gompers and his associates in the United States. As I argue in the following chapter, by this time in Germany the arenas of labor market and state were so closely entwined that the possibility of "pure and simple" unionism did not exist. Moreover, the legal position of trade unions was still ambiguous; until paragraph 153 of the 1869 Industrial Code was repealed in 1914, unions were rigorously prosecuted for "intimidation" during strikes and "coercion" of nonunionists in their attempts to establish closed shops.[29] Unions were also threatened, especially after 1908, by the efforts of employers' associations to

---

[28] Quoted in Steinberg, "Die Entwicklung des Verhältnisses von Gewerkschaften und Sozialdemokratie," p. 132.

[29] See Klaus Saul, *Staat, Industrie, Arbeiterbewegung im Kaiserreich* (Düsseldorf: Bertelsmann Universitäts-Verlag, 1974), pts. 3 and 4; Langerhans, "Richtungsgewerkschaft und gewerkschaftliche Autonomie, 1890–1914," p. 202; Mary Nolan, *Social Democracy and Society: Working-Class Radicalism in Düsseldorf, 1890–1920* (Cambridge: Cambridge University Press, 1981), pp. 62–63.

gain legislation restricting the right to strike. If for no other reason than this, German trade unions had to be deeply involved in politics to defend their precarious position under the law.

BRITAIN: AUTONOMOUS UNIONISM AND LABORISM

In the eighteenth century, British unions, like those in Prussia and the German states, were subject to traditional controls that applied to all combinations. Although trade unions were not specifically prohibited, an employer could take action against a combination "in restraint of trade" by privately promoting a bill in Parliament.[30] At the turn of the nineteenth century the Combination Acts extended the controls on combinations and simplified the procedures under which they could be prosecuted.[31] But state repression of trade unions in Britain did not last so long, and was never so severe, as repression in Prussia. First, combinations of artisans or laborers could legally be established to secure enforcement of the obsolete laws regulating wages. This provided journeymen with a legitimate reason for electing leaders and forming organizations that might later be put to more practical use in the labor market. Second, the boundary between legal and illegal activities was in any case a vague one, and in Britain it could not be policed by the kind of extensive state apparatus that existed in Prussia.[32] Finally, employers themselves had to initiate prosecution, and for various reasons they were often reluctant to do so.[33]

[30] Lujo Brentano, "Entwicklung und Geist der Englischen Arbeiterorganisationen," *Archiv für Sozialwissenschaft und Sozialpolitik* 8 (1895): 101–102; D. E. Macdonald, *The State and the Trade Unions* (London: Macmillan, 1976), pp. 15–17; Bendix, *Nation Building and Citizenship*, p. 96.

[31] Whether, and to what extent, the Combination Acts extended the scope and increased the severity of state repression in England has been the subject of an intensive debate. See J. L. Hammond and B. Hammond, *The Town Labourer* (London: Longmans, Green, 1925), chap. 7; M. D. George, "The Combination Laws Reconsidered," *Economic Journal* 1 (1926/1929), and "The Combination Laws," *Economic History Review* 6 (1935/1936); and E. P. Thompson, *The Making of the English Working Class*, pp. 546–555.

[32] See F. C. Mather, *Public Order in the Age of the Chartists* (Manchester: Manchester University Press, 1959), pp. 57, 227–230; Henry Pelling, "Trade Unions, Workers and the Law," in Pelling, *Popular Politics and Society in Late Victorian Britain* (London: Macmillan, 1968); Malcolm I. Thomis, *The Town Labourer and the Industrial Revolution* (London: Batsford, 1974), chap. 2.

[33] E. P. Thompson has pointed out that the probable costs to an employer who

This is not to say, however, that the repressive legislation of the first quarter of the nineteenth century in Britain was, in practice, only a mild yoke on union activity. Unions fortunate enough to be able to employ the subtle and covert method of unilateral regulation remained relatively undisturbed by the courts, but those unions that had to make explicit demands on employers, backed by the threat of openly coordinated strikes, proved easy targets for repression. Hence, unions in the secure London artisan trades flourished in these years, while those in the larger trades, such as weaving and framework-knitting, which relied on overt collective bargaining, were hard hit.[34]

The attempt by the state to suppress the right of artisans and laborers to combine in the labor market came to an end in 1824 when the Combination Acts were repealed. From this time onward trade unions were specifically allowed to deal with questions of wages and hours, while the right to strike was imputed to them. But legislation amending the Combination Acts Repeal Act the following year vaguely prohibited trade unions from using "threats, intimidation, molestation, and obstruction" and once more made them subject to common law with regard to conspiracies in restraint of trade.[35]

It was not until 1875 that trade unions secured legislation that appeared to remove the threat of persecution for conspiracy from their activities. In the intervening half century they existed in an often precarious position of semilegality, prone to the vagaries of judicial interpretation of the word "conspiracy." These years were marked by infamous trials and harsh sentences, but where it occurred, harassment of unions by the state was partial, intermittent, and uncoordinated. In contrast to the repression of workers' combinations in the German states before 1868 and after 1874, the legal disabilities suffered by trade unions under English common law were not, and were not intended to be, a means of outright suppression. By 1874 a peak of perhaps 1,200,000 workers be-

initiated prosecution were large, while there was no certainty of legal success (*The Making of the English Working Class*, p. 553).

[34] Sidney and Beatrice Webb, *History of Trade Unionism* (London: Longmans, Green, 1920), pp. 77–87; Macdonald, *The State and the Trade Unions*, p. 19.

[35] Macdonald, *The State and the Trade Unions*, chap. 2; Richard Price, *Labour in British Society* (London: Croom Helm, 1986), pp. 39–42. The best account of the passage of the Combination Acts Repeal Act (1824) and the Amendment Act (1825) remains that of the Webbs, *History of Trade Unionism*, chap. 7.

longed to a large collection of autonomous local and national unions of varying effectiveness in the labor market.[36]

Unions in Britain were not driven into revolutionary opposition of the state, nor were they forced to fight for their legal existence in the political arena. As in the United States, relative legal tolerance gave to unions the opportunity to defend the working conditions of their members in the labor market. Not all of them possessed the ability to do this effectively, but those that did were able to reap the sectional benefits of business unionism.

Before the establishment of the Trades Union Congress in 1868 a number of attempts were made to bring unions into horizontal organizations capable of providing mutual economic support and increased political leverage. But in the absence of a common threat powerful enough to counter the effects of labor market segmentation most unions were not prepared to sacrifice their autonomy to a central organization. The TUC differed from earlier horizontal organizations, such as Robert Owen's Grand National Consolidated Trades Union of the early 1830s and the National Association of United Trades of the mid-1840s, precisely because its horizons were limited; it made minimal economic demands on unions and required no sacrifice of their autonomy.[37] It began, in fact, as an annual debating society on the model of the British Association for the Advancement of Science and the Social Science Association. Only three years later, stimulated mainly by the 1871 Criminal Law Amendment Act, which extended the grounds under which picketing was an offense, did the TUC turn towards the organization of political agitation on behalf of its constituents.

In 1875, after an intensive political campaign, the Parliamentary Committee of the TUC was able to report the passage of the Conspiracy and Protection Act, which repealed the Act of 1871, legal-

---

[36] There are no accurate figures for trade union membership before the 1890s. For a comparison of estimates see W. Hamish Fraser, *Trade Unions and Society: The Struggle for Acceptance, 1850–1880* (London: Allen & Unwin, 1974), p. 16. The estimate of 1,200,000 for 1874 is that of Pelling, "Trade Unions, Workers and the Law," p. 72.

[37] As Hugh Clegg points out, the TUC was "established at a time when many of its constituents were already developed and mature. They wished to guard against any encroachment of their own autonomy and they had the strength to do so." See *The System of Industrial Relations in Britain* (Oxford: Rowman and Littlefield, 1972), p. 396. On the origins of the TUC see A. E. Musson, *The Congress of 1868: The Origins and Establishment of the Trades Union Congress* (London: Trades Union Congress, 1955), and V. L. Allen, *The Sociology of Industrial Relations* (London: Longman, 1971), chap. 11.

ized peaceful picketing, and exempted trade disputes from the law of conspiracy unless the acts concerned were criminal if committed by an individual. This success did not, however, spur unions to indulge in new and more ambitious political activity. Rather the reverse. George Howell, the secretary of the Parliamentary Committee, was satisfied that the TUC had fulfilled its purpose and resigned. His successor, Henry Broadhurst, was content to continue the organization in the limited role of a "watch-dog" over prospective legislation.[38] Up to 1882 the TUC had no regular source of income and apart from a full-time secretary, no administrative staff.[39]

The narrow basis of common political concern among unions in Britain is further revealed in the events leading to the establishment of the Labour party itself. With the growth of militant new unions in previously unorganized sectors of industry after 1889, socialism found a foothold in British trade unionism. But strong though the demand for socialist measures of governmental job regulation was in newly established and relatively ineffective trade unions, such as the Gasworkers' Union and the Dockers' Union, it was not widely enough shared to provide the basis for joint political action. Socialists who hoped that a labor party would become an active and radical voice for the working class as a whole were to be found mostly outside trade unions in the Social Democratic Federation. The overwhelming majority of unions viewed the Labour Representation Committee (established in 1900, and later renamed the Labour party) as a relatively innocuous means of achieving a limited and straightforward goal, that of "securing the return of an increased number of labour members to Parliament."[40] The previous arrangement with the Liberal party was found to be unsatisfactory, not on ideological grounds, but mainly because Liberal party constituencies failed to adopt enough workers as candidates, despite the favorable attitude of the Liberal leadership.[41] The Sec-

[38] John Lovell and B. C. Roberts, *A Short History of the T.U.C.* (London: Macmillan, 1968), p. 29.

[39] Allen, *The Sociology of Industrial Relations*, pp. 159–161. "Until 1902 ... [the T.U.C.'s] administrative work was done entirely by a part-time secretary" (p. 159).

[40] Lovell and Roberts, *A Short History of the T.U.C.*, pp. 37–38.

[41] In addition, the Liberal party failed to press for the payment of M.P.s. Both Pelling and Clegg et al. emphasize that the decision of the TUC to support the Labour Representation Committee was not so much due to Socialist drive as it was to the fact that the Lib-Labs did not organize its defeat. See Henry Pelling, *Origins of the Labour Party* (Oxford: Clarendon Press, 1965), p. 224 and Hugh Clegg, Alan Fox, and A. F.

retary of the LRC was an unpaid official, and Ramsay MacDonald
was chosen for the post partly because he had another source of
income.[42]

In its first year of existence the Labour Representation Committee could only gain the support of a minority of unions affiliated
with the TUC. But the year after came the Taff Vale case in which
the House of Lords held that unions were liable for damages
caused by their members during strikes. Alarmed by the threat to
their considerable funds, unions like the previously wavering Engineers, and even the conservative Lancashire Textile Workers, ral-
lied behind the political organization best equipped to gain reme-
dial legislation. The affiliated membership of the LRC jumped
from 375,000 in 1901 to 861,000 in 1903.[43]

After the 1906 election the ruling Liberal party, spurred by the
LRC, framed the Trades Disputes Act removing the liabilities on
striking unions conferred by the Taff Vale decision. In this year the
LRC was renamed the Labour party, but its subsequent activity up
to the First World War remained within the limited bounds of the
originally conceived body. Apart from its role as parliamentary de-
fender of union rights, the Labour party was little more than an
adjunct of the Liberal party, "uncommitted," in Henry Pelling's
works, "not merely to Socialism, but to any program whatsoever."[44]
But if the trade union presence in Parliament was narrow and re-
active, it was at least institutionalized. And if the Labour party had
no coherent philosophy by which it could initiate legislation, it at

---

Thompson, *A History of British Trade Unions since 1889* (Oxford: Clarendon Press,
1964), 1: 303.

[42] Pelling, *Origins of the Labour Party*, p. 210.

[43] Ibid., p. 215; Henry Phelps Brown, *The Origins of Trade Union Power* (Oxford:
Clarendon Press, 1983), chap. 4. On the conversion of trade unions to support for
the LRC see Pelling, *Origins of the Labour Party*, chap. 2; James Hinton, *Labour and
Socialism: A History of the British Labour Movement, 1867–1974* (Amherst: University of
Massachusetts Press, 1983), chap. 4; John Lovell, *British Trade Unions, 1875–1933*
(London: Macmillan, 1977), chap. 3; Clegg et al., *A History of British Trade Unions since
1889*, pp. 373–377; and Samuel H. Beer, *British Politics in the Collectivist Age* (New
York: Vintage Books, 1969), pp. 113–115.

[44] Pelling, *Origins of the Labour Party*, p. 38. To be sure, Pelling's argument has been
disputed. Clegg et al. claim that Labour party policies covered the badly organized
and poorer just as much as the organized and better off and "could be presented as
the beginnings of a reform of society as a whole" (*A History of British Trade Unions since
1889*, 1: 487). See also H. V. Emy, *Liberals, Radicals, and Social Politics, 1892–1914*
(Cambridge: Cambridge University Press, 1973), p. 124, for support of the Pelling
thesis.

least served to represent the legislative demands of individual unions, though Parliament itself was increasingly being bypassed by unions beginning to use more direct channels of corporatist leverage.

THE UNITED STATES: AUTONOMOUS UNIONISM
AND THE GROWTH OF POLITICAL LOBBYING

Unlike the countries of Western Europe, America did not enter the industrial era with a legacy of strict controls on all associations independent of the state. But though America lacked a feudal past, it shared with England the accumulated precedents of English common law concerning conspiracy "in restraint of trade" and conspiracy "to injure others."

The earliest judgment of combination in the labor market on grounds of conspiracy, the Philadelphia Cordwainers' Case of 1806, found the striking artisans guilty of both conspiring to raise wages and conspiring to injure others to maintain a closed shop.[45] Subsequent cases focussed less on the former grounds of conspiracy, which held unions illegal by virtue of purpose, and more on whether the means used in sustaining unions were "coercive and arbitrary," although as late as 1835 a union could be condemned on both grounds.[46]

These trials under common law, together with the constant threat of prosecution, severely hampered the activities of unions in the labor market and occasionally provoked vehement, and sometimes violent, reactions on the part of workers. The verdict of the 1806 cordwainers' trial, for instance, was followed by a tumultuous demonstration, and that of the 1835 Geneva shoemakers' trial and subsequent tailors' trial precipitated a mass meeting at which effigies of the presiding judges were burned and a resolution was passed calling for a state convention to form a workingmen's party.[47] But the doctrine of conspiracy was not systemized by statutory law as it was in England under the Combination Acts of 1799 and 1800, nor

[45] John R. Commons et al., eds., *Documentary History of American Industrial Society* (Glendale, Calif.: A.H. Clarke, 1911), 3: 135–138; Selig Perlman, *History of Trade Unionism in the United States* (New York: Macmillan, 1922), p. 147.

[46] Commons et al., *The History of Labor in the United States* (New York: Macmillan Company, 1926), 2: 405–408.

[47] Perlman, *History of Trade Unionism in the United States*, p. 150.

was it employed so harshly. Although some workers were sentenced to prison, most trials ended in acquittals or nominal fines.

In 1842 unions were released from the onus of prosecution for conspiracy under common law by the decision of the *Commonwealth v. Hunt* case, which held unions to be legal unless actual or intended harm could be attributed to their actions.[48] This ruling gave to American unions a modicum of security under the law that was only achieved by unions in Britain in 1875 and by unions in Germany during the First World War. The unions that developed in this climate of relative legal tolerance fought primarily, as Ira Katznelson has noted, "for the bread-and-butter issues of higher wages, a minimum wage, shorter hours, collective-bargaining rights, and the closed shop. Their activity was not part of a larger working-class movement; indeed, they excluded common laborers and did not involve their unions in attempts to build a workers' political party."[49]

Until the 1880s, when new applications for the law of conspiracy were found, American unions were left relatively free of state interference. These years saw the emergence of autonomous and sectional unions on much the same lines as in Britain. By the early 1870s, twenty-nine national unions and numerous local and regional unions were in existence with a total membership of about 300,000.[50] Like British unions, American unions were spared the kind of intense state repression that ushered German unions into the arms of the Social Democratic party.

By this time, however, one specifically nonsectional union of workers was successfully established. Composed largely of unskilled workers having no sectional advantages in the labor market to defend, the Knights of Labor was founded in 1869 on the ideal of

[48] Commons et al., *The History of Labor in the United States*, 2: 411–412; Neil W. Chamberlain and J. W. Kuhn, *Collective Bargaining*, 2d ed. (New York: McGraw-Hill, 1965), p. 273; Perlman, *History of Trade Unionism in the United States*, pp. 150–152. It is worth noting in this connection that as early as the 1830s debates about the role of law in labor disputes were funneled into party competition and provided a means for the Democratic party to appeal to workers and thereby encompass them in broad, nonclass coalitions. See Amy Bridges, *A City in the Republic: Antebellum New York and the Origins of Machine Politics* (Cambridge: Cambridge University Press, 1984), pp. 69–70.

[49] Ira Katznelson, *City Trenches: Urban Politics and the Patterning of Class in the United States* (New York: Pantheon Books, 1981), p. 61.

[50] Lloyd Ulman, *The Rise of the National Union* (Cambridge, Mass.: Harvard University Press, 1955), pp. 4, 19.

intercraft solidarity. The Knights rejected the trade assembly and the concept of job-territory, on which the existing occupational and industrial unions were based, in favor of the mixed assembly and the avowed goal of raising the "wage-earner above the narrow view of his class or trade, or job."[51] The unit of membership was the individual, not the union or trade assembly to which he belonged, and the preferred method of regulation was political rather than economic.

The general unionism of the Knights of Labor and the craft unionism of the sectional unions were fundamentally incompatible and, in 1886, after unsuccessful attempts to find some grounds for a working compromise, open war was declared. Later the same year a conference of national craft unions was called to coordinate and centralize their efforts to preserve their autonomy and protect their membership from the poaching of the Knights. The result was the creation of the American Federation of Labor.[52]

This organization stood in a similar relation to its constituent unions as did the British Trades Union Congress. Both functioned within limits that were staked out by the principle of union autonomy. The power of these bodies, short of their rarely used ability to expel a union, rested on subtle forms of influence and persuasion rather than compulsion. The activities of both the AFL and the TUC reflected the shared views of the lowest common denominator of their membership rather than those of any majority. As far as political activities were concerned, this meant that both organizations were poorly placed to mobilize their members behind broad political platforms but could act decisively in defending or improving their members' legal position.

By the 1870s and early 1880s many union leaders felt so secure under the law that they advocated legal incorporation of trade unions to better protect their funds. But from the late 1880s unions were faced with increasingly belligerent courts and the growth of powerful employer associations willing to go on to the offensive on the political front. The chief instrument of this offensive was the writ of federal injunction, issued by discretion of a federal judge at

[51] Quoted in Ulman, *The Rise of the National Union*, p. 349.
[52] See Philip Taft, *The A.F. of L. in the Time of Gompers* (New York: Harper, 1957), chaps. 1 and 2; Lewis L. Lorwin, *The American Federation of Labor: History, Policies, and Prospects* (Washington, D.C.: The Brookings Institution, 1933), chap. 1.

an employer's request, restraining a union from activities deemed injurious to the employer's business.[53]

As the pressure from the courts mounted, the AFL was dragged further and further into politics, despite the often-voiced preference of Samuel Gompers and other leading unionists for "pure and simple" unionism untrammeled by political activity. In 1890, when the injunction was still a novelty, a proposal at the AFL convention calling for a permanent lobby in Washington during congressional sessions was defeated. But the bout of strikes in 1893 and 1894 saw intensive use of the injunction, and two years later the infamous contempt case involving Eugene Debs extended the old common law doctrine of conspiracy to acts in "destruction of an employer's business."[54] From 1894 the AFL lobbied Congress at each session for passage of an anti-injunction bill, and in 1896 it set up a permanent lobbying committee.[55]

But by 1906 these limited methods of political activity had achieved little. Although it successfully mobilized the support of the House of Representatives in 1900, and again in 1902, for bills constraining the use of the injunction, the AFL could not move the Senate. And in 1905 President Theodore Roosevelt once again confirmed his opposition to a reduction of the courts' power of injunction.[56]

In the meantime two court decisions made the situation more urgent. In 1905 a circuit court in Connecticut allowed a lawsuit to be brought to trial against individual members of the United Hatters' Union in Danbury for damages resulting from a local boycott. Lawsuits against unions were by now commonplace, but to find that rank-and-file members were prone came as an unexpected shock. Moreover, the claim was a staggering $240,000, on the basis of triple damages under the Sherman Anti-Trust Act. The following year the AFL suffered another blow when the Chicago Typographical Union was restrained by an injunction during a strike that went

[53] Commons et al., *The History of Labor in the United States*, 2: 505–509; Perlman, *History of Trade Unionism in the United States*, pp. 154–157; C. Gregory, "Government Regulation or Control of Union Activities," in W. Haber, ed., *Labor in a Changing America* (New York: Basic Books, 1966), p. 225; S. Cohen, *Labor in the United States*, 3d ed. (Columbus, Ohio: C.E. Merrill Publishing Company, 1970), pp. 442–446.

[54] Commons et al., *The History of Labor in the United States*, 2: 501–503; Philip Taft, *Organized Labor in American History* (New York: Harper & Row, 1964), pp. 145–148.

[55] Marc Karson, *American Labor Unions and Politics, 1900–1918* (Carbondale: Southern Illinois University Press, 1958), pp. 29–30.

[56] Ibid., p. 32.

so far as to prohibit "peaceful picketing, any moral suasion whatever" and any "attempt by the printers to induce non-union printers to join the union."[57] Subsequently two of its officers were sentenced to prison, and the union was fined $1,500 for contempt of the injunction. This judgment was perceived to be all the more threatening because for the first time a court had struck at a bastion of the AFL, a union recognized to be a model of conservative unionism.

As we shall see in the next chapter, the ineffectuality of the previous political methods employed by the AFL and the increasingly antilabor stance taken by the courts were not the only concerns that led the AFL to extend the scope of its political activities. But there can be little doubt that these were the most compelling reasons for the change. The courts led the AFL into politics. Heightened political involvement was, as Marc Karson has argued, "a vital, practical requisite necessitated by the elementary principles of self-defense and self-preservation."[58]

In 1906 the federation drew up a bill of grievances, a wide-ranging legislative manifesto, and established a small, but permanent, labor representation committee in Washington, responsible for propaganda and the endorsement of federal candidates.[59] In 1906 the six House representatives who held union cards began meeting regularly as a group, and after the congressional elections of 1908 their number grew to seventeen. Despite prodding from unionists who wished to follow the British example, the AFL still refused to establish an independent political party, but now the traditional

---

[57] Taft, *The A. F. of L. in the Time of Gompers*, pp. 266–268; Karson, *American Labor Unions and Politics, 1900–1918*, pp. 36–37.

[58] Karson, *American Labor Unions and Politics, 1900–1918*, p. 41. Selig Perlman has argued from a similar perspective that "it thus came about that the Federation which ... by the very principles of its program wished to let government alone ... was obliged to enter into competition with the employers for controlling government; this was because one branch of government, namely the judicial one, would not let it alone" (*History of Trade Unionism in the United States*, pp. 202–203).

[59] On the "bill of grievances" and the AFL's change of course, see Christopher L. Tomlins, *The State and the Unions: Labor Relations, Law, and the Organized Labor Movement in America, 1880–1960* (Cambridge: Cambridge University Press, 1985), pp. 60–67; Karson, *American Labor Unions and Politics, 1900–1918*, pp. 42–49; M. R. Carroll, *Labor and Politics* (Boston: Houghton, Mifflin, 1923), pp. 42–47; John G. Rayback, *A History of American Labor* (New York: Macmillan, 1959), pp. 250–252; S. J. Scheinberg, "Theodore Roosevelt and the A.F. of L.'s Entry in Politics, 1906–1908," *Labor History* 3–4 (1962–1963): 131–137.

policy of rewarding friends and punishing enemies was intensively organized and nationally coordinated.

Results were not quickly forthcoming, however. In 1908 the Danbury Hatters' case went against the union, and one year later, Gompers, Mitchell, and Morrison, the three most prominent officials of the AFL, only escaped serving lengthy prison sentences for contempt of an injunction on a technicality.[60] Not until 1914, under the presidency of Woodrow Wilson, were unions afforded a measure of protection against the labor injunction by the Clayton Act.[61] But by this time the AFL was becoming increasingly immersed in other aspects of governmental policy making and had no intention of dismantling its political apparatus.

CONCLUSION

In this chapter I have explored the ways in which state repression or toleration of unions influenced their relations with political parties, their willingness to establish national federations, and their political orientation to the state. To the extent that the state repressed unions, so unions were faced with a common and overriding task, that of gaining the political rights necessary for effective combination in the labor market. And it was the political party, not the union itself, that was best equipped to meet this task. Hence, it was in precisely those countries where capitalist development went hand in hand with traditional absolutist controls suppressing worker combination—in Germany, Austria-Hungary, and Russia, for example—that unions were formed in the wake of exclusively political working-class organizations and subsequently existed in

---

[60] The best description of this case is that of Barry F. Helfland, "Labor and the Courts: The Common-Law Doctrine of Criminal Conspiracy and Its Application in the Buck's Stove Case," *Labor History* 18 (1977).

[61] Melvyn Dubofsky, "Abortive Reform: The Wilson Administration and Organized Labor, 1913–1920," in James E. Cronin and Carmen Sirianni, eds., *Work, Community, and Power: The Experience of Labor in Europe and America, 1900–1925* (Philadelphia: Temple University Press, 1983); Karson, *American Labor Unions and Politics, 1900–1918*, pp. 76–77; Carroll, *Labor and Politics*, pp. 156–158. The Clayton Act was hailed by Samuel Gompers as the unions' Magna Charta, though as it turned out the legislation achieved far less than anticipated. The provisions of the legislation against labor injunctions lacked teeth, and the right of workers to engage peacefully in assemblies, pickets, and boycotts without legal interference was later struck down by the Supreme Court.

subordination to them.[62] In these societies the link between unions and working-class political parties was strengthened by the existence of rigid status boundaries inherited from a feudal past that sharply separated artisans and other workers from higher status groups.[63]

When state repression was moderated, unions became less dependent upon the party. This hypothesis, and its converse, are illustrated by the responses of workers in Russia to changes in the legal climate before 1914. The easing of repression in 1906 and the first half of 1907 led several groups of workers to establish unions to press for better wages and hours. The printers, in Russia as elsewhere in the vanguard of reformism, actually managed to set up formal channels of collective bargaining with their employers. However, these efforts lapsed when repression was intensified after 1907. As Victoria Bonnell observes: "Above all, . . . the Bolsheviks struck a responsive chord among many union activists because the party's approach coincided with the workers' own experiences after 1912. The autocracy treated economic protest as political opposition, thereby creating the very conditions that eventually transformed the unions into revolutionary organizations."[64]

From the 1860s many German workers and their unions were led to socialism by the demand for basic political and economic rights. Later, when unions were given a little legal breathing room, most continued to support socialism, but the meaning had changed. From their perspective, socialism had to provide room for an autonomous union movement bent upon improving the condition of the worker in the most immediate way, that is, through the labor market. After the nonrenewal of the severely repressive Anti-Socialist Laws, increasingly effective and self-confident unions demanded freedom from party interference so that they could pursue a gradualist strategy of improvement within the existing wage system. After 1905, when there was a push within the SPD to revive

[62] See Isaac Deutscher, "Russia," in Walter Galenson, *Comparative Labor Movements* (New York: Prentice Hall, 1952), pp. 480–487; Charles A. Gulick, *Austria from Habsburg to Hitler*, vol. 1, *Labor's Workshop of Democracy* (Berkeley: University of California Press, 1948), chap. 1.

[63] See Seymour Martin Lipset, *The First New Nation* (New York: Basic Books, 1973), chap. 6.

[64] Victoria E. Bonnell, "Radical Politics and Organized Labor in Pre-Revolutionary Moscow, 1905–1914," *Journal of Social History* 12 (Winter 1978): 291.

the party's revolutionary stance, the unions were a zealous force on the side of reformism.

In those countries where repressive controls on worker combination were milder—in Britain, the United States, Australia, and the Scandinavian countries, for example—autonomous and sectional unions were established alongside or before working-class political parties.[65] Where unions were firmly entrenched before working-class political mobilization was underway, socialist or labor parties had to adapt to an already "formed" working class with its cultural ties and institutional loyalties. Unlike the parties that were established before the rise of trade unions, these parties could not integrate the working classes into a singular, inclusive, and politically oriented subculture of radical or revolutionary resistance against capitalism. In this important respect, the Social Democratic party, the early guardian and shaper of trade unionism in Germany, stands opposite the British Labour party.

These comparisons indicate that the duration and intensity of state repression of working-class organizations and the relative timing of the institutionalization of unions and working-class political parties are crucial influences on the political orientation of the working classes in the nineteenth century. Once the relationship between the union and party-political wings of the labor movements had been molded, it was difficult to break. Even though the Free Unions in Germany eventually succeeded in gaining formal autonomy from the SPD, they were still bound closely in the same movement by virtue of a shared and deeply rooted subculture. In Britain the relationship between the Labour party and the unions is still a function of its beginnings in the early years of the twentieth century. Recent reforms have moderated, but by no means eliminated, union domination of Labour party conferences, and unions still provide the bulk of members and funds for the party.

[65] See, for example, John T. Sutcliffe, *History of Trade Unionism in Australia* (Melbourne: Macmillan & Company, Ltd., 1921), pp. 54–65; Robin Gollan, "Nationalism, the Labour Movement and the Commonwealth, 1880–1900," in Gordon Greenwood, ed., *Australia: A Social and Political History* (Sydney: Angus and Robertson, 1974); Robin Gollan, *Radical and Working-Class Politics: A Study of Eastern Australia, 1850–1910* (Melbourne: Melbourne University Press, 1960); Walter Galenson, *Labor in Norway* (Cambridge, Mass.: Harvard University Press, 1949), pp. 56–64; Walter Galenson, *The Danish System of Labor Relations* (Cambridge, Mass.: Harvard University Press, 1952), pp. 18–26.

By the final decades of the nineteenth century unions were beginning to face a new set of issues that, like state repression, drew
them into politics. Startling developments in the organization of
capitalist production were changing the relationship of economic to
political activity in the core societies of Western Europe and North
America. As a result, unions and governments were faced with
choices that they had never conceived of before. It is to these developments in the context of industrial relations that we must turn
next.

CHAPTER 3

UNIONS AND
THE ORGANIZATIONAL REVOLUTION

Above and beyond variations in the strategies of unions in contemporary Western societies, it is possible to distinguish a fundamental orientation common to virtually all contemporary unions that sets them apart from unions in the nineteenth century. Contemporary unions are immersed in national politics to a degree unknown to unions a century ago. Even unions committed to collective bargaining in the labor market find it difficult not to take advantage of opportunities for political influence offered within liberal democratic societies. The range of union political interest and involvement is immense, encompassing virtually all government policies bearing directly or indirectly on their members, from minimum wage and health hazard legislation to fiscal and monetary policy, industrial and investment policy, and social welfare policy.

Perhaps the very ubiquity of this development is responsible for the fact that it has not been given more attention by those who write about unions.[1] The politicization of union strategy forms a necessary backdrop in any historical overview of union development but is neglected as a focus of investigation. Conceptualizations of union political activity in contemporary Western societies that have been elaborated by scholars of interest group/state relations have shed much light on contrasting modes of union politicization but have said little about the process of politicization itself and the changes that brought it about.[2]

---

[1] Notable exceptions are Evelies Meyer, *Theorien zum Funktionswandel der Gewerkschaften* (Frankfurt am Main: Europäische Verlaganstalt, 1973); Keith Middlemas, *Politics in Industrial Society* (London: Andre Deutsch, 1969); Ilse Costas, *Auswirkungen der Konzentration des Kapitals auf die Arbeiterklasse in Deutschland, 1800–1914* (Frankfurt: Campus Verlag, 1981); Hans Mommsen, "The Free Trade Unions and Social Democracy in Imperial Germany," in Wolfgang J. Mommsen and Hans-Gerhard Husung, eds., *The Development of Trade Unionism in Great Britain and Germany, 1880–1914* (London: George Allen & Unwin, 1985); Philippe Schmitter, "Modes of Interest Intermediation and Models of Societal Change in Western Europe," in Philippe Schmitter and Gerhard Lehmbruch, eds., *Trends toward Corporatist Intermediation* (Beverly Hills, Calif.: Sage, 1979).

[2] For an overview of this literature see Gary Marks, "Neocorporatism and Incomes

If we extend our view of union political activity back to the establishment of stable unionism in the nineteenth century as a baseline for comparison, it is possible to see fundamental commonalities, as well as contrasts, in the contemporary orientations of unions in societies as different as the United States, Britain, and Germany. Beyond differences in organizational structure, modes of participation in policy making, and party-political links, unions in Britain, and even the United States, share with those in Germany a profoundly politicized view of their legitimate role in society. One telling sign of this is the sheer breadth and depth of union political participation in these societies. It would demand at least a chapter simply to list the forums, agencies, councils, legislative committees, etc., on which unions in these countries are either directly represented or attempt to exert influence through a range of political strategies, from party-political and pressure group tactics to political strikes and public demonstrations.

Political involvement is not in itself novel. Unions in the nineteenth century, and especially those that were weak in the labor market, attempted to legislate improvements in wages and working conditions, or even to abolish the system of wage labor. But today the channels and forms of political activity have multiplied and diversified beyond recognition. The point of departure for this chapter is the belief that the scope of historical variation in union strategy over the last century is just as impressive and worthy of attention from the standpoint of comparative politics as variations across Western societies at individual points in time.

What are the sources of the routinization of intense political involvement on the part of unions? My thesis, which underpins this chapter, is that to answer this question we must explore a set of developments that shaped the most economically advanced societies from the last decades of the nineteenth century in arguably as profound a fashion as the Industrial Revolution shaped Western societies from the last decades of the eighteenth century. At the heart of this process was an unprecedented expansion in the application of organization to social life—a multifaceted attempt to exert purposeful control over political, social, and economic behavior on a scale beyond the dreams of the pioneers of the Industrial Revolu-

Policy in Western Europe and North America, 1950–1980," *Comparative Politics* 17 (April 1986).

tion. In describing this complex set of developments I have used the term "Organizational Revolution."

This process transformed unions, employers' associations, and their relations with each other and with the state. As organizations representing labor and capital vastly increased in size and scope, conflicts between them came to affect the entire society rather than just one sector, consequently taking on an explicitly political dimension. Governments found themselves impelled to intervene, either to find some grounds for compromise or to enforce union quiescence. At the same time governments were drawn into the substantive regulation of the labor market in response to newfound social responsibilities and growing pressures to protect those least able to survive the rigors of an impersonal labor market. As the state regulated the conditions of the sick, the aged, and the unemployed, so unions demanded, and received, a quasi-public role in the administration of those regulations. Finally, the tremendous growth in organization transformed the struggle between labor and capital into one that pitted hundreds of thousands or even millions of workers against corporations having vast financial resources. As each side tried to outflank the other in the political arena, both labor and capital searched for, and found, the means to convert their impressive market resources into political power.

These developments were bound together by a common element: each involved an interpenetration of state and market, a blurring of the boundaries separating the activities of the state, unions, and employers' associations. As with the Industrial Revolution, it does not seem possible to argue that the Organizational Revolution led to determinate outcomes for regime type or that it created specific constellations of class interests or union-party links. In substantive political terms the Organizational Revolution was open-ended. The strongest common influences have, I believe, to be understood at a higher level of abstraction, in terms of the meaning of politics and the vastly expanded role politics came to play in organized social life.

LAISSEZ-FAIRE AND THE ORGANIZATIONAL REVOLUTION

The Organizational Revolution was a major step in the process by which human beings have brought their own social relations under their collective control. In the words of Samuel Beer the Organizational Revolution was part of an increasingly "voluntarist"

conception of human affairs, based on the notion that "men ought
to design their environment, natural and social, to suit their own
purposes and wishes."[3] In terms of its consequences for union strategy perhaps the most crucial aspect of this development was the
introduction of purposive control in economic relationships that
were formerly governed by the impersonal forces of market competition. As unions, corporations, and employer associations grew
in size and scope, so decisions in the labor market increasingly became a function of relative power and purposeful strategy. This
development is at the core of the politicization of unions in the
twentieth century, and it is worthwhile to take a closer look at its
implications, particularly for the liberal political economy and its
foundations in laissez-faire and market competition.

   In its historical genesis, as well as in the political economy of
Adam Smith and David Ricardo, laissez-faire was buttressed by a
conception of economic activity based on competitive markets. The
doctrine of laissez-faire emphasized the benefits of market autonomy from state interference, while market competition posited a
logic of efficient allocation of resources that worked without any
conscious manipulation whatsoever. To the extent that market
competition fulfilled the criteria of "pure competition," economic
activity could be described as anarchic, the result of innumerable
decisions on the part of numerous individual buyers and sellers. In
place of political authority, or monopolistic power, or even of subtle
norms imposed through custom, pure competition describes an
economic world drained of all motives except the rational pursuit
of economic gain in a context where no one has power or authority
over anybody else. The role of the state, under this conception, is
to provide the legal context for market competition and to promote
certain minimal political goals, most essentially national security
and law and order.

   As an abstract theory of resource allocation, pure competition
was an elegant and powerful theory, but viewed from a larger so-
ciohistorical standpoint it contained an essential contradiction, for
it ignored entirely the incentives for market control through organization. In practice, the demand for economic security and fair-
ness, alongside inducements to take advantage of economies of
scale or provide collective goods, have led a variety of economic

[3] Samuel H. Beer, *Modern British Politics* (New York: Norton, 1982), p. 392.

actors to organize their response to market constraints and thus gain some purposive control over their economic fate.

This incentive was strongest in the market for the commodity that was the least mobile, storable, and most life sustaining—namely labor. For the artisan and domestic worker the growth of market competition and laissez-faire contained an immanent threat to their traditional communities, and sometimes to their physical survival. At a minimum, it meant the final disintegration of guilds and the breakdown of apprenticeship regulations, the growth of "dishonorable" work, increasing susceptibility to displacement through mechanical innovation, the cash nexus in place of paternalistic custom, and the dissolution of mercantilist state regulation of employment guaranteeing a "fair" wage and a measure of economic security in hard times. But at the same time the intensification of exploitation that accompanied these changes released artisans and domestic workers from the constraints of a traditional view of the reciprocal relationship between journeyman and master and opened the way—at least among those groups that had the necessary communal resources—for the creation of organization as a means of collective action and self-defense.

Although many unions, particularly in the Anglo-American societies, tacitly accepted laissez-faire, they could never accept market competition. Unions existed precisely to defend the worker against insecurity and exploitation in the labor market. And they attempted to do this by monopolizing as far as possible the supply of labor of their potential membership. Given sufficient control of the relevant labor supply they could replace the marginal product of labor as the determinant of the price employers were prepared to pay for additional amounts of labor, with a nonmarginal calculation involving total profits, the total wage bill, and the potential costs of a complete breakdown of business for the duration of a strike. Unions inevitably introduced considerations of power into an arena that under "pure competition" was determined solely by economic rationality.

As long as organization in the labor market was limited in extent, and the size of the bargaining unit was small, manipulation of the labor supply and its price had merely local effects. Power relations between unions and employers did not then much impinge on what we normally understand as politics, the authoritative allocation of values for society as a whole. But in the closing decades of the nineteenth century the scope and density of organization in the labor market increased greatly.

This had two vital consequences for the relationship between labor markets and the state. First, it drastically enlarged the economic consequences of conflict in the labor market. As industrial relations were coordinated at the interregional and national levels, disputes in certain industries could disrupt the economy as a whole. Governments could not afford to stand outside the labor market as impartial observers but were increasingly drawn into the process of conflict resolution itself. Second, the growth of organization in the labor market gave rise to an intense competition between economic groups that spilled out into the political arena. If the doctrine of market competition served to protect the market from the interference of the state, it also assumed the independence of the state from dominance by particular economic interests by postulating economic units that were too small to exercise decisive political leverage. But the emergence of large-scale industry and centralized associations representing, on the one side, thousands of employers and, on the other, hundreds of thousands of workers, allowed a ready transfer of leverage in the market to leverage in the political sphere.

The consequences of this development were already visible to Emil Lederer, the German sociologist, writing in 1913:

> All economic organizations . . . have a common purpose, that of organizing the market by restricting competition within a specific group. First and foremost, all of these associations represent a retreat from the liberal conception of the economy. . . . Further, these economic organizations attempt to express the common interests of their constituent groups, directly in the economy against other groups, whether they are organized or not, and indirectly through a far-reaching influence on the state, and particularly on those aspects of political life in which they attempt to represent their interests. Because these organizations go beyond economic life and the market to make society as a whole, the public realm, the arena of their activities, they experience an important internal change in that they demand for themselves influence on the development of state affairs.[4]

[4] Emil Lederer, *Die Wirtschaftliche Organization* (Leipzig: B.G. Teubner, 1913), p. 6.

The massive increase in the scale of industrial conflict and competition between economic organizations, which we can conceptualize as a growth in the political consequences of economic conflict, was matched by an expansion of state regulation of the labor market. As the economic foundations and ideology of the self-regulating market system were undermined, and as governments found themselves subjected to increasing pressures for various kinds of intervention in the economy, so the state was drawn into new regulative and integrative responsibilities that it could fulfill only with the advice and cooperation of functional economic groups. In return for this cooperation these groups demanded influence in the relevant policy-making and policy-implementing institutions.[5] The logic of this development can be seen in the role that unions began to play in administering welfare and labor market legislation in the late nineteenth and early twentieth centuries. During the First World War, the willingness of the state to enter into a political exchange with unions intensified under the pressures of assuring industrial peace and total mobilization, and governments in all the warring countries were eventually induced to invest unions with a wide range of quasi-public functions.

These, then, were the general developments in the context of constraints and inducements on union strategy associated with the decline of market competition and laissez-faire in the Organizational Revolution of the decades around the turn of the twentieth century. In the remainder of this chapter I shall examine the historical unfolding of these profound changes in the most economically advanced societies of the West—namely Britain, Germany, and the United States.

THE TRANSFORMATION OF INDUSTRIAL CONFLICT

The years from the last decade of the nineteenth century, when reliable figures for union membership are first available, to the eve of the First World War, saw a remarkable growth of unionism in Western Europe and the United States. In the United Kingdom union membership increased by more than 250 percent from 1892

[5] See Beer's epilogue in *Modern British Politics* and the now voluminous literature on neocorporatism, especially the collection of articles in Phillippe Schmitter and Gerhard Lehmbruch, eds., *Trends toward Corporatist Intermediation* (Beverly Hills, Calif.: Sage, 1979); Meyer, *Theorien zum Funktionswandel der Gewerkschaften*, chap. 1; and Timothy May, *Trade Unions and Pressure Group Politics* (London: Westmead, 1975).

to 1913, and by the latter date unions encompassed almost one worker out of four in industry and commerce.[6] In the United States the increase was more than fivefold in the shorter time span (1897–1913) for which reliable data are available.[7] By 1913 unions had more than 2.5 million members, about 10 percent of the nonagricultural workforce. In Germany the rate of increase was even greater: between 1891 and 1913 union membership increased more than eightfold to encompass roughly one-fifth of potential union members.[8]

Both the smaller and exclusive craft unions as well as the larger industrial and general unions grew in this period, but it was the latter that grew the most. This was partly the result of the disproportionate expansion in this period of communications and heavy industry in which the newer industrial and general unions predominated.[9] But it also reflected the breakthrough of what in Britain

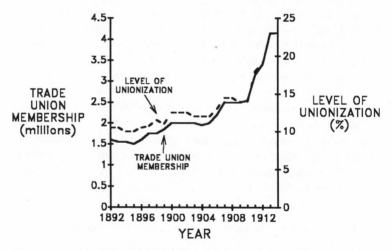

Figure 3.1 Trade Union Membership and Density in the United Kingdom, 1892–1914
SOURCE: Bain and Elsheikh, *Union Growth and the Business Cycle*, pp. 133–134.
NOTE: Level of unionization is union membership as a proportion of potential trade union membership excluding the agricultural sector.

[6] George Sayers Bain and Robert Price, *Profiles of Union Growth* (Oxford: Basil Blackwell, 1980), pp. 37–38.
[7] Ibid., pp. 88–89.
[8] Ibid., pp. 133–134.
[9] Hugh A. Clegg, Alan Fox, and A. F. Thompson make this point in *A History of*

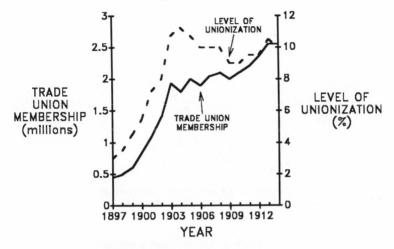

Figure 3.2 Trade Union Membership and Density in the United States, 1897–1914
SOURCE: Bain and Elsheikh, *Union Growth and the Business Cycle*, pp. 136–137.
NOTE: Level of unionization is union membership as a proportion of potential trade union membership excluding the agricultural sector.

was called "new unionism"—unionism catering specifically to unskilled groups of workers, such as dockers and railway workers, who were specifically excluded from the established craft unions.[10] As revealed in tables 3.1, 3.2, and 3.3, the shift in the balance between craft and industrial unionism was greater in Germany than in the United Kingdom or the United States, but in each of these countries unionism gained most ground among groups of workers situated at the heart of the economy, in industries such as mining,

---

British Trade Unions since 1889 (Oxford: Clarendon Press, 1964), 1: 467. See also J.H.A. Clapham, *An Economic History of Modern Britain* (Cambridge: Cambridge University Press, 1938), 3: 319–333. On German unions see Gerhard Bry, *Wages in Germany, 1971–1945* (Princeton, N.J.: Princeton University Press, 1960), pp. 24–25.

[10] On the growth of new unionism in Britain see James Hinton, "The Rise of a Mass Labour Movement: Growth and Limits," in Chris Wrigley, ed., *A History of British Industrial Relations, 1875–1914* (Amherst: University of Massachusetts Press, 1982); Clegg et al., *A History of British Trade Unions since 1889* vol. 1, ch. 2; Eric J. Hobsbawm "General Labour Unions in Britain, 1889–1914," in Hobsbawm, *Labouring Men* (London: Weidenfeld & Nicolson, 1964); on Germany see Gerhard A. Ritter and Klaus Tenfelde, "Der Durchbruch der Freien Gewerkshaften Deutschlands zur Massenbewegung in letzten Viertel des 19. Jahrhunderts," in Hans O. Vetter, ed. *Vom Sozialistengesetz zur Mitbestimmung* (Köln: Bund Verlag, 1975); on the United States see Leo Wolman, *The Growth of American Trade Unions, 1880–1923* (New York: National Bureau of Economic Research, 1924), chap. 2.

Figure 3.3 Membership and Density of German Free Trade Unions, 1891–1914
Sources: Trade union membership: Hirsch-Weber, *Gewerkschaften in der Politik*, p. 144. Potential trade union membership: Hoffmann, *Das Wachstum der deutschen Wirtschaft seit der Mitte des 19.Jahrhunderts*, pp. 196–199.
Note: Level of unionization is union membership as a proportion of potential trade union membership excluding the agricultural sector.

railroads, and engineering, where industrial conflict would have societywide consequences.[11]

This development was reinforced in Britain especially, and to a lesser extent in the United States and Germany, by the transition from local and regional to interregional and even national collective bargaining. Only one industrywide agreement existed in Britain in 1899, in the cotton weaving industry. By 1910 national agreements were signed in engineering, shipbuilding, cotton spinning, building, printing, iron and steel, and footwear.[12] In addition, interregional agreements were the rule in a number of other industries including coalmining and the railways. In the United States the first industrywide agreement, negotiated in the stove foundry industry in 1891, provided the impetus to similar agreements in ten industries before 1917, including iron and steel, bituminous coal, printing,

[11] See James E. Cronin, "Strikes and the Struggle for Union Organization: Britain and Europe," in Wolfgang J. Mommsen and Hans-Gerhard Husung, eds., *The Development of Trade Unionism in Great Britain and Germany, 1880–1914* (London: George Allen & Unwin, 1985).

[12] Clegg et al., *A History of British Trade Unions since 1889* 1: 471; E. H. Phelps Brown, *The Growth of British Industrial Relations* (London: Macmillan, 1959), p. 268; John Lovell, *British Trade Unions, 1875–1933* (London: Macmillan, 1977), pp. 41–44.

TABLE 3.1
Membership of Ten Largest Free Trade Unions in Germany, 1892–1913

1892		1913	
Metalworkers*	26,100	Metalworkers*	557,000
Saar coalminers*	22,400	Construction workers*	327,000
Carpenter (joiners)*	18,100	Transport workers*	230,000
Printers	16,000	Factory workers*	211,000
Westfalen coalminers*	15,300	Woodworkers*†	195,000
Masons	11,800	Textile workers*	142,000
Tobacco workers	11,100	Coalminers*	104,000
Shoemakers	10,200	Printers	69,000
Carpenters	8,400	Carpenters	62,000
Saxony coalminers*	7,200	Municipal workers	53,000

SOURCE: Fricke, *Die deutsche Arbeiterbewegung, 1869–1914* pp. 696–699.
NOTES: * Denotes industrial or general, as opposed to craft, union.
    † This union (Holzarbeiter) was the result of a merger of craft carpenters' unions, including the joiners (Tischler), into an industrial union. See Ritter and Tenfelde, "Der Durchbruch der Freien Gewerkschaften Deutschlands zur Massenbewegung in letzten Viertel des 19.Jahrhunderts," p. 103.

and machinery production.[13] The nationalization of collective bargaining in Germany was stunted by initial union opposition and the fierce resistance of employers. Only printing and four minor craft industries signed national agreements before 1914.[14] But the decade before the First World War did see a movement from collective bargaining at the level of the firm and locality to the region, and, perhaps more importantly, a sharp growth in the size of strikes and lock outs in industries where institutionalized means of conflict resolution were absent.[15]

[13] Neil W. Chamberlain and J. W. Kuhn, *Collective Bargaining*, 2d ed. (New York: McGraw-Hill, 1965), p. 35.
[14] H. Deckers, *Betrieblicher oder Überbetrieblicher Tarifvertrag* (Münster: Aschendorffsche Verlagsbuchhandlung, 1960), p. 18.
[15] See ibid., pp. 15–18. Paul Umbreit, *25 Jahre Deutsche Gewerkschaftsbewegung, 1890–1918* (Berlin: General Kommission der Gewerkschaften Deutschlands, 1915), p. 62; Theodore Cassau, *Die Gewerkschaftsbewegung, Ihre Soziologie und Ihr Kampf* (Berlin, 1920), pp. 178–181, 189–193; Siegfried Nestriepke, *Die Gewerkschaftsbewegung* (Stuttgart: E. H. Moritz, 1922), 1: 410–411. The growth in the size of strikes in Germany, shown in Table 3.6 is not reflected in the average size of strikes. But in this context

TABLE 3.2

Membership of Ten Largest Trade Unions in the United Kingdom, 1890–1910

1890		1910	
Engineers	67,900	Durham coalminers*	122,000
Yorkshire coalminers*	50,000	Engineers†	111,000
Durham coalminers*	49,000	Yorkshire coalminers*	88,300
Boilermakers	32,900	Railway workers*	75,200
Carpenters	31,500	Carpenters	55,800
Railway workers*	26,400	Boilermakers	49,400
Boot and Shoe workers	23,500	Postal workers*	37,900
Glass bottle makers	18,100	Northumberland coalminers*	37,400
Northumberland coalminers*	17,000	Boot and shoe workers	30,200
Tailors	16,600	Co-op employees	29,900

SOURCE: Webb and Webb, *The History of Trade Unionism*, pp. 745–750. Textile unions are not included in the Webbs' figures and are not listed in this table.

NOTES: * Denotes industrial or general, as opposed to craft, union.

† Although not an industrial or general union, the Amalgamated Society of Engineers expanded its membership among the unskilled and semiskilled from the last decade of the nineteenth century. See Pelling, *A History of British Trade Unionism*, p. 104; Zeitlin, "Craft Regulation and the Division of Labour: Engineers and Compositors in Britain, 1890–1914."

The disproportionate growth of unionism in basic industries, together with the widening of the bargaining area, changed the nature of the strike. Intensive strike activity was not uncommon before the 1890s, but even when strikes were well organized their economic impact was local, or regional at most. But a national strike in a heavy industry could threaten the welfare of the country as a whole. Even when a national strike was directed to limited economic ends, its impact was political, and governments, in one way or another, felt compelled to intervene. The logic of the situation was acutely perceived by the German socialist theoretician, Rudolf Hilferding, writing in 1910.

The development of employer and worker organization gives wage conflicts ever greater general social and political signifi-

the largest strikes, not the average, determined state policy. For statistics on average strike size see Heinrich Volkmann, "Modernisierung des Arbeitkampfes," in Harmut Kaelble et al., eds., *Probleme der Modernisierung in Deutschland* (Opladen: Westdeuscher Verlag, 1978).

TABLE 3.3
Membership of Ten Largest Trade Unions in the United States, 1897–1916

1897		1916	
Locomotive engineers	30,300	Coalminers*	318,000
Cigarmakers	28,300	Carpenters	213,000
Carpenters	28,200	Railway clerks	143,000
Printers	28,100	Machinists	101,000
Railroad trainmen	25,400	Locomotive firemen	93,600
Locomotive firemen	24,300	Garment workers*	85,100
Bricklayers	23,300	Bricklayers	73,800
Railway conductors	20,700	Switchmen	64,600
Machinists	14,000	Printers	60,700
Boot and shoe workers	12,500	Molders	50,000

SOURCE: Wolin, *The Growth of American Trade Unions, 1880–1923*, pp. 110–119.
NOTE: * Denotes industrial or general, as opposed to craft, union.

cance. The guerrilla war of the trade union against the individual employer gives way to mass conflicts which involve whole industrial spheres. If those conflicts extend to the most vital sectors within the division of labor, they threaten to bring the entire process of production in society to a standstill. Thus, the trade union struggle grows beyond its specific sphere and is transformed from a concern of those employers and workers who are immediately involved to a general concern of the society, that is to say into a political phenomenon.[16]

The parallel occurrence of huge strikes in Britain, the United States, and Germany in the decades around the turn of the twentieth century is evident from tables 3.4, 3.5, and 3.6.

The first national stoppage in Britain took place in the coal industry in 1893. The dispute severely affected production in other industries and, as a consequence, placed the government under

[16] E. H. Phelps Brown, "New Wine in Old Bottles: Reflections on the Changed Working of Collective Bargaining in Great Britain," in Brian Barrett et al., eds., *Industrial Relations and the Wider Society* (London: Collier Macmillan, Open University Press, 1975), p. 332; Edward Berman, *Labor Disputes and the President of the United States* (New York: Columbia University Press, 1924), pp. 7–8; Rudolf Hilferding, *Das Finanzkapital* (1910; reprint ed., Berlin: Dietz, 1955), pp. 548–549.

TABLE 3.4
Major Industrial Disputes in Britain, 1890–1914

Industry	Year	No. of Workers Involved	Duration
Coalmines	1893	300,000	5 months
Engineering	1897/1898	100,000	6 months
South Wales coalmines	1898	100,000	5 months
Textiles	1908	120,000	2 months
Railways	1911	200,000	2 weeks
Coalmines	1912	450,000	1 month
London docks	1912	80,000	2 months

SOURCES: Coalmines (1893): Wigham, *Strikes and the Government, 1893–1974*, p. 11. Engineering: Pelling, *A History of British Trade Unionism*, p. 112. South Wales coalmines: Wigham, *Strikes and the Government, 1893–1974*, p. 14. Textiles: Clegg et al., *A History of British Trade Unions since 1889*, pp. 459–460. Railways: Wigham, *Strikes and the Government, 1893–1974*, p. 25. Coalmines (1912): Phelps Brown, *The Growth of British Industrial Relations*, pp. 324–326. London docks: Wigham, *Strikes and the Government, 1893–1974*, p. 25; Webb and Webb, *The History of Trade Unionism*, pp. 502–503.

mounting public pressure to act.[17] In the end, William Gladstone, the Liberal prime minister, was moved, despite his deep-seated reluctance to interfere in the private economy, to propose a conference of trade union and employer representatives under the chairmanship of a cabinet minister. This was the first instance of government intervention to mediate an industrial dispute in Britain. Three years later the state's newfound role was institutionalized under the Conciliation Act, which empowered the Board of Trade to bring the parties of a dispute together. Although this act did not create the legal machinery to impose terms on either party, it was, as D. E. Macdonald has emphasized, "an official recognition that the State has an obligation to interfere, however delicately, in matters previously considered the exclusive province of employers and workers."[18]

[17] Eric Wigham, *Strikes and the Government, 1893–1974* (London: Macmillan, 1976), pp. 49–50; Clegg et al., *A History of British Trade Unions since 1889*, 1: 106–109; Phelps Brown, *The Growth of British Industrial Relations*, pp. 161–162.
[18] D. E. Macdonald, *The State and the Trade Unions* (London: Macmillan, 1976), pp.

TABLE 3.5
Major Industrial Disputes in the United States, 1890–1914

Industry	Year	No. of Workers Involved	Duration
Anthracite coalmines	1894	125,000	2 months
Bitumous coalmines	1897	100,000	2 months
Building trades	1900	55,000	1 month
Anthracite coalmines	1900	130,000	1 month
Anthracite coalmines	1902	150,000	5 months
New York building trades	1903	70,000	1 month
Anthracite coalmines	1912	180,000	1 month

SOURCES: Anthracite coalmines (1894): Taft, *Organized Labor in American History*, pp. 101–102. Bitumous coalmines: ibid., p. 170. Building trades: ibid., p. 208. Anthracite coalmines (1900): Berman, *Labor Disputes and the President of the United States*, pp. 46–47; Perlman, *History of Trade Unionism in the United States*, p. 175. Anthracite coalmines (1902): Berman, *Labor Disputes and the President of the United States*, pp. 49–50; Perlman, *History of Trade Unionism in the United States*, p. 176. New York building trades: Taft, *Organized Labor in American History*, p. 209. Anthracite coalmines (1912): Perlman, *History of Trade Unionism in the United States*, p. 179.

The first experience of the growth in the scale and consequences of industrial conflict was a watershed in government policy. Subsequently the state has been involved, whether through the existing machinery of conciliation or through ad hoc ministerial intervention, in every major strike or lock out that has taken place in Britain. Spurred into action by the recurring need to promote industrial peace in an increasingly interdependent economy, the state came to pursue a policy of intervention in the labor market that was never formulated coherently.[19] But the cumulative effect of this

49–50. See also Chris Wrigley, "The Government and Industrial Relations," in Wrigley, ed., *A History of British Industrial Relations, 1875–1914* (Amherst: University of Massachusetts Press, 1982); and V. L. Allen, *Trade Unions and the Government* (London: Longmans, 1960), pp. 51–54.

[19] Henry Pelling points out that the government "merely responded ad hoc to strikes as they took place, and its policy was shaped by external pressures from different directions, including, of course, that of the T.U.C. and of the Labour Party in the Commons." See *A History of British Trade Unionism* (London: Penguin, 1976), p. 144; James E. Cronin, "Strikes 1870–1914," in Chris Wrigley, ed., *A History of British*

TABLE 3.6
Major Industrial Disputes in Germany, 1890–1914

Industry	Year	No. of Workers Involved	Duration
Hamburg docks	1896/1897	18,000	2 months
Ruhr coalmines	1905	217,000	5 months
Construction industry	1910	180,000	1 month
Ruhr coalmines	1912	240,000	2 weeks

SOURCES: Hamburg docks: Griep, *Zur Geschichte der deutschen Gewerkschaftsbewegung, 1890–1914*, p. 60. Ruhr coalmines: Baudis and Nussbaum, *Wirtschaft und Staat in Deutschland am Ende des 19. Jahrhundert bis 1918/19*, p. 165. Construction industry: Griep, *Zur Geschichte der deutschen Gewerkschaftsbewegung, 1890–1914*, p. 122.

policy drift has been to reduce the autonomy of the labor market from the state even in substantive matters of wage setting. This was most clearly shown during the massive miner's strike of 1912. Once government attempts to conciliate the opposing sides failed, a bill giving the Miners' Federation most of what it wanted by establishing district minimum wages was rushed through Parliament.
The same pressures towards state intervention were present in the United States. Between 1894 and 1917, no less than thirteen strikes or threatened strikes in major industries—mainly coalmining and the railroads—occasioned direct presidential intervention. The most frequent response to large-scale strikes such as the Pullman strike of 1894 and the Coeur d'Alenes strike of 1899 was the introduction of police or troops to enforce court injunctions against union picketing, secondary boycotts, or more vaguely, "to protect property."[20] However, from the turn of the century, state intervention was almost always laced with federal mediation to induce the warring parties to find some middle ground. Conciliation and arbitration were supported by a number of middle-class reformers

Industrial Relations, 1875–1914 (Amherst: University of Massachusetts Press, 1982); Roger Davidson, *Whitehall and the Labour Problem in Late-Victorian and Edwardian Britain* (London: Croon Helm, 1985), pp. 258–264. On government policy in America, which was similar in this respect, see Berman, *Labor Disputes and the President of the United States*, pp. 251–252.

[20] See Berman, *Labor Disputes and the President of the United States*.

who sought to find corporatist solutions to labor problems. Moreover, such an approach was consistent with the sheer difficulty of coercing industrial peace from workers and the need on the part of the executive to advertise its even-handedness.[21]

The first attempt to set up federal machinery for mediating industrial disputes followed a sharp increase in strike activity in 1886. In that year President Cleveland followed the example of the New York and Massachusetts legislatures and established a three-man board under the commissioner of labor to investigate and arbitrate labor disputes.[22] The anthracite coal strike of 1902 set a new precedent for state intervention in the labor market. By the fourth month of the strike Americans were contemplating what President Theodore Roosevelt described as the "terrible nature of . . . a winter fuel famine."[23] The President expressed his predicament in a letter to Senator Mark Hanna, who had tried unsuccessfully to bring about a settlement of the strike:

> What gives me greatest concern at the moment is the coal famine. Of course we have nothing whatever to do with this coal strike and no earthly responsibility for it. But the public at large will tend to visit on our heads responsibility for the shortage of coal. . . . I do not see what I can do, and I know that the coal operators are especially distrustful of anything which they regard as in the nature of political interference. But I do most earnestly feel that from every consideration of public policy and good morals they should make some slight concession.[24]

The pressures on the President eventually compelled him into action, and he went so far as to threaten, without precedent and with doubtful legality, to seize the mines unless the coal operators accepted a plan of federal arbitration.[25] By 1913 state intervention was institutionalized on three levels: through the Federal Board of Conciliation, later the U.S. Conciliation Service under the Depart-

[21] William E. Akin, "Arbitration and Labor Conflict: The Middle Class Panacea, 1886–1900," *Historian* 29 (1966/1967).

[22] See ibid.

[23] Quoted in Berman, *Labor Disputes and the President of the United States*, p. 51.

[24] See ibid., p. 51.

[25] Good accounts of these events are given by Marguerite Green, *The National Civic Federation and the American Labor Movement, 1900–1925* (Washington, D.C.: Catholic University of America Press, 1956), pp. 53–55; J. Amsden and S. Brier, "Coal Miners on Strike," *Journal of Interdisciplinary History* 7, no. 4 (1977); Berman, *Labor Disputes and the President of the United States*, pp. 51–59.

ment of Labor (1913), through state boards of arbitration, and finally through legislation for setting up machinery for individual industries. By 1910 the National Association of State Boards of Arbitration represented eighteen states, and federal arbitration machinery existed for several industries, including, most notably, the railroads.[26] As in Britain the state became involved in every major strike that took place in the twentieth century.

In Germany state intervention frequently took an overtly repressive form. Prohibition of mass meetings, arbitrary arrests and deportations, curfews, and confiscation of membership lists were the methods generally used to deal with large strikes in sensitive industries.[27] But such a heavy-handed approach had its limitations, especially when it came to the largest strikes, some of which involved hundreds of thousands of workers, or strikes having the moral support of broad sections of the middle classes.

The first instance of such a strike was that of over two hundred thousand Ruhr coalminers in 1905. Lacking sufficient funds to outlast the financially powerful and united coal syndicate, the workers, according to Jutta Schmidt and Wolfgang Seichter, realized that "a battle against the employers alone was, from the outset, hopeless; instead, pressure was exerted against the entire economy and the state."[28] In the second month of the strike, Bülow, the chancellor of the Reich, set up a government commission to inquire into the causes of the unrest with the goal of bringing about a negotiated compromise. When the employers refused to cooperate with the commission, Bülow brought an end to the strike, which now threatened to cause a widespread shortage of coal for domestic heating, by rushing through a legislative amendment to the existing coalmining code granting the workers much of what they wanted.[29]

Despite this precedent, political mediation of industrial conflict

[26] See Edwin E. Witte, *The Government in Labor Disputes* (New York: McGraw-Hill Book Company, 1932), chap. 9.

[27] See Jutta Schmidt and Wolfgang Seichter, "Die deutsche Gewerkschaftsbewegung von der Mitte der neunziger Jahre des 19.Jahrhunderts bis zum Ersten Weltkrieg," in Frank Deppe et al., eds., *Geschichte der deutschen Gewerkschaftsbewegung* (Köln: Pahl-Rugenstein, 1977), pp. 74–82; Gerhard Griep, *Zur Geschichte der deutschen Gewerkschaftsbewegung, 1890–1914* (Berlin: Tribune, 1960), chaps. 2 and 5; Cassau, *Die Gewerkschaftsbewegung, Ihre Soziologie und Ihr Kampf*, pp. 255–258.

[28] Schmidt and Seichter, "Die deutsche Gewerkschaftsbewegung von der Mitte der neunziger Jahre des 19.Jahrhunderts bis zum Ersten Weltkrieg," p. 79.

[29] Dieter Baudis and Helga Nussbaum, *Wirtschaft und Staat in Deutschland am Ende des 19. Jahrhunderts bis 1918/1919* (Berlin/DDR: Topos, 1978), pp. 166–176.

was not institutionalized in the kind of government arbitration machinery that was created in Britain or the United States. Until the First World War, when the radical restructuring of German society, and of labor's role within it, induced the state into more even-handed intervention, strikers usually had to take on the repressive forces of the state as well as their employers.

THE GROWTH OF COMPETITION IN THE POLITICAL ARENA

The extension and concentration of organization in the labor market in these years was not limited to workers but was just as evident on the side of employers. In the most economically advanced societies the last years of the nineteenth century saw the beginning of a profound shift away from market competition to an "organized economy" increasingly dominated by some combination of oligopolistic and monopolistic corporations, trusts, and cartels.[30] The transformation was bound up with a variety of technological advances, amounting to what some economic historians have called "a second industrial revolution," consisting most notably of rapidly expanding marketing areas, cheaper and faster communications, the advent of electric power, and the discovery and exploitation of economies of scale in heavy industry and the new mass production industries.[31]

[30] Leslie Hannah, *The Rise of the Corporate Economy* (Baltimore: The Johns Hopkins University Press, 1976), chap. 1.

[31] On Britain: Clapham, *An Economic History of Modern Britain*, chap. 5; Eric J. Hobsbawm, *Industry and Empire* (London: Weidenfeld and Nicolson, 1968), pp. 177–178; G. C. Allen, *British Industries and Their Organization* (London: Longmans, 1970), pp. 10–13; W.H.B. Court, *A Concise Economic History of Britain* (Cambridge: Cambridge University Press, 1967), pp. 210–216. On the United States: Alfred D. Chandler, *The Visable Hand: The Managerial Revolution in American Business* (Cambridge, Mass.: Belknap Press, 1977); Harold U. Faulkner, *The Decline of Laissez-Faire, 1897–1917* (New York: Rinehart, 1951), chap. 8; Ida M. Tarbell, *The Nationalizing of Business, 1878–1898* (New York: The Macmillan Company, 1936); Howard N. Ross, "Economic Growth and Change in the United States under Laissez-Faire: 1870–1929," in Frederic C. Jaher, ed., *The Age of Industrialism in America* (New York: Free Press, 1978). On Germany: Hans-Ulrich Wehler, *Bismarck und der Imperialismus* (München: Deutscher Taschenbuch, 1976), pp. 96–97; Wilhelm Treue, "Wirtschafts und Sozialgeschichte Deutschlands im 19. Jahrhundert," in B. Gebhardt, *Handbuch der deutschen Geschichte* (Stuttgart: Union Verlag, 1960), vol. 3; Wolfgang Zorn, "Typen und Entwicklungskräfte deutschen Unternehmertums," in Karl E. Born, ed., *Moderne Deutsche Wirtschaftsgeschichte* (Köln: Kiepenheuer und Witsch, 1966); Wolfram Fischer, "Bergbau, Industrie und Handwerk, 1850–1914," in H. Aubin and W. Zorn, eds., *Handbuch der deutschen Wirtschafts und Sozialgeschichte* (Stuttgart: Ernst Klett, 1976), 2: 532–533.

In Germany and the United States, and to a lesser extent in Britain, the trend towards large-scale industry was consolidated in the years around the turn of the twentieth century by an outbreak of mergers and trade agreements. In Germany this movement typically took the form of agreed limitations of production between firms organized in cartels. By 1905 more than four hundred cartels were established, and they dominated most major industrial sectors, particularly the production of raw materials, including coal and iron and steel.[32] In the United States the enactment of legislation making cartels illegal precipitated an extensive merger movement. Between 1895 and 1905 the size of the one hundred largest American companies quadrupled, and by 1905 they controlled 40 percent of the nation's industrial capital.[33] In the five years between 1899 and 1904 the average size of American manufacturing firms increased by more than 25 percent. In Britain, where price-fixing agreements were legal, organized restraint of competition remained an alternative to amalgamation, and a government inquiry in 1918 found more than five hundred such associations.[34]

The efforts of employers to coordinate their activities in production and marketing led in many cases to coordination on similar, or even more explicit, lines against unions. Many trade associations, mergers, and cartels were, in any case, conceived with political as

TABLE 3.7
Cartels in Germany, 1865–1905

	1865	1870	1875	1879	1885	1890	1896	1900	1905
Number of cartels	4	6	8	14	90	210	260	351	400

SOURCES: 1865–1900: Kuczynski, *Die Geschichte der Lage der Arbeiter unter dem Kapitalismus*, 14: 130. 1905: Dobb, *Studies in the Development of Capitalism*, p. 3.

[32] This is the figure of the Kartell-Commission of 1905 reported in Maurice Dobb, *Studies in the Development of Capitalism* (New York: International Publishers, 1947), p. 310. See also Costas, *Auswirkungen der Konzentration*, pp. 25–37; Hans-Ulrich Wehler, *Das deutsche Kaiserreich, 1871–1918* (Göttingen: Vandenhöck & Ruprecht, 1973), pp. 48–53.

[33] Alan L. Friedman, *Industry and Labor* (London: Macmillan, 1977), p. 38; Harold U. Faulkner, *American Economic History* (New York: Harper, 1960), pp. 421–435.

[34] Clapham, *An Economic History of Modern Britain*, pp. 301–302, 316; Friedman, *Industry and Labor*, p. 38.

TABLE 3.8
Growth of American Manufacturing Establishments, 1899–1914

	1899	1904	1909	1914
Average product	$54,969	$68,433	$76,993	$87,916

SOURCE: Faulkner, *The Decline of Laissez-Faire, 1897–1917*, p. 155; computed from figures in Bureau of the Census, *Statistical Abstract of the United States*, 1921, table 482, p. 868.

well as economic goals in mind. The last two decades of the nineteenth century saw intensive debate in all industrialized countries on the issues of tariff reform and privileged spheres of foreign trade. Economic competition was increasingly carried on under the skirts of state power, whether in colonial or domestic markets, and employers with common interests were induced to combine to gain increased political leverage. Once employers had formed associations to influence political decisions related to protection and empire, it was a short step to put labor legislation on the agenda.

At the same time many employers, especially in those sectors most prone to international competition, mobilized to defend or extend their autonomy from workers' control on the shop floor. In these years labor management was increasingly viewed as a science demanding the subordination of individual craftsmen and laborers to rational methods of production, directly supervised through the management hierarchy. Employers who had long opposed the existence of unions as threats to their own paternalistic control could now argue—on apparently value-free grounds—that workers' organization on the shop floor was an impediment to efficiency and must be resisted accordingly. The only role that unions could usefully play under such a conception of workplace authority was in educating and disciplining workers in the rigors of rationally organized production.[35]

[35] This topic has been the subject of much fine recent research on the part of social and labor historians. On the United States see, for example, David Montgomery, *Workers' Control in America* (Cambridge: Cambridge University Press, 1979). On Britain see Jonathan Zeitlin, "The Labour Strategies of British Engineering Employers, 1890–1922," in Howard F. Gospel and Craig R. Littler, eds., *Managerial Strategies and Industrial Relations: Historical and Comparative Perspectives* (London: Heinemann Books,

With intensified and increasingly politicized competition among employers and their clashes with organized labor, organization itself passed a critical threshold to become a self-reinforcing phenomenon. Like the process of nuclear fission, which at some critical mass becomes self-sustaining, the most vital inducement to organization was the sheer existence of other, competing, organizations. The essential basis of organization was economic, but the vast resources that the resulting organizations commanded meant that their struggles were played out in society as a whole. The fundamental separation of economic and political activity that underpinned the theory of laissez-faire became increasingly irrelevant in the organized economy.

In Germany individual cartels in collaboration with the two major peak organizations, the Central Association of German Industrialists, representing heavy industry, and the League of German Industrialists, representing the new chemical and electrochemical industries, pursued a vindictive political campaign against the socialist Free Trade Unions.[36] Until the outbreak of the First World War, German employers successfully defended the de jure and de facto rights of nonunion labor and maintained, or in some cases even stiffened, the vague laws restricting strikes and picketing. They also attempted to contain the scope and cost of social welfare reforms and the role that unions played in their administration.

The efforts of these peak employers' organizations were vehemently supplemented by employers' associations based in individual industries or localities. Agitation for antiunion cooperation was strongest in Hamburg, where trade unionism was particularly well

---

1983); Richard Price, *Masters, Unions and Men* (Cambridge: Cambridge University Press, 1980); Richard Price, "The New Unionism and the Labor Process," and Alastair Reid, "The Division of Labour and Politics in Britain, 1880–1920," both in Wolfgang J. Mommsen and Hans-Gerhard Husung, eds., *The Development of Trade Unionism in Great Britain and Germany, 1880–1914* (London: George Allen & Unwin, 1985). On Germany see Dieter Groh, "Intensification of Work and Industrial Conflict in Germany, 1896–1914," *Politics and Society* 8, nos. 3–4 (1978).

[36] On the activities of German industrialists against the socialist Free Unions, see Karl Born, "Der soziale und wirtschaftliche Strukturwandel am Ende des 19. Jahrhunderts," *Vierteljahrschrift für Sozial- und Wirtschaftsgeschichte* 50 (1963); Born, *Staat und Sozialpolitik seit Bismarcks Sturtz, 1890–1914* (Weisbaden: F. Steiner, 1957), pp. 80–83; Paul Umbreit, *25 Jahre Deutsche Gewerkschaftsbewegung, 1890–1918*, pp. 106–107 and chap. 5; Wehler, *Das deutsche Kaiserreich, 1871–1918*, pp. 100–104; Max Präger, "Grenzen der Gewerkschaftsbewegung," *Archiv für Sozialwissenschaft und Sozialpolitik* 20 (1905): 240–241; Hans Rosenberg, *Grosse Depression und Bismarckreich* (Berlin: W. de Gruyter, 1967), pp. 154–168.

entrenched. In 1902 the newspaper of the local employer association argued at length that the most urgent need of industry was "the consolidation of organization on every side," so that the employer "is not made to stand powerless before trade union demands like a defenseless fish caught in a net whose mesh becomes ever narrower."[37] The chief functions of regional employer associations were to provide strike and lock-out funds and exclude union members from their firms by enforcing a system of certificates of employment. But the concern of many employers to eradicate unionism and remain "masters of their own houses" led the local associations to add their weight to the peak associations in their political campaigns against unions at the national level.[38]

Employers in the United States were not so united in their demands. The National Civic Federation, for example, brought together employers, mainly in the basic large-scale industries, and labor union leaders to promote industrial conciliation and, in some instances, legislation placing unionism on a sound footing.[39] But the National Civic Federation was vigorously opposed by the National Association of Manufacturers and a host of smaller corporations and local employer associations. These groups, acting in concert, effectively lobbied in defense of the "open-shop" and yellow unions and helped stymie proposed legal limitations on the use of the labor injunction.[40] The success of these political campaigns was summed up by the president of the National Association of Manu-

[37] Quoted in Klaus Saul, *Staat, Industrie, Arbeiterbewegung im Kaiserreich* (Düsseldorf: Bertelsman Universitäts-Verlag, 1974), p. 101.

[38] Quoted in ibid., p. 103. See also Rudolf Leckebusch, *Entstehung und Wandlungen der Zielsetzungen, der Struktur und der Wirkungen von Arbeitgeberverbänden* (Berlin: Duncker und Humbolt, 1966), pp. 128–134; Nestriepke, *Die Gewerkschaftsbewegung*, pp. 292–293; W. Simon, *Macht und Herrschaft der Unternehmerverbände BDI, BDA, und DIHT* (Köln: Pahl-Rugenstein, 1976), pp. 23–28.

[39] Green, *The National Civic Federation and the American Labor Movement, 1900–1925*; Philip Taft, *Organized Labor in American History* (New York: Harper & Row, 1964), pp. 195–197, 227–229; Lewis L. Lorwin, *The American Federation of Labor: History, Policies, and Prospects* (Washington, D.C.: The Brookings Institution, 1933), pp. 82–84.

[40] Little has been written on the orientation of the National Association of Manufacturers toward trade unions. The following deal with this topic tangentially: A. K. Steigerwalt, *The National Association of Manufacturers, 1895–1914* (Ann Arbor: Bureau of Business Research, Graduate School of Business Administration, University of Michigan, 1964); R. W. Gable, "Birth of an Employers' Association," *Business History Review* 33, no. 4 (1959); F. W. Hilbert, "Employers' Associations in the United States," in Jacob B. Hollander and George Barnett, *Studies in American Unionism* (New York: Holt & Company, 1905).

facturers in 1906: "Only a few years ago trades unionism unrestrained and militant was rapidly forcing the industries of the country to a closed shop basis. It was almost a crime to criticize the unions. . . . But a change has come and the Association is largely responsible for it. . . . What has brought these changes. The question can be answered in one word—Organization."[41]

The same pressures to organize were felt by employers in Britain. As the National Farmers' Union explained to their potential members in 1913: "The question we propose to ask you is whether you think you are safe, at a time when every trade is combining AGAINST EVERY OTHER, in remaining outside your own Farmers' Union. Against every other, mind you. Every trade in the world is combined against yours. Dare you risk isolation."[42]

At the national level the Employers' Parliamentary Committee (later Council) was established in 1898 to counter the political efforts of the Parliamentary Committee of the TUC. As one of its founders, Lord Weymiss, explained in *The Times*, "Those who profess through labour organization to speak collectively in the name of labour are listened to, while employers, as a body hitherto having no corporate organization, are consequently not listened to."[43] The committee proceeded to lobby for various legal restrictions on trade unions and provided backing for the largest of the "blackleg" agencies, the National Free Labour Association.[44]

 But the efforts of British employers against unions in the political arena lacked the intensity of those of their counterparts in Germany, or even in the United States, and the Employers' Parliamentary Council never became as influential as the National German Employers' Association or the National Association of Manufacturers. Until the establishment of the Federation of British Industries and the National Union of Manufacturers during the First World War, employers in Britain were generally content to exercise political leverage through sponsored or "interested" members of Parliament.

[41] Quoted in Faulkner, *The Decline of Laissez-Faire, 1897–1917*, p. 296.

[42] Quoted in Samuel H. Beer, *British Politics in the Collectivist Age* (New York: Vintage Books, 1969), p. 113.

[43] *The Times*, 18 November 1898. Quoted in Clegg et al., *A History of British Trade Unions since 1889*, pp. 174–175.

[44] Clegg et al., *A History of British Trade Unions since 1889*, chap. 4; K. G. Knowles, *A Study in Industrial Conflict* (Oxford: B. Blackwell, 1932), pp. 61–65; Phelps Brown, *The Growth of British Industrial Relations*, pp. 162–163, 270–272.

The years around the turn of the twentieth century saw a rapid and enveloping increase in competition between functional economic groups in the political arena. As one group mobilized its resources for political leverage, so competing groups had to do the same so as not to be left behind. This, like the nationalization of industrial relations and the changing character of the strike, led to a greater interpenetration of economy and polity. As economic organization outstripped the limitations of scope and size necessary for perfect competition, so laissez-faire was progressively undermined. Conflicts that were previously confined to local or regional labor markets increasingly spilled out into the national political arena, where they became the concern of collective organizations representing nationwide constituencies.

The individual, the chief actor under laissez-faire, was increasingly submerged under new organizational forms reflecting the increased scale of economic life. As Samuel Beer, describing developments in Britain, has pointed out: "If the rise of the large business corporation was the central thread in economic development, the rise of trade unions, trade associations, and indeed of cooperatives was part of the same general tendency away from individualism and toward collectivism."[45] Or as Karl Erich Born has summarized the "new order" that emerged in Germany in the Organizational Revolution of the decades around the turn of the twentieth century: "If one wishes to define this development in a concise formula, one could describe it, pointedly, as the change from the individualism of the middle-class liberal age to the group solidarity of the age of mass society."[46]

UNIONS AND WELFARE POLITICS

The politicization of union strategy was reinforced by an increased willingness on the part of governments in Britain, Germany, and the United States to accept responsibility for workers' welfare and to legislate improvements in unemployment, illness, and retirement compensation. Even when the influence of laissez-faire was greatest, the state had never completely retreated from its traditional paternalist moorings, but as the scope of its substantive

---

[45] Beer, *British Politics in the Collectivist Age*, p. 74.
[46] Born, "Der soziale und wirtschaftliche Strukturwandel am Ende des 19. Jahrhunderts," p. 364.

regulation of the labor market grew in the last decades of the nineteenth century, the context of union strategy was transformed. Unions that were weak in the labor market had long campaigned for political regulation of wages and working conditions, but now the opportunities for gaining legislation—and administering it—expanded greatly.

At first unions tended to be suspicious of the motives behind the state's growing role in welfare provision largely because they viewed the state as trying to usurp their own benefit functions in the labor market and thus weaken their own organizations. In retrospect, perhaps one of the most remarkable features of unions in these years is the reticence they displayed in campaigning for those broad measures of state support for the unemployed, the sick, the aged, and the nonunionized that became the basis for the welfare state.[47] However, once these new state responsibilities for welfare were legislated, unions came to play an important role in their administration. Business unions that had formerly kept their distance from politics gradually accepted an ever larger role in public administration, while radical socialist unions came to experience the potential benefits of gradualistic state intervention in the labor market.

The initial resistance of unions to state intervention was greatest in Germany. As Bismarck himself made clear, the purpose of the health, accident, and old-age and invalidity insurance legislation of the 1880s was not to create new rights but to preserve traditional

[47] On Britain see Hugh Heclo, *Modern Social Politics in Britain and Sweden* (New Haven, Conn.: Yale University Press, 1974), pp. 89–90; Henry Pelling, "The Working Class and the Origins of the Welfare State," in Pelling, *Popular Politics and Society in Late Victorian Britain* (London: Macmillan, 1968). On the United States see Vivian Vale, *Labour in American Politics* (New York: Barnes & Noble, 1971), pp. 39–40; Michael Rogin, "Voluntarism: The Political Functions of an Antipolitical Doctrine," *Industrial and Labor Relations Review* 15 (1961/1962); Gary M. Fink, "The Rejection of Voluntarism," *Industrial and Labor Relations Review* 26 (1972/1973). For a contrasting perspective that emphasizes the role of labor in gaining welfare legislation see Keith D. Brown, *Labour and Unemployment, 1900–1914* (Newton Abbot: David and Charles, 1971). Peter Flora and Jens Alber find that the percentage of votes gained in national elections by working-class parties is related to the timing of the introduction of welfare legislation. But, as they note, social insurance legislation was partly a defense by the established powers against working-class mobilization. See their "Modernization, Democratization, and the Development of Welfare States in Western Europe," in Peter Flora and Arnold J. Heidenheimer, *The Development of Welfare States in Europe and America* (New Brunswick, N.J.: Transaction Books, 1981), p. 58. This appears to be the case in Britain as well as in Germany.

political relationships by reconstituting the preindustrial dependence of the individual on the paternalistic state.[48] Unions reciprocated by denying that the reforms would lead to long-term economic gains for workers and protesting that, in the words of a unanimous resolution of the 1883 Social Democratic Congress, "the so-called social reform is nothing but a tactical means designed to lure the workers away from the correct path."[49]

But towards the end of the century the growing independence of trade unions from the Social Democratic party and the turn towards reformism led the unions to reverse their earlier refusal to participate in the administration of the welfare measures. Moreover, as time went on it became increasingly obvious that individual workers benefited from the social welfare reforms. State intervention in the labor market could neither be reversed nor ignored. From the Frankfurt Congress of 1899 unions in Germany were progressively drawn into corporatist bodies composed of worker, employer, and state representatives responsible for administering an increasingly complex system of welfare provision. Henceforth, the chief issue involved in this form of state regulation was not the legitimacy of welfare provision itself but the relative power of organized groups in its administration.

By 1914 the Free Unions had evolved an extensive and elaborate apparatus through which they could coordinate their participation in the social insurance system and pressure the government for increased representation and further legislation. A centralized union body was established to promote social reforms and monitor the welfare insurance system in 1902, and in the following years district workers' secretariats were set up to parallel the administrative structure of the state welfare system.[50] Over the next twelve years about one hundred such bodies worked in close liaison with the state bureaucracy. In 1911 the Central Association of German In-

[48] As Carl Janke has pointed out, "What Bismarck meant was thus not a federalist economic and social order independent of the idea of the state but a movement toward a corporate representation of interests which, despite a high degree of differentiation of occupations, groups, and strata in the modern economy, would be able to bring about public co-responsibility, national state feelings, and adaption and subordination to the interests of the whole as represented by the state." See *Der Vierte Stand* (Freiberg: Herder, 1955), p. 272; this passage is translated by Ralf Dahrendorf in *Society and Democracy in Germany* (New York: Anchor Books, 1969), p. 39.

[49] Gaston V. Rimlinger, *Welfare Policy and Industrialization in Europe, America, and Russia* (New York: John Wiley and Sons, 1971), pp. 124–125.

[50] See Umbreit, *25 Jahre Deutsche Gewerkschaftsbewegung, 1890–1918*, pp. 106–107.

dustrialists, in collaboration with the government, managed to reduce union representation on those boards where workers were in
the majority, but, despite this setback, the unions remained firmly
wedded to the administrative system. Union representatives served
on industrial courts concerned with disputes between employers
and individual workers, on courts of arbitration for the accident,
invalid, and old-age insurance, on artisan subcommittees of the
guild and handwork chambers, and on local labor exchanges.[51] In
the decades before the First World War the original socialist impetus of unionism was gradually diverted into bureaucratic channels.
Union leaders came to define their role in administrative terms, to
such an extent that, as Hans Mommsen has observed, "they could
not imagine society changing to a socialist order in any other way
than by a gradual integration of union institutions into the state
machine."[52]

In Britain, traditional mercantilist regulations of employment,
guild monopolies, and local welfare systems were swept aside by the
beginning of the nineteenth century by a strong and independent
middle class intent on drawing its labor supply from a competitive,
interregional market. New codes regulating the working conditions
of apprentices, children, and women were enacted early in the
nineteenth century and were extended by the factory legislation beginning in the 1830s and 1840s.[53] But until the twentieth century
and the coming into office of the great reforming Liberal government in 1906, state intervention in the labor market only margin-
ally compromised the dominant policy of laissez-faire.

The principal Liberal reforms of conditions in the labor market
were the establishment of trade boards, labor exchanges, and
health and unemployment insurance. Unions were involved in the
administration of each of these measures.

51 Gerhard A. Ritter, *Die Arbeiterbewegung im Wilhelminischen Reich* (Berlin-Dahlem:
Colloquium Verlag, 1959), chap. 6; Umbreit, *25 Jahre Deutsche Gewerkschaftsbewegung*,
chap. 9; Hans Josef Varain, *Freie Gewerkschaften, Sozialdemokratie und Staat: Die Politik
der Generalkommission unter der Führung Carl Legiens, 1890–1920* (Düsseldorf: Droste-
Verlag, 1956), p. 54.

52 Mommsen, "The Free Trade Unions and Social Democracy in Imperial Germany," p. 385.

53 Court, *A Concise Economic History of Britain*, p. 122; S. G. Checkland, *The Rise of
Industrial Society, 1815–1885* (London: Longmans, 1964), pp. 329–345; Allen, *Trade
Unions and the Government*, pp. 44–45. On the debate concerning the timing and he-
gemony of laissez-faire in Britain see the excellent essay by Arthur J. Taylor, *Laissez-
Faire and State Intervention in Nineteenth-Century Britain* (London: Macmillan, 1972).

With the passage of the Trade Boards Act in 1909, the state, for the first time in over a century, accepted responsibility for setting minimum wages. Under the act, trade boards were set up to enforce minimum rates for timework and piecework in any trade where the prevailing rate of wages was "exceptionally low as compared with that of other industries."[54] By 1914 eight such boards covered about half a million workers. As D. E. Macdonald has pointed out, "For the first time since the Tudor and Stuart legislation had gone, the State accepted a measure of direct responsibility for wage-fixing."[55]

When labor exchanges were established in 1909 trade unions were represented on the commission that appointed the senior administrative officers, of whom a number were union officials. At the same time, the Parliamentary Committee of the TUC was invited to act as a consultative subcommittee to the president of the Board of Trade on the operation of the new employment service.[56] Unions were further integrated into the administration of the state's new welfare responsibilities with the introduction of health and unemployment insurance in 1911. Instead of instituting a uniform state-controlled system of insurance on the German model, Lloyd George, the Liberal prime minister, agreed to make existing friendly societies and trade unions the "approved societies" for the operation of the state system.[57]

Surprisingly, unions were not unanimous in their support of these reforms. They were generally suspicious of the concept of the minimum wage embodied in the Trade Boards Act on the grounds that it might become the maximum, and they feared that the labor exchanges might become agencies for the supply of blackleg labor.[58] Although most union leaders welcomed the National Insur-

[54] Quoted in Allan Flanders, *Trade Unions* (London: Hutchinson, 1968), p. 87. See also Clapham, *An Economic History of Modern Britain*, 3: 427–428.

[55] Macdonald, *The State and the Trade Unions*, p. 70.

[56] John Lovell and B. C. Roberts, *A Short History of the T.U.C.* (London: Macmillan, 1968), p. 41. Good accounts of the establishment of labor exchanges are M. Bruce, *The Coming of the Welfare State* (London: Batsford, 1968), pp. 192–195 and J. R. Hay, *The Origins of the Liberal Welfare Reforms, 1906–1914* (London: Macmillan, 1975), pp. 47–52.

[57] Pelling, *A History of British Trade Unionism*, p. 129; Bruce, *The Coming of the Welfare State*, pp. 212–220.

[58] On trade union opposition to the Trade Boards Act see Lovell and Roberts, *A Short History of the T.U.C.*, p. 41. On opposition to labor exchanges see Pelling, *A History of British Trade Unionism*, pp. 128–129.

ance Act, their support of the measure was not decisive either in its inception or eventual passage through Parliament.[59] But the cumulative effect of the extension of state responsibility for welfare profoundly influenced unions, integrating them on a routinized basis into the administrative apparatus of the state. This process had not proceeded very far in Britain by 1914, but it was to provide a foundation for the more extensive development of union participation in the body politic during the First World War.

In the United States, where colonial mercantilist regulations of employment crumbled early under pressure of labor scarcity, laissez-faire in the labor market remained virtually undiluted from the beginning of the nineteenth century to almost its midpoint, although this varied to some extent by state. The first legislation of the labor market, regulating the instruction of employed children, was enacted in Massachusetts in 1836. At the end of the 1840s, the ten-hour day became law in New England's industrial states, and from that time onward there was a gradual, though discontinuous and geographically uneven, growth of government regulation of the labor market.[60]

Although state responsibility for welfare, and union participation in its administration, was not carried so far as in Germany or Britain, the direction of change was unmistakable. At the federal level the growth of state regulation of the labor market was accelerated after 1912, when legislation concerning federal workers, seamen, and railway workers that had been stalled during the previous Republican administrations was enacted by the Wilson administration.[61] In 1913 a new and independent Department of Labor was

[59] Hugh Heclo concludes that "in and out of parliament, the British Left had played no direct part in this fundamental extension of modern social policy" (*Modern Social Politics in Britain and Sweden*, p. 89). Henry Pelling, in his article "The Working Class and the Origins of the Welfare State," p. 13, points out that even National Insurance was unpopular among the working-class for some time after its enactment. See also H. V. Emy, *Liberals, Radicals, and Social Politics, 1892–1914* (Cambridge: Cambridge University Press, 1973), pp. 253–262.

[60] J. E. Anderson, *Politics and the Economy* (Boston: Little, Brown, 1966), pp. 224–228; J. G. Rayback, *A History of American Labor* (New York: Macmillan, 1959), chap. 8; Selig Perlman, *History of Trade Unionism in the United States* (New York: Macmillan, 1922), pp. 298–301.

[61] Marc Karson, *American Labor Unions and Politics, 1900–1918* (Carbondale: Southern Illinois University Press, 1958), chap. 4; M. R. Carroll, *Labor and Politics* (Boston: Houghton Mifflin, 1923), pp. 87–98; Faulkner, *American Economic History*, pp. 469–473; Perlman, *History of Trade Unionism in the United States*, pp. 206–207.

established, with William B. Wilson, a former Knight of Labor and official of the United Mine Workers, as secretary.

But it was at the state level that regulation proceeded most quickly. By the time the United States entered the First World War almost every state had enacted a comprehensive array of factory inspection laws, in addition to laws forbidding the employment of children under fourteen and prescribing maximum hours for women.[62] Thirty states, including all those in the North, provided voluntary accident insurance schemes, and a few were experimenting with unemployment compensation. Unions participated in the administration of these measures by influencing the political appointments to the inspectorates set up to oversee these codes through the spoils systems of their local party machines. Numerous union officials were involved in public policy implementation before 1917, although their participation was more fragmented than that of trade unionists in Germany or Britain, a reflection of the decentralized American political system.[63]

THE FIRST WORLD WAR

The First World War saw the complete disintegration of laissez-faire in the belligerent states and a sharp decline in the system of market competition that had formerly provided its foundation. The demand for state intervention in the labor market was straightforward and compelling. The attritional nature of trench warfare between developed industrial societies demanded an unprecedented mobilization of resources, human and physical, for the war effort. The recruitment of soldiers, the production of munitions, the rationing of scarce commodities—each of these led the warring

[62] James Weinstein, "Big Business and the Origins of Workmen's Compensation," *Labor History* 7–8 (1966–1967); T. C. Cochran and W. Miller, *The Age of Enterprise* (New York: Harper, 1961), pp. 276–280; Rayback, *A History of American Labor*, chap. 18; Vale, *Labour in American Politics*, p. 17; Anderson, *Politics and the Economy*, pp. 227–232.

[63] John R. Commons, "Labor and Municipal Politics," in Commons, *Labor and Administration* (New York: Macmillan, 1913); K. L. Bryant, Jr., "Labor in Politics: The Oklahoma State Federation of Labor during the Age of Reform," *Labor History* 11 (1970); Irwin Yellowitz, *Labor and the Progressive Movement in New York State, 1897–1916* (Ithaca, N.Y.: Cornell University Press, 1965); Edward J. Harpham, "Federalism, Keynesianism, and the Transformation of the Unemployment Insurance System in the United States," in Douglas E. Ashford and E. W. Kelley, eds., *Nationalizing Social Security in Europe and America* (Greenwich: JAI Press, 1986).

states to regulate the labor market to a degree beyond the furthest expectations of the prewar years. The logic of market competition was displaced by the logic of centralized planning and control.

Governments soon realized that the cooperation of unions was a vital requisite for the success of this mobilization. Cooperation was sought, first and foremost, to ensure industrial peace, an especially critical factor as union market power increased under labor scarcity. But as the organizational problems associated with the total mobilization of labor became apparent, union cooperation was sought more extensively to help administer the burgeoning system of state controls.

In the opening stages of the war the price exacted from governments by unions for this cooperation was a small measure of the costs they could incur by withholding it. The belligerent states entered the First World War with a fervent nationalism, and unions readily sacrificed their particularistic demands for national goals. But as the war went on union leaders came to recognize their potential economic and political weight and were increasingly willing to use it to gain at least a foothold in the policy-making process.

The political consequences of the First World War unfolded slowly, as the nature of the war itself, as a drawn-out struggle of attrition, became apparent after the failure of the initial German onslaught in 1914.[64] The immediate demand on the part of the state was for industrial peace, and soon after the outbreak of war, unions in Germany and Britain acceded this in the "Burgfrieden" and "Industrial Truce" of August 1914. These were one-sided declarations, committing unions to withhold their right to strike but demanding little or nothing in return. Later on, however, when labor shortages became acute and when unions were more keenly aware of their market power, the commitment to avoid aggressive strikes became part of formal and comprehensive agreements with governments and employer associations, placing some form of restriction on profits and establishing elaborate systems of binding ar-

[64] Gerald D. Feldman, *Army, Industry, and Labor in Germany, 1914–1918* (Princeton, N.J.: Princeton University Press, 1966), pp. 28–30; Kurt Pohl and Frauke Werther, "Die Freien Gewerkschaften im Ersten Weltkrieg," in Frank Deppe et al., eds., *Geschichte der deutschen Gewerkschaftsbewegung* (Köln: Pahl-Rugenstein, 1977), pp. 99–100; Fritz Klein, *Deutschland von 1897/98 bis 1917* (Berlin: Pahl-Rugenstein, 1977), pp. 268–277; Pelling, *A History of British Trade Unionism*, pp. 149–152; Lovell and Roberts, *A Short History of the T.U.C.*, p. 50; Macdonald, *The State and the Trade Unions*, pp. 83–85.

bitration, with workers represented on the relevant boards. By the end of 1916, after the enactment of the Auxiliary Service Law (Hilfdienstgesetz) in Germany, and the Munitions Act in Britain, the provisions for compulsory arbitration resulted in what was virtually state regulation of wages.[65]

The same general development, governed by the same need for industrial peace, took place in the United States in 1917.[66] State regulation of the labor market in America never reached the level of that in Germany or Britain, but it must still be considered extraordinary when set against the dominance of the doctrine of laissez-faire throughout most of the nineteenth century. With the hindsight of union experience in the warring societies of Western Europe, American unions did not volunteer restraint unconditionally when their country's involvement in the war was declared but stated in advance that they would agree to relinquish the strike only on condition that "the Government . . . recognize the organized labor movement as the agency through which it must cooperate with wage earners."[67]

This demand was, by and large, met. American trade unions subsequently were represented on the trilateral War Labor Conference Board, which exercised extensive responsibilities over working conditions. Guided by norms such as equal pay for equal work for women and the "right of all workers, including common laborers, to a living wage," the War Labor Conference Board and its successor, the War Labor Administration, directly contravened market considerations of supply and demand.[68] Neither had legal powers

[65] Feldman, *Army, Industry, and Labor in Germany, 1914–1918*, pp. 316–333; Paul Umbreit, *Die Deutsche Gewerkschaften im Weltkrieg* (Berlin: Verlag fur Sozialwissenschaft, 1917), chap. 9; Klein, *Deutschland von 1897/98 bis 1917*, pp. 350–358; Albin Gladen, *Geschichte der Sozialpolitik in Deutschland* (Weisbaden: F. Steiner, 1974), pp. 88–91; Bernd Otto, *Gewerkschaftsbewegung in Deutschland* (Kiel: Bund Verlag, 1975), pp. 62–63; Pelling, *A History of British Trade Unionism*, pp. 155–156; R. Lowe, "The Erosion of State Intervention in Britain, 1917–1924," *Economic History Review*, 2d series, vol. 31, no. 2 (1978); Lovell and Roberts, *A Short History of the T.U.C.*, p. 32.

[66] Perlman, *History of Trade Unionism in the United States*, pp. 233–236; Karson, *American Labor Unions and Politics, 1900–1918*, pp. 94–99.

[67] Quoted in Perlman, *History of Trade Unionism in the United States*, p. 233.

[68] John S. Smith, "Organized Labor and Government in the Wilson Era, 1913–1921: Some Conclusions," *Labor History* 3–4 (1962–1963): 277–278; Vale, *Labour in American Politics*, p. 41. One of the clearest cases of governmental intervention is reported by a lumber employer who testified to the Price Fixing Committee that "at the direct request of the President" the industry in the northwest went on a eight-hour

for the compulsory arbitration of labor disputes, but their interventions, backed by public opinion and the indirect powers of the president, were generally effective.[69] As in Germany and Britain, the impersonal, blind, mechanism of market competition was set aside in the attempt to produce a workable consensus in the labor market that would, it was hoped, reduce industrial strife.

As the regulative tasks of the belligerent states expanded, unions were drawn into wider spheres of policy implementation. The magnitude of state regulation of the economy during the First World War is suggested in the new vocabulary that surfaced to describe it: "state socialism," "war socialism," and "wartime collectivism." The sheer scope of the state's administrative task, coupled with the need to gain consensus and legitimacy in its expanded role, induced governments to bring trade unions into the political process. And unions themselves welcomed the legal recognition, substantive improvements in working conditions, and the share of the newly acquired decisional power that they received in return. In the First World War the "osmotic process," described by Philippe Schmitter, "whereby the modern state and the modern interest associations seek each other out" was, for the first time, a determining factor in their relationship.[70]

The pace at which unions were integrated into the state apparatus was swift, but at least up to 1916 this was an unplanned development, dictated primarily by the need to meet pressing problems of labor mobilization, rationing, and welfare, as they arose.

In Germany this process began in the fall of 1914 with union collaboration in relieving unemployment, caring for the families of soldiers and the war-wounded, and mobilizing urban labor to relieve the labor shortage that threatened the first wheat crop of the war.[71] But the unintended consequences of this development were profound. From organizations beyond the social and political pale of German society, unions were transformed into recognized up-

---

basis. Quoted in James Weinstein, *The Corporate Ideal in the Liberal State, 1900–1918* (Boston: Beacon, 1969), p. 227.

[69] Witte, *The Government in Labor Disputes*, pp. 246–249; Berman, *Labor Disputes and the President of the United States*, pp. 152–158.

[70] Phillippe C. Schmitter, "Still the Century of Corporatism," in Phillippe Schmitter and Gerhard Lehmbruch, eds., *Trends toward Corporatist Intermediation* (Beverley Hills, Calif.: Sage, 1979), p. 27.

[71] Pohl and Werther, "Die Freien Gewerkschaften im Ersten Weltkrieg," p. 101; Umbreit, *25 Jahre Deutsche Gewerkschaftsbewegung, 1890–1918*, pp. 142–143, 146–148; Umbreit, *Die Deutsche Gewerkschaften im Weltkrieg*, chaps. 2–6.

holders of economic and social stability. As Clemens von Delbrück, the minister of state for internal affairs, stated in the Reichstag in March 1915, "Trade unions are not by preference instruments of agitation, but, in the first place, have tasks to fulfill, without which our economic life is unthinkable."[72]

The longer the war lasted the more difficult it was for the authoritarian regime to deny unions a voice in the councils of policy making. By the last year of the war, under the "social partnership" between unions and the German War Office, union officials sat on numerous tripartite determination, draft, and arbitration committees, were elected to an ever-increasing number of workers' committees set up for the munitions and related industries, and formally participated in decisions relating to the supply and rationing of food. They were represented in the newly established Ministry of Labour and on the tripartite chambers of industry that were established to safeguard, and reconcile, the interests of workers, employers, and government.[73]

In Britain the barriers to the involvement of representatives of the working classes in government were not so high as in Germany. In mid-1915 the Labour party itself was accepted into a coalition government, and for the first time a number of Labour party members and trade unionists in their capacity as representatives of organized labor became government ministers. In December 1916, when the government was re-formed under Lloyd George, the role of labor was expanded. Arthur Henderson, chairman of the Parliamentary Labour party, served in the inner War Cabinet, and two new ministries were formed, for labor and pensions, to be headed by union card-carrying Labour MPs. Altogether eight union officials were appointed junior ministers in the last three years of the war.[74]

Alongside this highly publicized and symbolically important development at the top went a far-reaching and systematic integration of unions into the state at the middle level. Wherever the govern-

---

[72] Quoted in Heinz Josef Varain, *Freie Gewerkschaften, Sozialdemokratie und Staat: Die Politik der Generalkommission unter der Führung Carl Legiens, 1890–1920*, p. 78.

[73] Feldman, *Army, Industry, and Labor in Germany, 1914–1918*, p. 320; Umbreit, *25 Jahre Deutsche Gewerkschaftsbewegung*, pp. 149–154; Cassau, *Die Gewerkschaftsbewegung, Ihre Soziologie und Ihr Kampf*, pp. 271–275.

[74] Allen, *Trade Unions and the Government*, pp. 28–30, 56–57; D. F. Macdonald, *The State and the Trade Unions*, pp. 82–87; Pelling, *A History of British Trade Unionism*, pp. 154–155.

ment extended its field of operation into the labor market and industry it set up committees, and on almost every committee union representatives were present in equal proportion to those of employers and the state. The committee system appropriated spheres of decision making that were formerly the jealously guarded prerogative of employers. In the mines, for example, the competence of the committees stretched from labor disputes, working hours, and recruitment to output, transport costs, and retail coal prices.[75] The impact of this development on the political orientation of unions was dramatic. As the president of the TUC put it in 1917, "The man in our ranks to-day who is neither a Government official nor a member of some Government Committee is unknown to the movement. . . . [T]he prejudice of trade unionists against politics has hitherto held us back . . . but the events of the last three years have taken the scales from our eyes."[76]

The experience of the First World War allowed unionists in Britain to set their sights on goals that before 1914 would have seemed utterly impracticable. This was well illustrated at the TUC conference held in mid-1918, five months before the end of the war, in which British unions proclaimed their allegiance to socialism by demanding the further extension of wartime controls, "of retaining after the war and of developing the present system of organizing, controlling and auditing the processes, profits and prices of capitalist industry."[77]

Shortly after America declared war in 1917 Walter Lippman stated that his country stood "at the threshold of a collectivism which is greater than any as yet planned by the Socialist Party."[78] Socialist principles concerning the distribution of power and resources were, of course, not realized in the war, but in terms of the

[75] Allen, *Trade Unions and the Government*, p. 30.

[76] Quoted in Ross McKibbin, *The Evolution of the Labour Party* (Oxford: Oxford University Press, 1974), p. 105.

[77] Quoted in ibid., p. 104. McKibbin argues that "if collectivism amounted to not much more than preserving those controls established under emergency regulations, it was still a very considerable advance." Jay M. Winter, in *Socialism and the Challenge of War* (London: Routledge & Kegan Paul, 1979), emphasizes the continuity of socialist thought before, during, and after World War I, and argues that "it was not the theory but rather the political activity and influence of British socialism which changed under the impact of the First World War" (p. 270). This interpretation is consonant with that developed in this chapter.

[78] Walter Lippman to J. G. Stokes, 1 May 1917; quoted in Weinstein, *The Corporate Ideal in the Liberal State, 1900–1918*, p. 214.

collectivization of resources by the state for "national" ends Lippman was right. The United States was actively involved in the First World War for less than twenty months, but in this relatively short time industries of direct concern to the war effort, water and rail transport, the mines, the telephone and telegraph systems chief among them, were brought under direct state control, while various others, including the munitions industries, were subject to extensive regulation.[79]

Apart from its pivotal role on the Advisory Commission of the National Council of Defense and the numerous district exemption boards that handled matters specific to labor, the AFL appointed members to a wide range of government boards, including the Emergency Construction Board, the Fuel Administration Board, the Women's Board, the Food Administration Board, and the War Industries Board.[80] At the same time the Department of Labor, under William B. Wilson became, in Selig Perlman's words, "the Federation's arm in the Administration."[81] As the *New Republic* reported in September 1918, "no important measure vitally affecting labor is now taken without consultation with the leaders of the American Federation of Labor."[82]

The growth of such institutionalized channels of conflict regulation created intense discontent among certain groups of workers who were excluded, for one reason or another, from these channels and the benefits, in terms of job security and conditions of employment, that they brought. Moreover, as union leaders participated in government they were saddled with responsibility for compromises that they previously would have attacked.

The kinds of workers encompassed in these revolts were extremely heterogeneous. Vagrant farm workers, lumberers, hard rock miners in America who were excluded from the established unions of the AFL; skilled engineering workers in Britain who were threatened by state-sponsored policies of labor dilution during the

[79] Stanley Shapiro, "The Great War and Reform: Liberals and Labor, 1917–1919," *Labor History* 11 (1971): 326; C. W. Wright, *Economic History of the United States* (New York: McGraw-Hill Book Company, 1949), chap. 42.

[80] Lorwin, *The American Federation of Labor*, pp. 155–173; Karson, *American Labor Unions and Politics, 1900–1918*, pp. 96–100; Taft, *Organized Labor in American History*, pp. 311–319; Rayback, *A History of American Labor*, pp. 273–276.

[81] Perlman, *History of Trade Unionism in the United States*, p. 236.

[82] Shapiro, "The Great War and Reform: Liberals and Labor, 1917–1919," p. 333. See also Weinstein, *The Corporate Ideal in the Liberal State, 1900–1918*, p. 226.

First World War; munitions workers in Berlin who rebelled against union leaders implicated in repressive state policies: each of these groups were drawn into open revolt against the existing system of industrial relations and the cooption of union leaders into economic and political institutions of the status quo.

At first the tensions within union movements were contained by the willingness of workers to sacrifice their immediate economic interests in the war effort. But as the war continued, the unifying and restraining influence of nationalism declined. In each of the warring countries the unrest was focused in those industries most subject to state control, especially the munitions industries. In these industries union officials found themselves in the position of "urging the Government to make labour restrictions more palatable and entreating their own members to accept the restrictions necessary for the war effort."[83] In short, they became "brokers and intermediaries between the Government and labour," in Ralph Miliband's words, or "semi-official agents of the government," as Gerald Feldman has pointed out for Germany.[84]

The potential for such conflict was particularly great in Germany. The harsh demands placed on the work force, severe labor shortages, the authoritarian character of the regime in which union leaders participated, and its declining legitimacy from 1917 as defeat became imminent created tensions within unions that could not be contained by the organizational resources available to union leaders. If the First World War gave a preview of extensive cooperation at the national level between unions and the state, it also showed the strains between leaders and rank and file that could attend this.

At the same time the developments in the organization of the labor market that were underway in the decades before 1914 continued apace. The scope of organization was extended on both sides of industry. Between 1913 and 1918 union membership increased by 13.5 percent in Germany and 58.0 percent in the United Kingdom. In the United States the increase between 1916 and 1918 was 23.7 percent. The smaller growth in union membership in Ger-

[83] Ralph Miliband, *Parliamentary Socialism* (London: Merlin Press, 1973), p. 47. See also Ross M. Martin, *T.U.C.: The Growth of a Pressure Group, 1868–1976* (Oxford: Clarendon Press, 1980), p. 147; S. J. Hurwitz, *State Intervention in Britain: A Study of Economic Control and Social Response* (New York: Columbia University Press, 1949).

[84] Miliband, *Parliamentary Socialism*, p. 53; Feldman, *Army, Industry, and Labor in Germany, 1914–1918*, p. 520. See also Marwick, *Britain in the Century of Total War* (Boston: Little, Brown, 1968), pp. 99–100.

many was largely the result of the more intensive mobilization of the labor force for active duty in the armed forces there.[85] In all three countries the pattern of disproportionate growth of unionism in industries vital to the economy as a whole continued. During the First World War, the metal, shipbuilding, and engineering industries—the industries most crucial for the supply of war materials—showed the greatest relative increase in union membership. In the United Kingdom and Germany the increase between 1913 and 1918 was 74.4 percent and 44.2 percent respectively.[86] In the United States the increase was 48.3 percent for the shorter period from 1916 to 1918.[87]

There was a parallel extension of organization among employers in the same period. This development was driven, as it was before the war, by competition with the organized forces of labor. But during the war years, the expanded role of the state in economic planning and coordination provided an additional incentive to association. Writing in 1930, Joseph Foth pointed out that in the United States during the First World War, "the government was compelled to deal with groups, and needed the information concerning industry which only an organization could furnish. On the other hand, unorganized industry was helpless in dealing with the numerous government agencies of the first period of control, and found no place whatsoever in the machinery, as set up under centralized control. The government machinery of control was not complete without a corresponding organization in industry."[88]

In Britain a new and more effective national employers' organization was established, the Federation of British Industries. At the first general meeting of the FBI in March 1917 its membership in-

---

[85] The levels of mobilization in Germany, Britain, and the United States during World War I were as follows:

	Total No. Mobilized	No. Mobilized per 100 Inhabitants
Germany	13,250,000	19.7
England	5,700,000	10.5
United States	3,900,000	3.8

[86] *19th Abstract of Labour Statistics of the United Kingdom*, 1928, Command 3140, vol. 25, pp. 166–167; *Correspondenzblatt der Generalkommission der Gewerkschaften Deutschlands*, 1915, no. 4; 1919, no. 3.

[87] Wolman, *The Growth of American Trade Unions, 1880–1923*, pp. 112–113.

[88] J. H. Foth, *Trade Associations* (New York: The Ronald Press Company, 1930), p. 27.

cluded 50 employer associations. At the end of its first year of operation the number of member associations increased to 78, and by late 1918 there were 129.[89] In Germany the two national employer federations, the Central Association of German Industrialists and the League of German Industrialists, merged in 1913. The resulting organization, the Federation of German Employer Associations, grew steadily over the next five years, while the number of employer associations at the industry level increased from 61 to 76 over the same period.[90]

In Britain the growth of organization in the labor market was accompanied by another development that was evident before the war, industrywide collective bargaining. From 1916 a number of union federations, such as the Transport Workers' Federation and the National Federation of General Workers, were established to coordinate bargaining at the national level. Industrywide regulation of working conditions was extended to workers in the railway, docking, coal, gas, chemical, aluminum, and aircraft industries.[91] In Germany voluntary collective bargaining was inhibited during the war by the greater role of the military authorities in compulsorily determining working conditions for large sections of munitions-related industry. But once the state withdrew from this task, the scope of collective bargaining and its centralization increased sharply. In 1919 the number of workers covered by collective bargaining was almost 6 million compared to 1.4 million in 1913, and the average number of firms encompassed per agreement was 24.7 compared to 13.1 in 1913.[92]

---

[89] *Industrial Trade Associations: Activities and Organization, Political and Economic Planning* (London, 1957), p. 14; Steven Blank, *Industry and Government in Britain: The Federation of British Industries in Politics, 1945–1965* (Lexington: Lexington Books, 1973), pp. 14–17; Keith Middlemas, *Politics in Industrial Society*, pp. 111–114.

[90] Hans Mottek, Walter Becker, and Alfred Schröter, *Wirtschaftsgeschichte Deutschlands* (Berlin/DDR: Deutsche Verlag der Wissenschaft, 1974), 3: 88–105; Leckebusch, *Entstehung und Wandlungen der Zielsetzungen, der Struktur und der Wirkungen von Arbeitgeberverbänden*, pp. 61–68; Simon, *Machte und Herrschaft der Unternehmerverbände BDI, BDA, und DIHT*, pp. 28–31. Lenin summed up this development as follows: "If individual capitalist property is characteristic of the pre-imperialist epoch, so the present system of finance capitalism is characterized by the collective property of mutually organized capitalists. . . . This is today the most recent stage of the development which has manifested itself particularly clearly in the war years. The most important aspect of this is the fusion of bourgeois state organizations with economic organizations." (V. I. Lenin, *Werke*, 5th ed., (Moscow: Marx-Lenin Institute, 1969), 35: 334.

[91] Lovell, *British Trade Unions, 1875–1933*, pp. 50–51; Lovell and Roberts, *A Short History of the T.U.C.*, p. 52.

[92] Deckers, *Betrieblicher oder Überbetrieblicher Tarifvertrag*, table 1, p. 109. See also

Once the war was over the apparatus of state intervention in the economy and the corporatist institutions through which unions participated in policy making and policy implementation were largely dismantled. The consequences of this for unions in Germany were offset by the foundation of a democratic republic in which the SPD became the largest party. But in Britain and the United States the end of the First World War saw a wholesale retreat from "war socialism" and an attempt to return to the "normalcy" of the prewar era. However, the underlying development in the organization of the labor market could not be turned back, nor could laissez-faire be reconstituted. As R. H. Tawney, writing of developments in Britain, has argued: "The period of war economy accelerated the demise of the individualist, competitive phase of British capitalism. It stimulated organization and combination among manufacturers; advertised rationalisation; strengthened the demand for tariffs; and encouraged, in another sphere, the settlement of wages and working conditions by national rather than by local agreements."[93]

In addition, as Eric Hobsbawm has pointed out, the First World War subtly altered perceptions of the proper limits of state regulation of the economy.

> It [the war economy] was dismantled with unseemly haste after 1918. . . . Nevertheless, nothing could be quite the same again. The apparatus of government remained larger and more comprehensive than before. The protection of "key" industries was no longer a theoretical issue. The compulsory rationalization and amalgamation of industries by government, or even their nationalization, was not a matter of practical policy. Above all, the possibilities of government action had been tested. It would henceforth be possible to have state intervention, but no longer to claim reasonably that it could not work.[94]

In a similar vein, Jonathan Hughes has seen an important legacy of the First World War for the United States in the "pervasive yet sub-

Cassau, *Die Gewerkschaftsbewegung, Ihre Soziologie und Ihr Kampf*, pp. 193–196; Adolf Weber, *Der Kampf zwischen Kapital und Arbeit*, 5th ed. (Tübingen: J.C.B. Mohr, 1930), p. 488.

[93] R. H. Tawney, "The Abolition of Economic Controls, 1918–1921," *Economic History Review* 13 (1943). See also A. S. Milward, *The Economic Effects of the Two World Wars on Britain* (London: Macmillan, 1970). Allan Flanders and Alan Fox, "Collective Bargaining: From Donovan to Durkheim," in Flanders, *Management and Unions* (London: Faber, 1970), place the development of industrial relations between 1914 and 1918 in a broad historical context.

[94] Hobsbawm, *Industry and Empire*, pp. 240–241.

tle change in an increasing acceptance of federal nonmarket control."[95]

With the growth of organization in the labor market and the decline of pure market competition, the "classical" order of industrial relations, based on an acceptance of market constraints as the objective arbiter over working conditions, could not be revived. Market outcomes, even in peace time, came to have ever clearer political consequences, and political solutions were increasingly sought for market-generated externalities, such as poverty, unemployment, illness, and economic insecurity. In terms of the perspective that has been developed in this chapter, that of the relationship between state and labor market, the First World War extended and deepened a development that was underway in the decades before 1914 and continued, although interruptedly, in the decades after 1918.

CONCLUSION

The interrelated set of changes I have described in terms of the Organizational Revolution in the most economically advanced societies in the decades around the turn of the twentieth century transformed the expression of class conflict. Capitalism and the Industrial Revolution created the distinctive class basis of Western society, but it was not until the last decade of the nineteenth century that class conflict took an organizationally coherent form. A supposition of this chapter is that in understanding the critical historical junctures in the development of Western society, we should pay as much attention to the Organizational Revolution as to the Industrial Revolution itself.

As it is described here the Organizational Revolution refers to the rapid increase from the decades around the turn of the twentieth century in the size, bureaucratization, and complexity of those institutions responsible for the coordination of human activity in society, particularly in the economic sphere. This is a development that appears to have been common to the leading industrialized societies of the West. But blanket statements about divergence or convergence miss the point. To the extent that our focus is on the po-

---

[95] J.R.T. Hughes, *The Governmental Habit: Economic Controls from Colonial Times to the Present* (New York: Basic Books, 1977), p. 137. See also Smith, "Organized Labor and Government in the Wilson Era, 1913–1921: Some Conclusions," pp. 279–280, on the retainment of the war labor administration after 1918.

litical, as contrasted to the technological, aspects of this development, we find remarkable contrasts as well as similarities. The substantive political consequences of the Organizational Revolution were governed by the particular historical circumstances of the societies in question. With respect to political regimes, the Organizational Revolution was as indeterminate a development as the Industrial Revolution itself: both were consistent with a remarkable variety of regime types. To the extent that the Organizational Revolution had some common set of political consequences in different societies, it was in the way it enlarged the scope of politics to include spheres of human activity that were presumed to be governed by the market or to be beyond human control altogether. Perhaps no social phenomenon reveals more clearly the elasticity of the meaning of politics itself. In this fundamental respect the Organizational Revolution did not merely change the context in which politics took place; more precisely, it transformed the way people conceived of politics and of how they could shape society through their own concerted efforts.

CHAPTER 4

PRINTING UNIONS AND
BUSINESS UNIONISM

Printing unions have a special place in the history of labor movements, for in most countries where trade unionism has developed
printing unions have been in the vanguard. As Seymour Martin
Lipset, Martin Trow, and James Coleman observe in their study of
the International Typographical Union, "In France and England
printers were negotiating with and sometimes striking against their
employers as early as the sixteenth century. And there is clear evidence that printers were either the first or among the first two or
three crafts to organize into unions in Belgium, Germany, Sweden,
Norway, Italy, Switzerland, Spain, Ireland, Russia, Austria, Australia, Canada, Chile, Argentina, and Mexico."[1]

Printers were unusual on other grounds that make them particularly interesting for the purposes of this study. They formed exceptionally cohesive occupational communities and were able to
sustain very strong unions. Printers were skilled, craft workers, and
they were able to turn their occupational community and organization to good use in defending their niche in the division of labor.
In other words, printers had some unusual resources that allowed
them to adapt to economic change in their industry. This logic of
union organization and effectiveness appears to be generalizable
across societies. Printing unions are not only fascinating in their
own right but they thus serve as a particularly appropriate case for
illustrating the sources of union political orientation and exploring
commonalities in union orientation from a comparative perspective.

In this and the following chapter, which compares coalminers'
unions, I examine the sources of union political activity from an
unfamiliar perspective by comparing the same kind of union across
countries. These chapters provide an opportunity to think through
the effects of similar labor market conditions in differing national

[1] Seymour Martin Lipset, Martin A. Trow, and James S. Coleman, *Union Democracy:
The Internal Politics of the International Typographical Union* (New York: Doubleday,
1965), pp. 27–28.

contexts. To what extent are common patterns of union political orientation found in Western societies? Do similar constraints and opportunities in the workplace, occupational community, and labor market condition similar political responses in different societies? These questions have far-reaching implications, not just for gauging the causal weight of variables influencing union political activity, but, beyond this, for how we should study working-class politics. Without trying to minimize the sources of commonality among unions within countries, this and the following chapter provide evidence for the existence of sectoral patterns across countries that are rooted in the experiences of occupational groups in particular labor markets. To explore such patterns we need to combine cross-national comparison with comparison at the level of the individual union.

These chapters are posed as case studies of printing and coalmining unions in the United States, Britain, and Germany. I should emphasize that these unions are not meant to be representative of the entire population of unions in these countries. They are illustrative cases, selected because they provide instances of broadly contrasting orientations to political activity over the period of this study.[2] The extent to which the syndrome of factors associated with each case is representative of other unions within a particular society is a matter for empirical investigation. My interest here is in the prior question of whether there are patterns of similarity at the level of individual unions that hold up across different national contexts and, if so, how we can explain them.

THE SOCIAL BASES OF UNIONISM

Union organization is oriented to the future: workers organize to gain some collective capacity for strategy so as to defend or improve their conditions of employment and their working lives. But the ability to organize usually depends on the strength and stability of social ties developed in the past. In particular, groups of workers

[2] My approach here is informed by Alexander L. George, "Case Studies and Theory Development: The Method of Structured, Focussed Comparison," in Paul G. Lauren, ed., *Diplomatic History: New Approaches* (New York: Free Press, 1979); Harry Eckstein, "Case Study and Theory in Political Science," in Fred I. Greenstein and Nelson W. Polsby, eds., *Handbook of Political Science* (Reading: Addison-Wesley, 1975), vol. 7; Arendt Lijphart, "Comparative Politics and the Comparative Method," *American Political Science Review* (1971).

forming cohesive occupational communities have the capacity to
enforce union membership as a social norm. No group of workers
was better placed in this respect than printers. They formed extraordinarily close-knit occupational communities, based on the
Chapel, a self-governing shop floor organization that regulated just
about every aspect of the printer's working life, from who works
when and how to who should buy beer for which occasions. The
Chapel was a multifaceted resource in the workplace that allowed
printers to sustain unionism as an expression of preestablished
group loyalty.

The Chapel has been a remarkably durable institution, structur-
ing the daily working lives of printers from medieval times to the
present day. Its historical roots go back as far as printing itself. By
the time the first historian of the printers, Joseph Moxon, was writing in 1682, the origins of the Chapel and the source of its name
were already clouded in mystery.[3] The encompassing character of
the Chapel in the lives of printers was rooted in its role as medieval
guild. As Willi Krahl observed in one of the first histories of German printing unions:

> It was the bond that embraced all those who belonged to the
> craft, as well as being the dam against arbitrariness and oppres-
> sion. The Chapel's influence accompanied the apprentice
> throughout his apprenticeship. The master's rights against ar-
> tisan disturbances were embodied in the Chapel. It protected
> him from ruinous competition, but also compelled him to con-
> sider, as the profession demanded, his journeymen as compan-
> ions, his equals within the craft and therefore entitled to the
> same expectations in life. In this way, the Chapel maintained
> order in all that concerned the printing industry, regulating

[3] J. Moxon, *Mechanick Exercises* (London, 1683), 2: 356. On the origins and functions of the Chapel see Charles Sabel, *Work and Politics* (Cambridge: Cambridge University Press, 1982); F. C. Avis, *The Early Printers' Chapel in England* (London: Avis,
1971); E. Howe and H. E. Waite, *The London Society of Compositors* (London: Cassell,
1948), pp. 30–41; Willi Krahl, *Der Verband der Deutschen Buchdrucker* (Berlin, 1916), 1:
81–98; George A. Stephens, *New York Typographical Union No. 6* (New York: New
York State Department of Labor, 1912), pp. 114–130. Sociological analyses of the
Chapel are A.J.M. Sykes, "Trade-Union Workshop Organization in the Printing Industry—The Chapel," *Human Relations* 13, no. 1 (February 1960); A.J.M. Sykes, "The
Cohesion of a Trade Union Workshop Organization," *Sociology* 1, no. 2 (May 1967);
Philip Sadler, "Sociological Aspects of Skill," *British Journal of Industrial Relations* 8, no.
1 (March 1970).

every minor detail. The influence of the Chapel extended to all members of the craft: masters, journeymen, and apprentices.[4]

With the growth of capitalism and the decline of the guilds the Chapel lost its broad-based character. As the interests of masters and journeymen were split further and further apart by the emergence of competitive labor markets and increasing capital requirements, the Chapel lost its hold over masters and came to represent only wage earners. But the Chapel remained a self-contained, self-governing body exerting profound influence over the printer's working life. As the name itself suggests, the Chapel continued to encompass both the mystical and the mundane. Apprentices were initiated in elaborate ceremonies full of ancient rites with inexplicable verses repeated over and over. Yet Chapels also institutionalized practical democratic procedures among their members for adjudicating personal and collective grievances and enforced a complex web of regulations concerning the quality and pace of work.

Chapels existed throughout the societies of Western Europe and North America, and they would make for a fascinating comparative study. From our standpoint they were the focal point of the printers' sense of occupational solidarity, sustaining the printers' job control by resisting any attempt by employers to divide, compartmentalize, or dilute the work force. But they were more than rational job protection dressed in mystical disguise, for the aura of mystery and otherworldliness was, by all contemporary accounts, an essential and enduring part of their existence. The meaning of the Chapel was quasi-religious as well as instrumental.

In such intimate surroundings printers had formidable resources to enforce group norms. Those who did not comply with those norms were vulnerable to all the kinds of pressures that small, close-knit groups can apply. Naturally, even these were regulated by Chapel custom. Benjamin Franklin, who worked in London as a printer in 1725, recalled in his autobiography his experiences with what was called the Chapel ghost or devil:

> Watts, after some weeks, desiring to have me in the composing-room, I left the pressmen, a new bien venu for drink was demanded of me by the compositors. I thought it an imposition, as I had paid one to the pressmen; the master thought so, too,

[4] Krahl, *Der Verband der Deutschen Buchdrucker*, 1: 90–91.

and forbad my paying it. I stood out two or three weeks, was accordingly considered as an excommunicate, and had so many little pieces of private malice practiced on me, by mixing my sorts, transposing and breaking my matter, etc. if I ever slept out of the room, and all ascribed to the chapel ghost, which they said ever haunted those not regularly admitted; that notwithstanding the master's protection, I found myself obliged to comply and pay the money; convinced of the folly of being on ill terms with those one is to live with continually.[5]

Few groups of manual workers can boast a Benjamin Franklin, Horace Greeley, Stephan Born, William Morris, or Pierre Joseph Proudhon. Printers, as many historians have observed, had personal qualities that facilitated their early organization. Their craft encouraged literacy, and many unmarried printers were journeymen in practice as well as in name, traveling from town to town in search of work and experience. Printers were the intellectual elite among workers, and their literacy and worldly experience no doubt made them sensitive to the benefits of organization and aided their efforts to create financially sound unions.

ORGANIZATIONAL STABILITY AND THE BENEFIT SYSTEM

Printers had certain other qualities that helped them create stable and effective unions. They usually earned enough to put by a surplus for hard times and were thus able to pay the monthly dues for the benefit system offered by their union.[6] In addition, printers had

---

[5] *Memoirs of the Life and Writings of Benjamin Franklin* (London, 1818), 1: 69; quoted in Howe and Waite, *The London Society of Compositors*, pp. 39–40.

[6] On the income of printers in Germany see Jürgen Kuczynski, *Die Geschichte der Lage der Arbeiter unter dem Kapitalismus* (Berlin/DDR: Akademie-Verlag, 1961), 1: 376; 2: 225; 3: 423; Gerhard Beier, *Schwarze Kunst und Klassenkampf* (Frankfurt am Main: Europaische Verlaganstalt, 1966), 1: 90–91; Diedrich Saalfeld, "Methodische Darlegungen zur Einkommensentwicklung und Sozialstruktur 1760–1860 am Beispiel einiger deutscher Städte," in H. Winker, ed., *Vom Kleingewerbe zur Grossindustrie* (Berlin: Duncker und Humbolt, 1975), table 3, p. 239; K. Abraham, *Der Strukturwandel im Handwerk in der ersten Hälfte des 19.Jahrhunderts* (Köln: S.N., 1955), p. 136. On the income of printers in Britain see John Child, *Industrial Relations in the British Printing Industry* (London: Allen & Unwin, 1967), pp. 7, 32; Howe and Waite, *The London Society of Compositors*, chap. 18. On the income of printers in the United States see Clarence D. Long, *Wages and Earnings in the United States, 1860–1890* (Princeton, N.J.: Princeton University Press, 1960), chap. 4 and app. A; Albert Rees, *Real Wages in Manufacturing* (Princeton, N.J.: Princeton University Press, 1961), pp. 11, 19, 20, 25.

relatively low levels of occupational mobility. They tended to remain in their occupation long enough to have the prospect of gaining a satisfactory return on their investment of union dues.

The provision of benefits to their members provides a key to understanding the strategy and stability of printing unions. The benefits that were offered fall into two broad categories. First were the so-called "friendly benefits," insuring the union member against illness, old-age, or death. Once a worker started to pay the dues on friendly benefits, he could only realize his investment if he became unfit for work. This kind of benefit, therefore, provided an important means of assuring organizational continuity by binding the member to the union by long-term economic ties. The second category consisted of various "out-of-work" benefits paid to union members when they were traveling in search of work. This kind of benefit preserved union control of the labor supply by allowing the union to unilaterally stipulate acceptable terms of employment while paying benefits to workers who could not find jobs at the union wage rate. Employers who paid "illegal" wages, that is, wages lower than the union rate, were denied a steady pool of labor until they agreed to the conditions set down by the union.[7]

Although printing unions were most visible when they carried out local or regional strikes, the expenditure on friendly and out-of-work benefits dwarfed that on strike support. In the major printing unions—the Verband der Deutschen Buchdrucker in Germany, the Typographical Association and the London Society of Compositors in Britain, and the International Typographical Union in America—the total expenditure on nonstrike benefits for the period up to 1913 was more than fives times that spent on strike support.[8] This is not to say that printing unions were pacific; on the

Information on wages in the first quarter of the nineteenth century is sketchy, but see G. A. Stephens, *New York Typographical Union No. 6*, pp. 4, 11, 112, 132.

[7] On union "legislation" see David Montgomery, *Workers' Control in America* (Cambridge: Cambridge University Press, 1979), chap. 1.

[8] For the Verband der Deutschen Buchdrucker, see Willi Krahl and Klaus Hemholz, *Der Verband der Deutschen Buchdrucker, 1866–1924* (Leipzig: Verband der Deutschen Buchdrucker, 1924), p. 26; Max Präger, "Grenzen der Gewerkschaftsbewegung," *Archiv für Sozialwissenschaft und Sozialpolitik* 20 (1905): 146–149; for the Typographical Association and the London Society of Compositors, see A. E. Musson, *The Typographical Association: Origins and History Up to 1949* (London: Oxford University Press, 1954), app.; Howe and Waite, *The London Society of Compositors*, app. 1; for the International Typographical Union see Ethelbert Stewart, *A Documentary History*

contrary, they fiercely defended their members' conditions of employment and, above all, their niche in the division of labor. Rather, it tells us something important about the strategy adopted by printing unions. Instead of relying on the brute force of the strike, these unions preferred to control the supply of labor at its source by encompassing as much of the work force as possible; monopolizing the tasks performed by labor, and unilaterally denying employers a supply of cheap nonunion labor. An extensive system of benefits, if it could be institutionalized, did this on a day-by-day basis while at the same time providing a private economic incentive for membership.

Figures 4.1, 4.2, and 4.3 show the membership of the major printing unions in Germany, Britain, and the United States up to 1913. The information available on the level of union membership (i.e., the ratio of membership to potential membership) in these years is fragmentary, but it is likely that the growth of membership of printing unions resulted mainly from their geographical expansion into nonunion areas. Many urban centers, even in the early

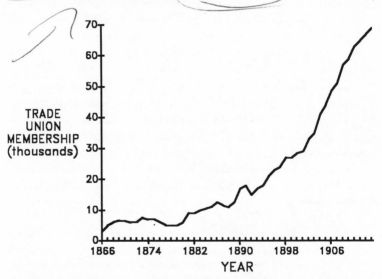

Figure 4.1 Membership of the Verband der Deutschen Buchdrucker, 1866–1913
SOURCE: Krahl and Hemholz, *Der Verband der Deutschen Buchdrucker, 1866–1924*, p. 26.

of the Early Organizations of Printers, Bulletin of the Bureau of Labor, no. 61 (1905), p. 885; Stephens, *New York Typographical Union No. 6*, p. 510.

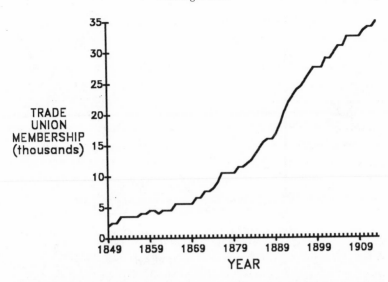

Figure 4.2 Membership of the Typographical Association and the London Society of Compositors, 1849–1913

SOURCES: Musson, *The Typographical Association*, appendix; Howe and Waite, *The London Society of Compositors*, p. 338.

nineteenth century, were relatively highly unionized. Unionism was particularly strong in the newspaper side of the industry, which was centered in the cities and larger towns where patriachal relations between master and journeymen had disappeared earliest. It was weakest among those employed in small, and sometimes geographically isolated, jobbing printing firms where an independent master might be working with a handful of printers who, in all likelihood, had never undergone a full apprenticeship.

Growth came mainly as printing unions spread from urban centers to outlying towns and rural areas. The first interregional printing unions began as a loose alliance of local unions situated in larger towns or cities. Because they were based on a preexisting form of workplace organization, the Chapel, such local unions could be strongly organized. In Germany we hear that by 1867, only five years after it was founded, the Berlin Buchdrucker-Gehilfen-Verein (which later merged into the Verband der Deutschen Buchdrucker) encompassed about 50 percent of all Berlin printers within its ranks.[9] In England the Northern Typographical Union

[9] Reported by Ulrich Engelhardt, *"Nur Vereinigt sind wir stark": Die Anfänge der*

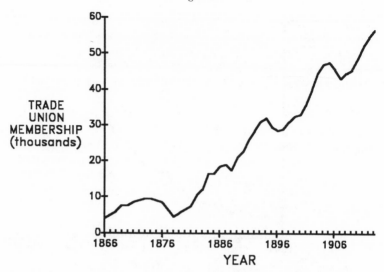

Figure 4.3 Membership of the International Typographical Union, 1866–1913
SOURCES: 1866–1897: Barnett, *The Printers: A Study in Trade Unionism*, appendix 7.
1898–1913: Wolin, *The Growth of American Trade Unions, 1880–1923*, pp. 110–119.

actually encompassed four out of every five printers in the towns
connected with it by 1842, twelve years after it was established.[10]
The International Typographical Union in America was founded
by local societies in just six cities, each of which had considerable
control over the supply of labor in their respective localities.[11]

Printing unions tended to have relatively stable memberships, a
testament to the strong social ties they were able to draw upon. A
good way of examining this quantitatively would be to take actual
lists of members and calculate the rate of individual membership
turnover from year to year. Sadly, most membership lists are in-
complete or lost. But we can gain fair insight into organizational
stability by analyzing year-to-year changes in aggregate membership. I have calculated an index of organizational stability for the
major printing and coalmining unions in the United States, Britain,

deutschen Gewerkschaftsbewegung, 1862/3 bis 1869/70 (Stuttgart: Klett-Cotta, 1977), pp.
182–183.

[10] Reported by A. E. Musson, *The Typographical Association*, p. 39. See also Lloyd
Ulman, *The Rise of the National Trade Union* (Cambridge, Mass.: Harvard University
Press, 1955), pp. 20–21.

[11] See Philip Taft, *Organized Labor in American History* (New York: Harper & Row,
1964), pp. 35–56; Ulman, *The Rise of the National Trade Union*, pp. 20–21.

and Germany from their establishment to 1913.[12] It is particularly
sensitive to the proneness of unions to sharp decreases in membership and is calculated by averaging the yearly declines as a percentage of total membership and dividing by the number of years in the
relevant time period. Thus, the lower the index, the more stable a
union's membership.[13]

Calculating this index for printing unions yields some very low
scores. For the Verband der Deutschen Buchdrucker in the period
covered by Figure 4.4, the index is 1.4; for the Typographical Association, it is a remarkable 0.16, for the London Society of Com-

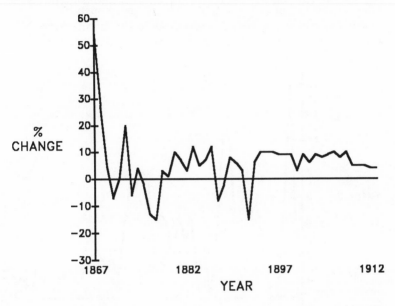

Figure 4.4 Annual Change in Membership of the Verband der Deutschen Buchdrucker, 1867–1913

[12] The index of organizational stability is defined mathematically as

$$\Sigma \, \frac{Y_{t+1} - Y_t}{Y_t} \quad \text{when } Y_{t+1} < Y_t$$

$$\Sigma \, \frac{Y_{t+1} - Y_t}{Y_t} = 0 \text{ when } Y_{t+1} > Y_t$$

[13] For example, over a ten-year period declines of 10 percent, 20 percent, and 30
percent in three years, and an increase or no change in seven years, results in an
index of organizational stability of 6. If the declines were, instead, 5 percent in each
case, the index would be 1.5.

positors, 0.88 (the T.A. and L.S.C. combined – 0.28); and for the
International Typographical Union, the index is 1.7. For purposes
of comparison, the indices of organizational stability for the major
coalmining unions in Germany, Britain, and the United States are
8.3, 1.9, and 6.0, respectively.

BARGAINING POWER AND TECHNOLOGY

Printing unions in the United States, Britain, and Germany were
perhaps the most outstanding examples of unions that were able to
adapt to their economic and technological environment.[14]

Printers had a number of advantages in the labor market. Although capital ownership in the printing industry became more

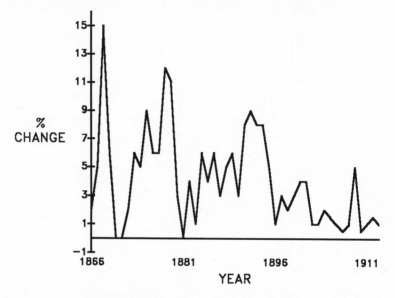

Figure 4.5 Annual Change in Membership of the Typographical Association and the
London Society of Compositors, 1866–1913

[14] On workers' control see Jonathan Zeitlin, "Craft Regulation and the Division of
Labour: Engineers and Compositors in Britain, 1890–1914" (Ph.D. diss., University
of Warwick, 1981); Robert Max Jackson, *The Formation of Craft Labor Markets* (New
York: Academic Press, 1984), pp. 168–177; and more generally, Richard Price, "The
New Unionism and the Labour Process," in Wolfgang J. Mommsen and Hans-Gerhard Husung, eds., *The Development of Trade Unionism in Great Britain and Germany,
1880–1914* (London: George Allen & Unwin, 1985).

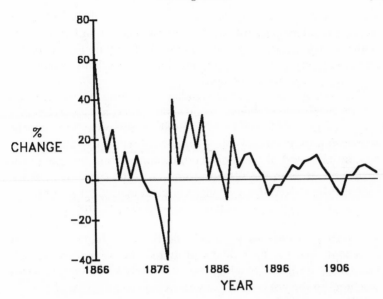

Figure 4.6 Annual Change in Membership of the International Typographical Union, 1866–1913

concentrated as the nineteenth century progressed, the gap between employee and employer never became as great as in heavy industry. Many employers in the early nineteenth century had themselves advanced through the craft and sympathized with the printers' collective effort to sustain their autonomy in the workplace.

The capacity of employers to collectively resist printing unions was weakened by the highly competitive character of the industry. This was especially true in newspaper printing where competition for circulation and advertising was intense. In this side of the industry printers also had the considerable advantage of producing a highly perishable product; news cannot be stored, and consequently a work stoppage or slowdown meant an immediate loss of revenue for employers. Given the highly volatile loyalty of newspaper readers, even a brief strike could have damaging repercussions for an employer. Book printing firms were in a stronger position, for they could stockpile their product in preparation for an industrial dispute, and they tended to take a correspondingly harder line on union demands.

Neither newspaper proprietors nor book and jobbing employers faced much foreign competition. The market for all kinds of printing increased steadily throughout the nineteenth and early twentieth centuries, and employers could be confident that their concessions to unions would not be undercut by foreign firms using cheap labor or more efficient methods.

But perhaps the most important key to the effectiveness of printing unions was their ability to control the impact of new technology on the division of labor. Printers, unlike many other artisans who practiced traditional skills, were not severely challenged by technology until the end of the nineteenth century. From the time of the first hand press in the fifteenth century to the early years of the nineteenth century, the technology of printing remained essentially unchanged.[15] When steam power was applied to the craft in the 1820s, its use was confined to the pressing stage of the operation. Typesetting or composing, which was the main ingredient of the craft and used the bulk of the printer's time, remained virtually unaffected until the development of various kinds of composing machines in the last two decades of the nineteenth century.

When composing machines were introduced, it was widely predicted that they would displace a significant proportion of unionized printers, and take, as one American printer put it, "the bread and butter out of workingmen's mouths."[16] But printing unions were able to maintain their niche in the division of labor by controlling the introduction of new technology. In the first place, the employment of the new machinery was limited for economic reasons to high volume work, mainly in newspapers, and this was precisely where the unions were strongest. Second, the fall in the price of typesetting led, through increased demand for the product, to a sizeable growth in the demand for labor. The Linotype could do the work of three or four compositors, but the demand for newspapers and printed matter was rapidly increasing, and this took up much of the slack in the labor market. Third, the skills developed by printers in their manual work of hand composition were found to be useful in operating the new machines. Finally, and this takes us back to occupational community and the Chapel, printers were

[15] See Elizabeth F. Baker, *Printers and Technology* (New York: Columbia University Press, 1957), pp. 3–30; Musson, *The Typographical Association*, pp. 16–21, 96–103; George E. Barnett, *Machinery and Labor* (Cambridge, Mass.: Harvard University Press, 1926), pp. 3–4.
[16] Quoted in James M. Lynch, *Epochal History of the International Typographical Union* (Indianapolis: ITU, 1924), p. 42.

not threatened by large numbers of semiskilled workers who were available to operate the new machines. The printers' occupational community encompassed all those regularly employed in the print room, a situation unlike that in engineering, for example, where previous mechanization created a class of semiskilled "handymen" who were denied entry into the craft.[17]

The first reaction of printing unions in each of the countries we are concerned with was opposition to the introduction of the new technology. But they came to realize that it was better to try to adapt to change rather than resist it.[18] Under the favorable circumstances outlined above, printing unions accepted the inevitability of labor-saving innovation, helped retrain hand operators on composing machines, insisted that apprenticeship regulations limiting the intake of new labor be retained, and, most important of all, managed to encompass the new tasks within their job territory.

PRINTING UNIONS IN GERMANY

The first German printing unions were formed in the early nineteenth century at a time of fundamental change in the organization of industry. Relations among masters, journeymen, and apprentices that had traditionally been determined by custom, law, and religion were increasingly subject to market relations.[19] Guilds,

[17] See Zeitlin, "Craft Regulation and the Division of Labour: Engineers and Compositors in Britain, 1890–1914."

[18] The classic analysis of union policy in the face of the introduction of labor-saving innovation is Barnett, *Machinery and Labor*; chapter 1 deals with the printers. On the policy of the International Typographical Union see also Jackson, *The Formation of Craft Labor Markets*; Ulman, *The Rise of the National Union*, pp. 34–35; H. Kelber and C. Schlesinger, *Union Printers and Controlled Automation* (New York: Free Press, 1967), chap. 1. On the policy of the Verband der Deutschen Buchdrucker, see F. C. Beyer, *Die volkswirtschaftliche und sozialpolitische Bedeutung der Einführung der Setzmaschine im Buchdruckgewerbe* (Karlsruhe: B.G. Braun, 1910), pt. 3. On the policy of the Typographical Association and the London Society of Compositors see W.E.J. McCarthy, *The Closed Shop in Britain* (Berkeley: University of California Press, 1964), pp. 136–140; *Report of the Quinquennial Delegate Meeting of the Typographical Association* (Liverpool, September 1898), pp. 36–42.

[19] See Werner Sombart, *Der moderne Kapitalismus* (München: Dunker, 1921), vol. 1, especially pp. 86–96; Werner Sombart, *Die deutsche Volkswirtschaft im neunzehnten Jahrhundert* (Berlin: G. Bondi, 1921), pp. 53–60; Gustav Schmoller, *Zur Geschichte der deutschen Kleingewerbe im 19.Jahrhundert, Statistische und Nationalökonomische Untersuchungen* (Halle: Buchhandlung des Waisenhauses, 1870), especially chap. 3; Jürgen Kuczynski, "Einleitung: Die wirtschaftlichen und sozialen Voraussetzungen der Rev-

which had organized production in the cities for centuries, were drastically weakened in most of the German states from the first decade of the nineteenth century. The status, conditions of work, and prospects of artisans were transformed. The traditional expectation of the journeyman that in time he would become an independent master of his own establishment was shattered. As market competition encouraged the exploitation of economies of scale in production and marketing, so the capital requirements of viable economic independence grew beyond the reach of most journeymen. The journeyman became, in other words, a lifelong employee. At the same time, the traditional defenses of the journeyman were broken down. From the early nineteenth century, detailed guild regulation of quality, price, and living standards increasingly gave way to the impersonal rule of the market.

The first unions formed by printers appealed to the state to reintroduce the traditional order of corporatist regulation. In the years up to 1848, artisans in a variety of industries submitted petitions to the kaiser and reichstag bemoaning economic "chaos" and its unsettling social consequences.[20] Their pleas were not entirely ignored; the Industrial Code of 1848 made some attempt to retain certain guild forms while extending market competition. But it became increasingly evident that the guilds, and the economic ideal they represented, were an anomaly. In the decades after 1848 printers came to accept that the system of traditional rights and obligations could never be recaptured and that attempts to improve their working lives would have to begin on the basis of capitalist market competition.

olution 1848/49," in Elisabeth Todt and Hans Radant, *Zur Frühgeschichte der Deutschen Gewerkschaftsbewegung, 1800–1849* (Berlin/DDR: Die Freie Gewerkschaft, 1950); Abraham, *Der Strukturwandel im Handwerk in der ersten Hälfte des 19.Jahrhunderts*; Wolfram Fischer, "Das Handwerk in den Frühphasen der Industrialisierung," in his *Wirtschaft und Gesellschaft im Zeitalter der Industrialisierung* (Göttingen: Vandenhöck & Ruprecht, 1972); J. Bergman, *Das Berliner Handwerk in den Frühphasen der Industrialisierung* (Berlin: Colloquium Verlag, 1973), pp. 307–321; Theodore S. Hamerow, *Restoration, Revolution, Reaction: Economics and Politics in Germany, 1815–1871* (Princeton, N.J.: Princeton University Press, 1958), chap. 2; Karl Heinrich Kaufhold, "Handwerk und Industrie, 1800–1850," in Hermann Aubin and Wolfgang Zorn, eds., *Handbuch der deutschen Wirtschafts—und Sozialgeschichte* (Stuttgart: Klett-Cotta, 1976), vol. 2.

[20] See Elisabeth Todt and Hans Radant, *Zur Frühgeschichte der Deutschen Gewerkschaftsbewegung, 1800–1849* (Berlin/DDR: Die Freie Gewerkschaft, 1950), pp. 169–185.

Early attempts by printers to create unions faced stiff state repression. Labor historians have recorded a handful of strikes on the part of printers before 1848, but their unions were small and ephemeral institutions.[21] The Chapel provided printers with an organic basis for local organization, but fear of repression prevented its consolidation on a regional or national scale.

Printing unions repeatedly petitioned the public authorities during and immediately after the 1848 revolution to revoke the clauses of the Industrial Code that specifically banned worker combination to raise wages. In this effort the early printing unions enthusiastically supported national worker organizations, especially the Arbeiterverbrüderung (Brotherhood of Workers) led by the printer Stephan Born.[22] Legal constraints applied to all workers, and in this respect the printers were no different from any other group.

The printing unions' concern with political freedom was tinged with some desperation in the years leading up to the explosion of discontent in the Revolution of 1848. According to a proclamation of the first National Conference of German Printers in 1848:

It is not political freedom alone that is so painful for the worker to do without; his call for bread and shelter is much stronger still. At issue is not only his political, but also his material existence. . . . The absence of political freedom makes it impossible for the worker to express his grievances openly. When whole workshops rose in revolt to improve working conditions, the police forcefully stepped in. The censor made public communication of the situation through the press impossible.[23]

But compared to other unions, the early printing unions were known for their political pragmatism. As Ludwig Rexhäuser, who later became the editor of the national union newspaper, the *Correspondenzblatt*, observed in the first history of the printers' unions:

[21] See ibid., pp. 68–79.

[22] See Frolinda Balser, *Sozial-Democratie 1848/49–1863: Die erste deutsche Arbeiterorganisation "Allgemeine Arbeiterverbrüderung" nach der Revolution* (Stuttgart: E. Klett, 1962), p. 57. On relations between the printers and the Arbeiterverbrüderung after mid-1848 see P. H. Noyes, *Organization and Revolution: Working-Class Associations in the German Revolutions of 1848–1849* (Princeton, N.J.: Princeton University Press, 1966), pp. 311–312.

[23] From the circular sent to masters in the printing industry by the National Conference of German Printers meeting in Mainz, June 1948, reprinted in Eduard Bernstein, ed., *Dokumente des Socialismus* (Berlin: Sozialistische Monatshefte, 1902), 1: 430.

"Of all trades it was the printers who began to draw from the altered political relations of 1848 consequences for practical life. While all of Germany revelled in a sea of republican dreams, the printers were intent on securing material advantages."[24] The extent to which the printing unions would subordinate their autonomy in collective working-class organization had narrow limits. The national printers' union established at the national conference in 1848, the Deutsche Nationale Buchdruckervereinigung, kept its distance from the Arbeiterverbrüderung when the workers' party became more radical. Rather than pursue a broad political strategy of radical change, printing unions focussed their efforts in the labor market where they had direct influence on the working conditions of their members.

Because unions of printers were among the first worker organizations to be established on a firm footing, they were never dependent upon the organizational support of the workers' political parties, the Lassallean Allgemeiner Deutscher Arbeiterverein and the Marxist-leaning Sozialdemokratische Arbeiterpartei.[25] Printers were represented in the congresses held in 1868 by these parties to gain union support, but they never extended their commitment to the comprehensive programs set out by either party. As in the past they steadfastly supported political efforts to gain amelioration of legal constraints, but, in the words of the Leipzig union of printers, they "considered the theories propounded for the improvement of the condition of workers as essentially and for all practical purposes unrealizable."[26] In contrast to unions that had to wait for the support of the socialist parties for their establishment, the printers leaned towards the self-help conceptions of Schultze-Delitsch and the liberal reformism of the labor economist Lujo Brentano.[27] As Ulrich Engelhardt observes in his monumental study of German trade unions in the decade of the 1860s, "Instead of forming a plan of revolutionary or even reactionary change, the printers confined

---

[24] Ludwig Rexhäuser, *Zur Geschichte des Verbandes der deutschen Buchdrucker* (Berlin: Verband der deutschen Buchdrucker, 1900), p. 10.

[25] See Dieter Fricke, *Die deutsche Arbeiterbewegung, 1869–1914* (Berlin: Dietz Verlag, 1976).

[26] Quoted in Engelhardt, *"Nur Vereinigt sind wir stark": Die Anfänge der deutschen Gewerkschaftsbewegung, 1862/3 bis 1869/70*, p. 169.

[27] See Beier, *Schwarze Kunst und Klassenkampf*, 1: 497–503. Robert Michels provides data on the relatively low SPD membership of printers in "Die deutsche Sozialdemokratie," *Archiv für Sozialwissenschaft und Sozialpolitik* 23 (1906): 499–501.

themselves to demands that could be fulfilled under the given circumstances, so that printers would at least have a sufficient wage."[28]

The determination of printing unions not to commit themselves
to broad working-class political organizations frequently led to
charges that they held themselves above the mass of workers. The
printers themselves did not do much to discourage this notion. In
fact, an invitation to printing unions to attend a national congress
in Heidelberg in 1848 claimed that "the printer, if we speak
frankly, belongs to the highest rank of the proletariat, the proletariat meaning here all those who are not able to establish their own
household, but are lifelong dependent on the good will or good
humor of an individual."[29] The term "aristocracy of the working
class," used pejoratively by later socialist leaders such as Karl Kautsky and Lenin, was actually a self-designation of printers themselves and crops up in their literature as early as the 1840s.[30]

Differences between the orientation of the printers' union and
other socialist unions survived even the period of repression under
the Anti-Socialist Laws of 1878 to 1890. Richard Härtel, the leader
of the Verein der Deutschen Buchdrucker, anticipated the suppression of socialist unions and reorganized the union into a benefit
society, the Unterstützungsverein Deutschen Buchdrucker. While
the remaining sixteen socialist Free Unions strengthened their in-
formal ties to the Socialist party, the UVDB preserved its legality by
adhering to the dictates of political neutrality. In these years the
printers extended and refined the economic functions of their association, adding, for the first time in Germany, unemployment
benefits for members who because of family commitments could
not take advantage of traveling benefits. Between 1878 and 1890
the UVDB more than doubled its membership, quadrupled its benefits, and increased its dues by 70 percent.[31]

In the 1890s, after the nonrenewal of the Anti-Socialist Laws, the
reconstituted printers' union, the Verband der Deutschen Buchdrucker, joined with the socialist Free Unions in forming a peak

[28] Engelhardt, *"Nur Vereinigt sind wir stark": Die Anfänge der deutschen Gewerkschaftsbewegung, 1862/3 bis 1869/70*, p. 186.
[29] *Typographia* 25, no 7 (March 1848); quoted in Todt and Radant, *Zur Frühgeschichte
der Deutschen Gewerkschaftsbewegung, 1800–1849*, p. 178.
[30] See Beier, *Schwarze Kunst und Klassenkampf*, pp. 141–148.
[31] See Krahl, *Der Verband der Deutschen Buchdrucker*, vol. l, chap. 5, and conclusion,
p. 17; Beier, *Schwarze Kunst und Klassenkampf*, pp. 490–497; A. Gerstenberg, *Die neuere
Entwicklung des deutschen Buchdruckgewerbes* (Jena: G. Fischer, 1892), pp. 108–122.

organization, the General Commission of German Trade Unions (Generalkommission). As other unions rebuilt their organizations and gained some leverage in the labor market, the printers' union was gradually transformed from an outcast among socialist unions to their vanguard. Criticism of the printers' demand for union autonomy from the party was muted as other unions gained in size and confidence. Collective bargaining agreements, which were first entered into in the printing industry in the 1890s, were gradually tolerated, and even copied, by other unions. The rapprochement between the printers and the other Free Unions resulted not because the printers compromised their former orientation but because the Free Unions turned towards what was described as a "practical economic strategy."[32] Typically, the printers were not reticent in taking pride in their new role in the union movement. As Emil Döblin stated in his presidential address at the printers' congress in 1908: "The feeling and the consciousness that we have attained what other organizations still vainly fight for, should, I think, contribute to the appreciation within our ranks of this success. . . . The path that we have come forward along is also the path that can serve the interests of the whole working class."[33]

With the ascendancy of "reformism" in the Social Democratic party and the perceptible shift in influence from the party to the unions, formalized in the Mannheim Agreement of 1906, the printers found themselves in the mainstream of the union movement. At the same time, events were making the printers more aware of the necessity of joint union political activity at the national level. Before 1914 the chief impetus in this direction was the legal offensive of the national employer associations in conjunction with the employers' organization in the printing industry, the Deutsche Buchdrucker-Verein. From 1905 the printers felt their position under the law to be more and more precarious as employers demanded greater restrictions on the right of unions to strike and use benefit funds in supporting strikers.[34]

[32] The term is Heinrich Öhme's; see Alfred Förster, *Die Gewerkschaftspolitik der deutschen Sozialdemokratie während des Sozialistengesetzes* (Berlin/DDR: Verlag Tribune, 1971), pp. 192–193.

[33] *Protokoll der Generalversammlung des Verbändes der deutschen Buchdrucker* (Köln, 1908), p. 3.

[34] See Hans-Peter Ullman, *Tarifverträge und Tarifpolitik in Deutschland bis 1914* (Frankfurt am Main: Lang, 1977), pp. 159–171; Thomas von der Vring, "Der Ver-

With the outbreak of the First World War and the decision on the part of the unions to give whole-hearted support to the war effort by unilaterally relinquishing strikes, the pressure on union legal status diminished. Mobilization and the ensuing reliance of the state on union cooperation in the war effort gave the Free Unions long-denied legitimacy in the social order. Incorporation into policy-making institutions was not as rapid for printing unions in Germany as it was in Britain or the United States, but by 1917 representatives of the printing union sat with government and employer officials on draft committees, arbitration committees, and on the chamber of industry established for the printing industry.[35] Just as the threat from employers' organizations led the printers into more intensive political activity, so regulation in the state arena of working conditions formerly determined in the labor market induced printers, alongside other unions, to focus more and more on national politics, while extending the de facto authority of their chief representative there, the Generalkommission.

PRINTING UNIONS IN BRITAIN

The emergence of unions among printers in Britain from the mid-eighteenth century occurred at a time of dynamic change in productive relations in their industry. The demise of guilds from the seventeenth century; the creation of permanent wage labor in place of the life-cycle progression of apprentice to independent master; the intrusion of the cash nexus into the employment relationship; the extension of competition into every sphere of the industry; and the consequent use of nonapprenticed labor: each of these created insecurity for the artisan and dashed his expectation of economic independence.[36] In the first half of the nineteenth cen-

band der Deutschen Buchdrucker im Ersten Weltkrieg, in der Revolution und in der Inflationszeit, 1914–1924" (Ph.D. diss., Frankfurt am Main, 1964), pp. 42–45.

[35] Thomas von der Vring, "Der Verband der Deutschen Buchdrucker im Ersten Weltkrieg, in der Revolution und in der Inflationszeit, 1914–1924," pt. 2. On the early printers' attitude towards the war see Emil Kloth, "Graphische Gewerbe," in F. Thinne and K. Legien, eds., *Die Arbeiterschaft im Neuen Deutschland* (Leipzig: S. Hirzel, 1915).

[36] See Lujo Brentano, "Entwicklung und Geist der Englischen Arbeiterorganisationen," *Archiv für Sozialwissenschaft und Sozialpolitik* 8 (1895): 83–101; Sidney and Beatrice Webb, *The History of Trade Unionism*, 2d ed. (London: Longmans, Green, 1920), chap. l; Karl Polanyi, *The Great Transformation* (Boston: Farrar & Rinehart, 1944), pp. 70, 82–83; E. P. Thompson, *The Making of the English Working Class* (London: Penguin

tury the skilled trades, as Edward Thompson has pointed out, "are like islands threatened on every side by technical innovation and by the inrush of unskilled or juvenile labour."[37]

The initial reaction of artisans, in Britain as in Germany, was to demand reconstitution of the old economic order and the protection it gave them. The Spitalfields silk weavers, for example, managed to maintain state regulation of their wages until the 1820s.[38] But for the majority of workers petitions demanding a return to traditional conceptions of reciprocity between master and journeyman could make no dent in the laissez-faire notions of their governors. The development of the artisans' strategy is summed up by Sidney and Beatrice Webb in their classic history of British trade unionism:

> The artisans of the seventeenth and eighteenth centuries sought to perpetuate those legal or customary regulations of their trade which, as they believed, protected their own interests. When these regulations fell into disuse the workers combined to secure their enforcement. When legal redress was denied, the operatives, in many instances, took the matter into their own hands, and endeavoured to maintain, by Trade Union regulations, what had once been prescribed by law.[39]

In the first quarter of the nineteenth century combinations "in restraint of trade" were illegal, both under common law and the Combination Acts. But legislation suppressing unions was never as comprehensively enforced in Britain as it was in Germany. Small unions based on cohesive communities continued to operate much as before. We hear of criminal charges being brought against journeyman printers in 1798 and again in 1810, but, according to the Webbs, the level of organization in the skilled handicraft trades of London actually increased in the first two decades of the nineteenth century.[40]

Along with many other groups of skilled artisans, printers were

Books, 1968), chap. 8; R. J. Morris, *Class and Class Consciousness in the Industrial Revolution, 1780–1850* (London: Macmillan, 1979), chap. 7.

[37] Thompson, *The Making of the English Working Class*, p. 269.

[38] See D. J. Rowe, "Chartism and the Spitalfields Silk-Weavers," *Economic History Review*, 2d ser., vol. 20 (1967), p. 491.

[39] Webb and Webb, *The History of Trade Unionism*, p. 21; see also Child, *Industrial Relations in the British Printing Industry*, chap. 3.

[40] Webb and Webb, *The History of Trade Unionism*, pp. 78–83.

active in protesting against the restrictive laws and spent considerable sums of money in collecting and presenting evidence of their
harmful effect to select committees of the House of Commons dealing with trade union legislation. But, in contrast to unions that had
little leverage in the labor market, printing unions were wary of
subsuming their organizations in working-class movements with
broad political goals. As A. E. Musson observes, "There was a
strong sentiment that trade unionism was one thing, politics another, and that trade societies should confine themselves to trade
affairs, unless politics obviously impinged upon them, as in the case
of the Combination Acts."[41]

The printing unions generously supported other unions on a
number of occasions when they appealed for funds in time of
strike; we find them making grants to builders, engineers, miners,
curriers, hatters, gold-beaters, boot and shoe workers, cotton spin-
ners, tin-plate workers, bookbinders and typefounders.[42] But they
were not associated with Robert Owen's famous attempt to build a
general union of all trades in the early 1830s, nor did they provide
much support for Chartism a decade later.[43] As Iowerth Prothero
points out:

> In London the highest-paid trades tended to be aloof from all
> kinds of joint working-class activity. The compositors, for in-
> stance, had a highly impressive union, but tended to keep to
> themselves. The view that they were prominent in London
> working-class activity is false. . . . The compositors, Robert
> Hartwell was later to write, were always isolated and conserva-
> tive, were rarely at meetings of the London Trades, and had a
> horror of anything political. This was a national and even an
> international phenomenon.[44]

Printers had the group-dependent capacity to form relatively stable unions, and for a variety of reasons their unions were able to
defend the printers' skills and nourish their sense that they had a

[41] A. E. Musson, *British Trade Unions, 1800–1875* (London: Macmillan, 1972), p. 37.
See also Malcolm I. Thomis, *The Town Labourer and the Industrial Revolution* (London:
Batsford, 1974), chap. 7.
[42] See Musson, *The Typographical Association*, p. 78.
[43] Iowerth Prothero, "Chartism in London," *Past and Present* 42–45 (1969), especially pp. 103–104; Iowerth Prothero, "London Chartism and the Trades," *Economic
History Review*, 2d ser., vol. 24 (1971); Musson, *The Typographical Association*, p. 77.
[44] Prothero, "London Chartism and the Trades," p. 209.

job territory within the existing division of labor that was worth defending. Printers were among those groups of workers who could adapt to the challenges of capitalist economic development. Unlike groups of workers who had no organizations to defend themselves, or no stake in the existing society, printers tended to shy away from violent methods. As Musson summarizes in his standard history of the Typographical Association:

> There is almost no trace among typographical societies of the blind rage and violence which characterized the lower grades of labour, the handloom weavers, the frame-work knitters, and the Chartist "physical force" men, in periods of social distress. Printers tended to more practical measures, to apprenticeship restriction, exclusion of "foreigners," curtailment of hours and overtime, agitation against the newspaper stamp, paper, and advertisement duties, tramp relief and unemployment funds, schemes of co-operative production, and assisted emigration.[45]

Printers always thought of themselves as superior to the mass of unskilled laborers who were unable to provide themselves with even the most elementary organizational defense in the market. They referred to their craft as a "profession" and, with the same metaphor used by printers in Germany, referred to themselves as "worthy of being ranked as the aristocracy of the working classes."[46] These feelings of superiority doubtless contributed to their moderation and aloofness from general working-class political movements. But, as in the case of the German printers, status consciousness never inhibited joint efforts with other groups of workers to gain freedom from legal constraints or legislation of working conditions for which activity in the labor market was unsuited.

Printing unions were active in campaigning for full legal recognition of their activities when a Royal Commission on Trade Unions was appointed in 1867, and in 1872, in response to the Criminal Law Amendment Act, they joined the Trades Union Congress.[47] Printing unions also lobbied to secure "fair wages" in public contracts and, in the process, petitioned Parliament, issued posters and circulars, and sent several deputations to ministers. In 1900 the Ty-

---

[45] Musson, *The Typographical Association*, p. 21.

[46] Ibid., p. 22.

[47] G.D.H. Cole, "Some Notes on British Trade Unionism in the Third Quarter of the Nineteenth Century," *International Review for Social History* 2 (1937): 14–18; Musson, *The Typographical Association*, pp. 341–342.

pographical Association and London Society of Compositors affiliated with the Labour Representation Committee, and in 1902 the Scottish Typographical Association followed suit.[48] Thus the printing unions, in Musson's words, were "carried along on the broad current of labour politics."[49]

Their commitment, however, remained a narrow one. In the debate at the 1872 Typographical Association Congress on whether to join the Trades Union Congress, H. Slatter, the general secretary of the union, supported the motion while claiming at the same time that he "could fairly take some little credit to printers generally for the care they took to steer clear of the political element in all their movements."[50] The arguments used at the 1891 Typographical Association Congress for affiliating with the Labour Representation Committee were pragmatic ones: "If we are granted votes," one delegate asked, "why should we not use them to our advantage?"[51] The benefits of legislation likewise were viewed along practical lines, one delegate arguing that it "would leave no chance for an unscrupulous employer in any branch to go back from an arrangement made possible after a long and expensive struggle with that branch."[52]

In the decades around the turn of the twentieth century the printers' concern with political activity intensified. On the one hand, the extension of the franchise in 1884 opened new possibilities for political influence. On the other, the inception of state welfare policies and the growth of employer organizations were reducing the autonomy of the labor market from the state. From the mid-1880s the Typographical Association threw its newfound political weight behind the campaign for "fair wages"—the demand that public contracts should embody the principle of a "fair day's wage for a fair day's work" and thereby favor employers who paid union rates to their workers. A "Fair Wages Resolution" was passed by the House of Commons in 1891, and by the end of the decade the principle was accepted by the majority of town councils in Britain. The success of the campaign convinced even skeptical unionists that po-

[48] S. Gillespie, *A Hundred Years of Progress: The Record of the Scottish Typographical Association, 1853 to 1952* (Glasgow: R. Maclehose, 1953), p. 135.

[49] Musson, *The Typographical Association,* p. 355.

[50] *Report of the Proceedings of the Meeting of Delegates from the Provincial Typographical Association and Mileage Relief Association* (Manchester, December 1872), p. 5.

[51] *Proceedings of the Delegate Meeting of the Typographical Association* (Manchester, September 1881), p. 19.

[52] Ibid.

litical activity could usefully complement union efforts directly in
the labor market. From the turn of the century the organ of the
Typographical Association, the *Circular,* reflected this shift in orientation by featuring articles on a variety of political issues alongside its traditional industrial concerns, including the eight-hour
day, factory legislation, workmen's compensation, old-age pensions,
education, health, and political representation.[53] In a by-election
held in 1904 the Typographical Association managed to elect an
official representative, G. H. Roberts, to the House of Commons "to
watch over the interests of the trade and all labour."[54]

As the stakes of political competition grew, employers responded
by concerting their own organizations. In the last decade of the
nineteenth century three national employers associations, the London Master Printers' Association, the British Federation of Master
Printers, and the Linotype Users' Association, were established in
the printing industry to counter the political influence of the Typographical Association and the London Society of Compositors.[55]
By 1901 these were joined by thirty-six local employer associations
representing the major provincial centers.

Union involvement in political activity was deepened during the
First World War. The complex reliance of the state on union restraint, advice, and consent led it to open doors in policy making
and policy implementation that were previously closed to trade
unions. The state was vitally concerned to forestall the strikes that
were feared under conditions of acute labor shortage, and from
1916, as mobilization in the armed services intensified, there was
the demand for the relaxation of union rules so that apprenticed
men could be replaced by unapprenticed, mostly women, workers.
In return for their cooperation, representatives of the printers,
along with those of many other groups of workers, were brought
into the framework of government. By the end of the war union
officials participated on a wide range of government committees,
including the National Service Committees, Labour Exchange Ad-

[53] Musson, *The Typographical Association,* chap. 14.

[54] *Report of the Quinquennial Delegate Meeting of the Typographical Association* (Birmingham, May 1903), p. 53.

[55] Hugh Clegg, Alan Fox, A. F. Thompson, *A History of British Trade Unions since
1889* (Oxford: Clarendon Press, 1964), pp. 145, 345; Child, *Industrial Relations in the
British Printing Industry,* p. 199; Eric Howe, *The British Federation of Master Printers,
1900–1950* (London: British Federation of Master Printers, 1950), chaps. 1 and 2;
Howe and Waite, *The London Society of Compositors,* p. 6.

visory Committees, and War Pensions Committees, while Roberts, the parliamentary representative of the Typographical Association, eventually sat in Lloyd George's cabinet as minister of labour.

PRINTING UNIONS IN THE UNITED STATES

Guild and state controls over working conditions were far weaker in eighteenth-century America than in either Germany or Britain. Although there were local state-aided monopolies alongside other practices taken over from the Old World, such as indenture and wage fixing, these were never deeply rooted in America.[56] By the early nineteenth century, state intervention in the labor market in the form of guild controls was considered so foreign to the American experience that the fledgling combinations of artisans never proposed it as a solution to their problems.

But basic economic developments involving the extension of markets, the exploitation of economies of scale in production and marketing, and the demise of the self-sufficient artisan were found in the New World as in the Old. In common with his counterpart in Britain and Germany the American journeyman was transformed into a permanent employee—a wage worker—who if he was to safeguard his interests had to act jointly with others in the same position. The dynamic of this change is described by David Saposs in the first volume of John Commons' classic, *History of Labour in the United States*:

Evidently the wide extension of the market in the hands of the merchant-capitalist is a cataclysm in the condition of the journeymen. By a desperate effort of organizations he struggles to raise himself back to his original level. His merchant-employers, who have now become sweatshop bosses, at first sympathize with him and endeavour to pass over to their customers, the merchant-capitalists, his just demand for a higher wage. But they are soon crushed between the level of prices and the

[56] See Ulman, *The Rise of the National Trade Union*, pp. 594–603; Leonard Bernstein, "The Working People of Philadelphia from Colonial Times to the General Strike of 1835," *Pennsylvania Magazine of History and Biography* 94 (1950): 323–324. For general analyses of the early absence of feudalism and the predominance of liberalism and liberal values in America, see Seymour Martin Lipset, *The First New Nation* (New York: Basic Books, 1963); Louis Hartz, *The Liberal Tradition in America* (New York: Harcourt, Brace, 1955); and Clinton Rossiter, *Conservatism in America* (New York: Knopf, 1962).

level of wages. . . . The journeymen now have no alternative but to organize into trade unions in order to resist the encroachments upon their standard of life. Since the skilled mechanics were the first to feel this pressure, it was quite natural that they should also be the founders of the early labour organizations.[57]

The need for effective organization in the labor market was rarely matched by the ability to create it. Tailors and shoemakers, for example, were hopelessly squeezed between the small sweatshop and the large factory producing for a rapidly developing mass market.[58] Their wages were inexorably forced downward by the influx of child and female labor in a craft formerly the preserve of skilled and independent artisans. Printers, in contrast, were never condemned by such drastic economic change. Their craft retained its essentially skilled and exclusive character, while their extraordinary occupational communities, encapsulated in the Chapel, gave an anchor to their organization in an era of great social flux. The general demands of printers, as expressed in the preambles of their union constitutions, were often couched in radical phraseology attacking the "oppression of the capitalists,"[59] "intolerance and aristocracy,"[60] and viewing their efforts in terms of "a perpetual antagonism between capital and labor."[61] But their activity was generally directed to pragmatic goals in the labor market. The

[57] John R. Commons et al., *The History of Labor in the United States* (New York: Macmillan Company, 1926), 1: 107. Frank Tannenbaum conceptualizes these changes as the decline of community and views the trade union as an attempt on the part of workers to re-create it, in his book *A Philosophy of Labor* (New York: Knopf, 1951).

[58] See Commons et al., *The History of Labor in the United States*, 1: 30–66.

[59] From the preamble of the *Report of the First Convention of the Federation of Organized Trades and Labor Unions of the United States and Canada*, 1881; quoted in Philip Taft, *The A.F. of L. in the Time of Gompers* (New York: Harper, 1957), p. 12. The curious mix of radicalism and conservatism that epitomized the printer's business unionism is noted by Norman J. Ware, *The Labor Movement in the United States, 1860–1895* (New York: D. Appleton and Company, 1929), p. 13. Ware quotes from a letter written by John Collins, the secretary of the ITU, calling for an Industrial Congress and promising that the proposed organization would not "deteriorate into a political party . . . but shall to all intents and purposes remain a purely industrial association, securing to the producer his full share of all he produces."

[60] From the address of the printer, Ely Moore, labor's first Congressman, to New York City unionists, 1835; quoted by Stephens, *New York Typographical Union No. 6*, p. 166.

[61] From the *Address to the Journeyman Printers of the United States* at the National Convention of Journeymen Printers held in New York, December 1850.

small local printing unions formed in the early decades of the nineteenth century were concerned above all with practical matters: how to restrict the number of apprentices, limit the number of female laborers and "two-thirders" (workers who had not finished their apprenticeship), collect and disemburse benefits, organize strikes, and circulate lists of "rats," or workers who had been caught working for less than the wage stipulated by the union. These unions generally kept their distance from political movements. In typical fashion the New York Typographical Society responded in 1829 to a circular sent by Robert Owen's Association for the Protection of Industry and for the Promotion of National Education with the statement that the "object, character and intentions" of their union was "entirely at variance with Owen's cooperative socialist views" which, they argued, would find little response "in the midst of a people enjoying liberty in its fullest extent, that liberty which was sealed by the blood of their fathers, and has descended to them in all its purity."[62]

An emphasis on labor market activity was characteristic of the International Typographical Union in the second half of the nineteenth century. This union was, in fact, selected by Selig Perlman as a model of "business unionism."[63] In their initial address to workers in the printing industry the founders of the ITU emphasized that there was a great disparity in the power of employers and workers, but they declared the remedy to be not "political activity" but "combination of mutual agreement in maintaining wages which has been resorted to in many trades, and principally our own. Its success has abundantly demonstrated its utility."[64]

The philosophy of the working man that underlay the strategy of business unionism was well expressed by the president of the ITU, William Bodwell, speaking at the 1878 congress. Attacking radicals who by "their vociferous assertions that they represent the laboring classes of America . . . have been the means of retarding greatly the legitimacy and thorough organization of workingman," Bodwell went on the state that "the workingmen desire no division of property and overthrow of the social structure. . . . What work-

---

[62] As reported in the New York *Mercury*, 16 December 1829; quoted in Commons et al., *The History of Labor in the United States*, 1: 249–250.

[63] See Selig Perlman, *A Theory of the Labor Movement* (New York: Augustus M. Kelley, 1949), pp. 272–279.

[64] From the *Address to the Journeyman Printers of the United States* at the National Convention of Journeymen Printers held in New York, December 1850.

ingmen desire is that they shall have the same right to form associations for the protection and advancement of their interests that businessmen of all professions have."[65]

This philosophy has been described by the term "voluntarism," a concern with economic gains in the labor market to the exclusion of political activity. But printing unions were far too pragmatic to observe the principles of voluntarism to the letter. The labor market was the chief arena of their activities, but they had no compunction about entering politics when their immediate goals were served by doing so. Thus we hear of the New York Typographical Society lobbying for a tax on imported printed matter in 1803 and pressuring city and state governments on a number of occasions to institute boycotts against employers who refused to accede to the unions' demands.[66] Typical of their efforts was the threat made by the New York Typographical Union after failing to gain a city boycott of a recalcitrant printing company: "That as the members of this union, in common with the workingmen of the City of New York freely cast their votes in favor of the members of said Boards of Aldermen, . . . we are determined to maintain the right of withholding our votes in future from all and every member of said Corporation Boards and not be deceived again by their claptrap of 'workingmen's friend'."[67]

Such incursions into the political arena were a straightforward extension of the union's activity in the labor market. They were limited in aim and scope, quite different from the more encompassing political activity demanded by radical or reformist bodies such as the Workingmen's party of the New England states in the late 1820s and early 1830s or the National Labor Congress of 1870. The latter organization was described in a report by a visiting ITU delegation as "made up of delegates, with few exceptions, who openly avowed the object to be the formation of a political party. Played-out politicians, lobbyists, women-suffragans, preachers without flocks, representatives of associations in which politics are made a qualification for membership, and declaimers on the outrages perpetrated on

[65] *Twenty-Sixth Annual Session of the International Typographical Union*, 1878, p. 19.
[66] See George E. Barnett, *The Printers: A Study in Trade Unionism* (American Economic Association Quarterly, 1909), pp. 268–273; Commons et al., *The History of Labor in the United States*, 2: 317, 365–366.
[67] Quoted in Stephens, *New York Typographical Union No. 6*, p. 389.

poor labor, formed the major part of the congress."[68] The only aspect of the congress that interested these self-designated "pure and simple" unionists from the ITU was a report of a committee on "abnoxious laws." Indeed, a concern with the legal framework of trade unionism was a recurring feature of printing unionism in America as it was in Germany and Britain. As the president of the ITU, James Lynch, wrote in his history of the union, politics in general were eschewed except "when it was felt that the union's toes were being trod upon specifically and deliberately."[69] Thus local printing unions allied with the Equal Rights, later the Loco-foco, party in the 1830s to secure the repeal of the conspiracy laws and pursued an ongoing and determined policy of opposition to the labor injunction through the American Federation of Labor from the late 1880s.[70]

Although the International Typographical Union was generous in aiding other striking unions, it remained aloof from broad cooperation in peak organizations. This began to change, however, in the final decades of the nineteenth century. Two developments channeled the ITU's interests towards cooperation with other unions at the national level. First, the establishment in 1887 of a peak organization of printing employers, the United Typothetae of America, and its declaration that it aimed "to secure uniform action . . . to resist any . . . unjustifiable encroachments of labor organizations upon the rights of employers" brought home to printers the need for organized interunion economic support.[71] It was argued that the centralized power of employers could be resisted only by joint efforts on the part of workers in different occupations. Sec-

[68] From the report to the 1871 International Typographical Union Convention by the delegates to the National Labor Congress of 1870. Quoted in *A Study of the History of the International Typographical Union, 1852–1963* (Colorado Springs: Executive Council, ITU, 1964), p. 309.

[69] Quoted by Lynch, *Epochal History of the International Typographical Union*, p. 37.

[70] See Stephens, *New York Typographical Union No. 6*, p. 166; Taft, *The A.F. of L. in the Time of Gompers*, pp. 266–268; Marc Karson, *American Labor Unions and Politics, 1900–1918* (Carbondale: Southern Illinois University Press, 1958), pp. 36–37.

[71] Quoted in Jacob Loft, *The Printing Trades* (New York: Ferrar & Rinehart, 1944), p. 175. On the growth and policies of the United Typothetae of America see Leona Margaret Powell, *The History of the United Typothetae of America* (Chicago: University of Chicago Press, 1926); George E. Barnett, "Collective Bargaining in the Typographical Union," in Jacob H. Hollander and George E. Barnett, eds., *Studies in American Trade Unionism* (New York: H. Holt & Company, 1905), pp. 167–181. The membership of the United Typothetae of America rose from 506 member firms in 1887, its first year of existence, to 1,450 in 1912 (Powell, p. 192).

ond, unions were spurred into cooperation by the perceived threat from the Knights of Labor, a general union that espoused a broad political program and attempted to recruit all wage earners regardless of craft jurisdiction.[72]

The American Federation of Labor, of which the ITU was a founding member, was a peak organization designed to safeguard the autonomy of its constituents rather than subordinate them to common projects. The AFL was itself a reflection of the limited political goals of its member unions. Although it could galvanize the defenses of unions in the legal sphere and against the recurring threat of dual unions, it was constrained by the principle of voluntarism in dealing with its constituents and was more an expression of labor sectionalism than it was of working-class unity.

Socialists, both in the ITU and in the AFL at large, tried to change this and create a more class-conscious, politically oriented labor movement. Max Hayes, an official of the ITU and member of the Socialist party, was particularly active in pressing socialist causes in AFL conventions in the early 1900s. But Hayes' influence within the ITU was slight. He served the union in the capacity of a local official and recruiter, apparently with skill, without ever moving into one of the leading positions of the union, president, vice-president or secretary-treasurer, and he usually found himself in a minority of one among ITU delegates on socialist issues.

With the first Wilson administration of 1912 to 1916 and the introduction of state regulation of working conditions in fields that were formerly the preserve of the market, the interest of the ITU in influencing the course of social legislation greatly increased. While still focussing its activities in the labor market, it could no longer afford to neglect the national political arena nor leave politics to larger unions, such as the coalminers and the railroad workers. As *The Typographical Journal* noted in an editorial in October 1916:

> During the past legislative year congress and state legislatures have passed ninety-two labor laws. Limitation or prohibition of child labor, amelioration of conditions of female employment, shorter hours for all kinds of labor, stricter regulation for haz-

[72] On the Knights of Labor see Ulman, *The Rise of the National Trade Union*, pp. 348–377. On the reaction of the ITU see *A Study of the History of the International Typographical Union, 1852–1963*, pp. 298–299, and George Tracy, *History of the Typographical Union* (Indianapolis: ITU, 1913), pp. 383–388.

ardous occupations, strengthened compensation laws and various forms of industrial insurance constituted the bulk of the subjects treated in these laws. . . .

And what has brought about this improvement in conditions? Nothing more or less than constant agitation by militant labor organizations.[73]

Even as the ITU engaged in broader pressure group activities within the AFL, it was still evident that there were limits to its cooperation with other unions. As one printer complained, "the fact that we continue aloof and bind ourselves in isolation from them certainly will cost us the respect, if not indeed the very sympathy, of fellow workers in other trades."[74]

But this aloofness was, in fact, declining in the face of the demands for joint political activity. During the First World War, these demands intensified. Although American involvement lasted less than two years, the ITU along with other AFL unions participated on numerous boards and committees covering wide areas of public policy. The wartime involvement of the ITU in national politics and administration was viewed as a temporary expedient, but its effect on union strategy was actually profound and long lasting. The change in union orientation was incremental, the result of adaption to a continually evolving political context. The cumulative result was that business unionism became increasingly alloyed with continuous and institutionalized activity at the various levels of government, from local, through state, to national politics.

CONCLUSION

The story of the printing unions begins not with industrialization and the factory but with the growth of capitalism and the changes in productive life associated with it. For artisans, capitalism meant the breakdown of the guilds, the loosening of traditional ties between master and journeyman, the growth of competition in the labor market, a more intense search for, and adoption of, labor-saving innovations, and the exploitation of economies of scale in larger, more capital intensive productive units. In short, the journeyman printer was faced by the disintegration of customary practices and mercantilist controls that assured him a measure of eco-

[73] *The Typographical Journal*, October 1916, pp. 458–459.
[74] Ibid., February 1917, p. 114.

nomic security and the promise of independence and enhanced status when he, in his turn, became a master.

As a result, journeymen were thrown back on their own resources. But those resources varied greatly from occupation to occupation. In the first place, as Max Weber emphasized in his discussion of the complexities of class position, workers bring differing types and levels of skill to the marketplace. The labor market is segmented into a variety of markets for diverse and often unsubstitutable kinds of labor, resulting in widely differing wage rates and life chances. Second, the organizational defenses of groups of workers varied decisively. Printers were not merely skilled; more crucially, they were among a select few who had the social resources to create and sustain unions. Their occupational community, institutionally based in the Chapel and expressed in their sense of exclusiveness, their occupational pride, and their relatively low rates of occupational mobility gave them the capacity to respond creatively to the challenge of capitalist innovation. Organization gave them the chance to shape their own collective destiny, to extend their repertoire of response beyond that of individual improvement, apathy, or rebellion. Because the study of trade unions is the study of organization, it is perhaps worth reminding ourselves that it is inherently focussed on rather exceptional groups of workers.

Printers not only sustained strong unions but were able to use them effectively in the labor market. They had several advantages when compared to most other groups of workers. The low degree of substitutability of their labor, intense competition among employers, the invulnerability of employers to foreign competition, and, especially in the newspaper side of the industry, the extreme perishability of the product gave printers a favorable economic context to exercise their organizational leverage.

Within their respective union movements printing unions were found on the political right. They wished to operate within the system of wage labor because they believed that they had something worth defending, namely their niche in the division of labor. But political accommodation should not be confused with economic moderation: printing unions defended their job control just about as militantly as socialist unions demanded the abolition of wage labor.

Similarly, their sectionalism should not be confused with selfishness. The printers' sectionalism was not so much a rejection of working-class unity as it was an instrumental response to the specific opportunities and constraints that faced them. There is plenty of evidence that printing unions were concerned about those who were in less favorable circumstances. On numerous occasions they buttressed the strike funds of less fortunate unions and gave generously to those in need. As individuals, printers were prominent among the leadership of their labor movements and were to be found on all parts of the working-class political spectrum. Paradoxically, the extraordinary group solidarity that printers exhibited in the workplace seems to have promoted *both* consciousness of class *and* sectional business unionism oriented to the defense of particularistic advantages in the labor market.

Sectionalism was by no means inherent in the strategy of printing unions. In fact, it rested on certain legal rights that were achieved through classwide mobilization. Under conditions of state repression discussed in Chapter Two, printing unions were impelled into the stream of broader working-class political activity by the overriding desire to gain basic legal freedoms. In Germany, where state repression was particularly severe, printing unions took a leading role in demanding basic political rights that would allow them to operate effectively in the labor market. In the United States and Britain printing unions were founding members of the AFL and the TUC, federations that were concerned to defend the legal position of unions. As literate workers in relatively strong unions, printers in all Western societies were deeply involved in establishing national organizations to gain a freer legal climate.

From the decades around the turn of the twentieth century printing unions were affected by fundamental changes in the relationship of political to economic activity that resulted from the Organizational Revolution. They were drawn, along with other unions in the United States, Britain, and Germany, towards a recognition that political power and state policies had a growing systematic effect on the substantive regulation of conditions of employment in particular labor markets. As the possibility of pure business unionism receded with the interpenetration of economy and polity in the decades around the twentieth century, printing unions, even in the United States, came to adjust their strategy to include interest group political activities that were sensibly conducted jointly with other unions at the national level.

National differences in the legal context of industrial relations and the effects of the Organizational Revolution created national and international commonalities in the political orientations of unions. But labor market factors were responsible for sectoral commonalities across Western societies. All workers, by definition, sell their labor power for the means to survive. But their skills, the degree to which their labor is substitutable, and above all, the organizational strategies that are open to them, differ decisively. The labor market, abstractly conceived, is a source of essential commonality among workers, but workers in different occupations and industrial sectors have contrasting capacities to defend themselves within it. The possibilities of creating organization, and the uses to which it could be put, vary systematically across occupations and industries in Western societies. In this light, the remarkable pattern of common orientation among printing unions is merely one instance of a more general phenomenon. In the next chapter I argue that a similar logic underlies commonalities among coalmining unions in the United States, Britain, and Germany, although the outcome to be explained is politicized unionism rather than business unionism.

CHAPTER 5

COALMINING UNIONS AND
POLITICAL UNIONISM

Coalminers formed the largest occupational grouping among trade unionists in Britain and the United States in the last quarter of the nineteenth century and beyond, and were a significant force in Germany, ranking first in 1892 and third behind the metalworkers and construction workers in 1913. In each of these countries coalminers' unions were to be found in the forefront of their union movements as the standard bearers of political action. In the United States, Britain, and Germany, as well as in various other Western societies, coalmining unions were among the first unions to campaign for legislation of safety conditions, maximum hours, and a "living wage," and were in the vanguard of the movement to gain political representation to press their demands directly in the legislature.

The classic explanation for the political forwardness of coalminers is based on Clark Kerr and Abraham Siegel's analysis of strike-proneness. They argue that coalminers, alongside certain other highly strike-prone groups, "form isolated masses, almost a 'race apart.' They live in their own separate communities . . . , [which] have their own codes, myths, heroes, and social standards. There are few neutrals to mediate the conflicts and dilute the mass. All people have their grievances, but what is important is that all of the members of these groups have the same grievances."[1]

The distinctiveness of coalminers has been noted by numerous writers from the first decades of the twentieth century. In 1915 the economist Stanley Jevons pointed out that "homogeneity of the population as regards employment is a factor which has a far-reaching effect on the character of the individuals of mining communities. There is not such diversity of aims, ambition and character amongst miners, as is found in towns where several kinds of indus-

---

[1] Clark Kerr and Abraham Siegel, "The Inter-Industry Propensity to Strike," in A. Kornhauser, R. Dubin, and A. Ross, eds., *Industrial Conflict* (New York: McGraw-Hill, 1954), pp. 191–192.

tries are carried on."[2] A similar observation was made by G.D.H.
Cole, writing in 1923.

The miner not only works in the pit: he lives in the pit village,
and all his immediate interests are thus concentrated at one
point. The town factory worker, on the other hand, lives often
far from his place of work and mingled with workers of other
callings. The townsman's experience produces perhaps a
broader outlook and quicker response to social stimuli coming
from without; but the miners' intense solidarity and loyalty to
their Unions is undoubtedly the result of the conditions under
which they work and live. They are isolated from the rest of
the world—even the rest of the Trade Union world; but their
isolation ministers to their own self-sufficiency and loyalty one
to another.[3]

These observations have sustained a view of coalminers as quin-
tessential proletarians, as class-conscious workers living and working under the harshest conditions, whose concern with political regulation of their working conditions reflects their communitarian
way of life and their militancy in the workplace.

However, the argument linking physical isolation and entrenched community to political forwardness is doubtful when we
consider the case of the printers alongside the coalminers. As I observed in the previous chapter, printing unions were based on extremely strong occupational communities yet pursued a strategy of
business unionism with minimal reliance on the political regulation
of their members' working conditions. The case of the printers suggests that we have to ask a further set of questions before we can
derive hypotheses about union political orientation from statements
about working-class community: What were the constraints on the
use of union organization to defend or improve the position of
workers, and, in particular, how could union organization be used
to pressure employers directly in the labor market? Printers, as we
have seen, were advantaged in this regard by their ongoing ability
to control their job territory as the division of labor evolved in their
industry. Coalminers, in contrast, faced far greater obstacles in the
labor market. Even when they were able to unionize a sizeable pro-

[2] H. S. Jevons, *The British Coal Trade* (London: Kegan Paul, 1915), p. 625.
[3] G.D.H. Cole, *Labour in the Coal-Mining Industry, 1914–1921*; quoted in Roy Gregory, *The Miners and British Politics: 1906–1914* (Oxford: Oxford University Press,
1968), p. 3.

portion of their huge work force—no mean feat—they were faced by militant and strongly entrenched employers who competed intensely in interregional, or even international, markets and who could store their product in anticipation of industrial conflict.

But there is another compelling reason for the insufficiency of the isolation argument. Coalminers and their communities in the nineteenth and early twentieth centuries rarely approximated the ideal type suggested by Kerr and Siegel. The classic explanation of coalminers' militancy appropriately turns our attention to the social bases of unionism, but we must look more closely at the experience of occupational community in the years before the First World War when the coalmining industry was rapidly growing into a modern colossus.[4]

COALMINERS AND OCCUPATIONAL COMMUNITY

The most decisive influence on the situation of workers in the coalmining industry in the United States, Britain, and Germany before 1914 was that the massive expansion of output was generated not by technological advance but by the mobilization of labor on a vast scale. Efforts were made to mechanize various jobs in coalmining from the 1870s, but the results had little impact on the labor intensity of production before the First World War.[5] Increases in coal production were achieved by even larger increases in the number of workers employed in and around the mines. In many cases the demand for labor outstripped the local or even regional supply. The rapid growth of coal production demanded the massive influx of agricultural laborers and immigrants into the industry: the English in the Welsh coalmines, the Irish in the Scottish coalmines,

[4] In a comparison of coalminers in the Ruhr and southern Illinois, Eric Weitz argues that the isolation of southern Illinois miners contributed to the divorce between industrial militancy and political radicalism. This is a plausible line of argument, although much of its force is lost when Weitz contends that the Ruhr miners, who were less isolated, had a coherent set of values and a coherent ideological conception of their place in society. See Eric D. Weitz, "Class Formation and Labor Protest in the Mining Communities of Southern Illinois and the Ruhr, 1890–1925," *Labor History* 27, no. 1 (Winter 1985–1986).

[5] Per capita production actually declined in the decades preceding the First World War. See Max Jürgen Koch, *Die Bergarbeiterbewegung im Ruhrgebiet zur Zeit Wilhelm II, 1889–1914* (Düsseldorf: Drost-Verlag, 1954), p. 139, and John Benson, *British Coalminers in the Nineteenth Century: A Social History* (New York: Holmes and Meier, 1980), pp. 216–217.

Poles in the coalmines of the Ruhr, and successive waves of immigrants in America: English, Scots, Welsh, and later Irish, and then Italians, Poles, and Slavs. The history of coalmining is also a story of human uprooting and resettlement on a huge scale.

Rapid demographic flux did not end with the movement of new workers into mining towns and villages. Once they were there, new workers tended to be extremely mobile in response to changes in the relative demand for labor in neighboring industries and coalmines. Information about individual coalmines reveals that turnover rates in excess of 50 percent per year were not uncommon.[6] The picture that we are left with is one of coalmining communities that were dynamic, transient, and heterogeneous rather than stable, fixed, and homogeneous.

This point is emphasized by Rowland Berthoff in his discussion of the Pennsylvania anthracite region from the middle decades of the nineteenth century: "Community ties were weak, even within towns and villages. Apart from a nucleus of shopkeepers, professional men, and what passed for old families in the few places in the Wyoming Valley that dated from the eighteenth century, the

Table 5.1
Labor Force in the Coalmining Industry

Year	United Kingdom*	Germany	United States
1870	517,000	209,000	186,000
1880	604,000	222,000	296,000
1890	751,000	295,000	435,000
1900	931,000	465,000	677,000

SOURCES: United Kingdom: Mitchell and Deane, *Abstract of British Historical Statistics*, p. 60. Germany: Hoffmann, *Das Wachstum der deutschen Wirtschaft seit der Mitte des 19. Jahrhunderts*, table 14, pp. 194–197. United States: *Comparative Occupation Statistics for the United States, 1870 to 1940*, Sixteenth Census of the United States, table 8, pp. 104–107.

NOTE: * Figures are for 1871, 1881, 1891, and 1901 respectively.

[6] See, for example, Robert J. Waller, *The Dukeries Transformed: The Social and Political Development of a Twentieth-Century Coalfield* (Oxford: Clarendon Press, 1983), pp. 28–29; Stephen H. F. Hickey, *Workers in Imperial Germany: The Miners of the Ruhr* (Oxford: Clarendon Press, 1985), p. 63.

population of most mining towns was too mobile, too transient, too quickly gathered and easily scattered again."[7]

Cultural, religious, and linguistic identifications were not easily submerged under occupational or class loyalties. The English and the Welsh were deeply split in the coalmines of South Wales. In the Ruhr a religious cleavage coincided with a political cleavage which was so deep that it was institutionalized in two separate unions, the socialist Alter Verband and the Catholic Christlicher Gewerkverein. Later, with the migration of Polish workers into the mines an exclusive Polish union was established. In a passage describing German coalminers in the Ruhr that could almost equally well describe coalminers in the United States, Steven Hickey observes:

> Religion did not stop workers from experiencing social injustice or from participating in industrial and political conflict: but many workers did so within a linguistic and social framework which isolated them from other confessional groups and particularly from the "atheistic" social democrats. Loyalties for many remained focused on particular groups, often defined in terms of ethnic origins or religious allegiance, and not on a broader concept of the workers at large.[8]

These cultural divisions meant that cohesive occupational communities were not inherent features of the coalminers' social situation but had to be created in the process of dynamic economic change. That unitary unions were established in the United States and Britain is a testament to the malleability of even ethnic identifications into wider occupational loyalty. But before we inquire into the conditions that facilitated this some further obstacles to union organization should be noted.

In the first place, we should not overlook an obvious but consequential fact: the sheer scale of the coalmining industry made it particularly difficult to build strong unions. Although the coalmining industry was based on the kind of small, close-knit groups in the workplace that formed the backbone of unionism in the printing industry, the size of the organizational task confronting the early coalmining unions was vastly greater. Coalminers outnumbered those employed in the printing industry by three to more

[7] Rowland T. Berthoff, "The Social Order of the Anthracite Region, 1825–1902," *Pennsylvania Magazine of History and Biography* 79 (July 1965): 263.

[8] Hickey, *Workers in Imperial Germany*, pp. 290–291.

than five to one in the United States, Britain, and Germany.[9] The
contrast becomes sharper if one compares the number of coalminers to compositors, who were the chief target group of the
printing unions and who numbered roughly half of those employed in the printing industry.[10]

Coalmining unions were subject to a further disadvantage that
set them apart from printing unions. The latter were able to aggregate relatively stable groupings of workers, tied to the social institution of the Chapel, into small unions that could operate effectively in individual cities and localities. The national printing
unions were formed as marriages of convenience between autonomous unions that were able to prosper alone. Coalmining unions,
on the other hand, were compelled, even at the beginning, to organize far broader aggregations of workers if they were to stand
any chance of success in the labor market.

The reasons for this difference lie in the size of the respective
product markets in printing and coalmining. The sphere of competition in the printing industry in the nineteenth century was local
in the case of newspapers and regional for job printing. With the
exception of a limited number of national newspapers and period-
icals, and the nationalization and regionalization of certain aspects
of job printing from the late nineteenth century, the situation has
not changed up to the present. The market for coal, on the other
hand, was limited less by product diversification than by natural obstacles that made transportation expensive. Although different
types and grades of coal can be distinguished, coal is a relatively
homogenous product, far more so than that of most other industries. As transportation became cheaper, so regional markets gave
way to national markets, and national markets to international markets. This process was already under way in each of the countries
under review by the second half of the nineteenth century.[11]

---

[9] The size of the labor force in printing in 1900 in the United States was 185,000,
in the United Kingdom 212,000, and in Germany 146,000. The sources are those for
Table 5.1.

[10] The United States Census gives separate figures for the number of compositors,
linotypers, and typesetters from 1910, when these categories accounted for 54 percent of the total number employed in the printing industry. The percentages in 1920
and 1930 were 54 percent and 57 percent respectively ("Occupation Statistics for the
United States 1870 to 1944," *Sixteenth Census of the United States*, table 8, pp. 104–107).

[11] On Britain see T. S. Ashton, *An Economic History of England: The Eighteenth Century*
(London: Methuen, 1966), p. 93; H. S. Jevons, *The British Coal Trade*, pp. 309–310
and chap. 24. On the United States see W. J. Ashley, *The Adjustment of Wages: A Study*

This meant that local coalmining unions, and eventually regional unions, were bound to face stiff resistance from employers. Coalmining unions found that unless all the competing firms in the relevant product market were unionized, and thus subject to the union's claims, unionized employers could not give higher wages and compete. Only by unionizing the bulk of firms in a given product market could the resistance of employers be dampened by their ability to pass on higher wages in prices. The importance of this consideration was sharpened by the fact that wages account for a high percentage, generally around 60 percent, of the cost of extracting coal.[12]

This inherent obstacle led local or regional coalmining unions to try to coordinate their organizations at the interregional or national level. The institutional history of coalmining unions in most Western societies is a complicated web of mergers and splits between unions attempting to submerge particular ethnic, religious, political, or institutional loyalties to form more encompassing, and therefore more effective, alliances. At every step they were opposed by employers who wished to maintain their sole authority in the workplace and who refused to tolerate workers' organizations that diminished their relative competitiveness in national or international markets.

COALMINERS IN THE WORKPLACE

It is only when we consider the immense obstacles in the path of unionism in coalmining that we can appreciate the strength of the social resources of coalminers and the intensity of their struggles to gain some influence over their working lives. Coalminers were never able to control the supply of labor into their occupation in the way printers did through the Chapel. The character of their industry made that impossible. But their work-group identity was

---

of the Coal and Iron Industries of Great Britain and America (London: Longmans, Green & Company, 1903), p. 103. On Germany see Jürgen Kuczynski, *Zur Frühgeschichte des deutschen Monopolkapitals und des staatsmonopolistischen Kapitalismus* (Berlin/DDR: Akademie-Verlag, 1962), chap. 2, pt. 1.

[12] Keith Burgess makes the additional point that the large role of wages in the cost of coal meant that employers could close their mines when demand was slack, or in time of strike, with relatively small losses due to idle capital. See *The Origins of British Industrial Relations* (London: Croom Helm, 1975), pp. 177–178.

extraordinary, and this gave them a foundation in the workplace, on which to build unions.[13]

Coalminers were set apart from other groups of workers by the character of their job. Even when they did not live in homogenous or isolated communities, all miners who worked underground shared uniquely severe and extremely dangerous working conditions. No matter what else separated them, they all worked in abysmal conditions in virtual darkness. Their work marked them in the most obvious way possible, by blackening them to the pores of their skin. Physically, as well as socially, they were truly a caste apart.

Coalmining was an extremely dangerous occupation. A few other industries had injury and job mortality rates that were about as high, but the sheer scale of disasters in the coalmining industry, the grisly death of those involved, and the community efforts to save those who were buried created a unique camaraderie among coalminers. Their shared sense of danger, group dependence for survival, and memories of past disasters were weaved into the miners' folklore, sustaining a common sense of history among established communities and helping to create one among new communities.

As soon as we enter the world of the miner's work itself, it becomes very hard to generalize about job control and worker/employer relations. These varied from region to region and even from mine to mine in the same locality depending on the depth of the shaft, the width of the seam, the softness the coal, etc.[14] But there were some generally shared features of mining that reinforced the group-centeredness of the miner's working life.

In the first place, the dispersion of working areas within the mine made it difficult to supervise the miner on a regular basis. This was particularly true under the standard method of mining up to the last decades of nineteenth century, room and pillar (sometimes called bord and pillar or stall and pillar), in which men would be scattered about the mine singly or in pairs. Coal would be extracted from the bottom of the pit shaft around pillars left to support the

[13] Michael Pollard, *The Hardest Work under Heaven: The Life and Death of the British Coal Miner* (London: Hutchinson, 1984); Wolfgang Köllmann, "Vom Knappen zum Bergarbeiter: Die Entstehung der Bergarbeiterschaft an der Ruhr," in Hans Mommsen and Ulrich Borsdorf, eds., *Glück auf, Kameraden! Die Bergarbeiter und ihre Organisationen in Deutschland* (Köln: Bund-Verlag, 1979).

[14] See John Benson, "Coalmining," in Cris Wrigley, ed., *A History of British Industrial Relations, 1875–1914* (Sussex: Harvester Press, 1982), pp. 188–189; Burgess, *The Origins of British Industrial Relations*, pp. 158–161.

roof, after which the pillars themselves would be pared down or "robbed." The second and newer method, longwall mining, concentrated miners into teams that would work on continuous sections of coal face along roadways driven from the pit bottom. But supervision remained difficult because the teams were usually widely dispersed about the mine.

Under these conditions the chief form of managerial control had to be exercised indirectly, through the cash nexus, in the form of piece rates. A particularly distinctive characteristic of mining was the continual friction between management and labor in the ongoing process of determining the actual piece rate in terms of the difficulty of the conditions in various parts of the mine. Because conditions were so variable, labor and management were thrust into constant and highly decentralized wage bargaining. National and regional agreements simply served as frameworks in which such bargaining could take place. Payment was by tonnage as measured in good trucks of coal, and what constituted a good truck—that is, one free of dirt and rocks—was a source of additional friction, even after coalminers managed to gain legislation constraining the arbitrary authority of management to disqualify an entire truck on account of its having too much rubble.[15]

The physical demands of coalmining emphasized the work group as the unit of organization and survival, but contrary to the myth of equality underground, coalmining was organized on a highly hierarchical basis. In most mines hierarchy reflected age, seniority, and experience, and was therefore consistent with a considerable degree of solidarity among widely different grades of workers. Even those at the bottom could, in time, expect to reach the lofty position of hewer. But where job distinctions reflected ethnicity, divisions among miners could be exacerbated in the workplace.

UNION ORGANIZATION

Two sets of figures illustrate the struggle for unionization among coalminers in Germany, Britain, and the United States in the years before 1914. The first set (figures 5.1, 5.2, and 5.3) shows the absolute growth in the membership of major coalmining unions. Given the obstacles in the path of coalmining unionization, it was

[15] The German name for this practice was particularly descriptive—*nullen*—literally, to negate.

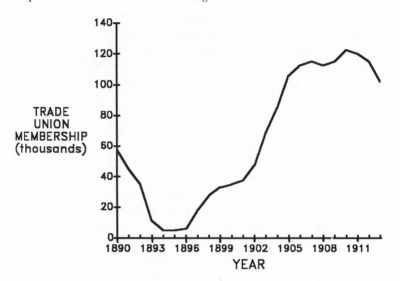

Figure 5.1 Membership of der Alte Verband, the Christlicher Gewerkschaft, and the Polnische Berufsvereinigung, 1890–1913

SOURCES: 1890–1912: Hue, *Die Bergarbeiter*, 2: 736–737. 1913: *Correspondenzblatt der Generalkommission der Gewerkschaften Deutschlands* 4 (1914): 183, 204.

not until the beginning of the twentieth century that unions were firmly entrenched in the industry. In the decade immediately prior to the First World War the proportion of coalminers unionized in Britain was around 60 percent, in the United States between 40 and 50 percent, and in the Ruhr between 30 percent and 40 percent.[16]

In these years coalmining unions grew into the massive organizations characteristic of our modern age. But their growth was far from smooth. In this respect coalmining unions contrast sharply with printing unions. While printing unions grew at an even pace, increasing their membership steadily from year to year, the membership of coalmining unions was subject to sudden fluctuations, downwards as well as upwards. This is shown in figures 5.4, 5.5, 5.6 and 5.7, which illustrate the annual percentage changes in union membership for the major coalmining unions in Germany, Britain, and the United States.

[16] Hickey, *Workers in Imperial Germany*, p. 243; Hugh A. Clegg, Alan Fox, and A. F. Thompson, *A History of British Trade Unions since 1889* (Oxford: Clarendon Press, 1964), 1: 468; Leo Wolman, *Ebb and Flow in Trade Unionism* (New York: National Bureau of Economic Research, 1936), appendices.

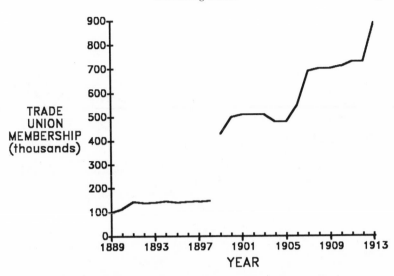

Figure 5.2 Membership of the Major Coalmining Unions in the United Kingdom, 1889–1913

SOURCES: 1889–1898: *6th Abstract of Labour Statistics, 1898/1899: United Kingdom Census Reports*, Cd. 119, lxxxiii. 1899–1913: *17th Abstract of Labour Statistics, 1914–1916: United Kingdom Census Reports*, Cd. 7733, lxi.

NOTE: Data for 1889–1898 include the Northumberland Miners' Mutual Confident Association, the Durham Miners' Association, the Yorkshire Miners' Association, and the Nottinghamshire Miners' Association. Data for 1899–1913 are for all coalmining unions.

The impression of flux that we gain from these figures is born out by comparing these unions on the index of organizational stability.[17] The German socialist coalminers' union, the Alter Verband, stands as the most unstable union with an index of 8.3, followed by the United Mine Workers of America with 6.0. These indices are several times higher than those for printing unions in Germany, the United States, and Britain which score 1.4, 1.7, and 0.3 respectively. When we confine the comparison to the years from 1890 to 1913, and ignore the preceding decades for which we have statistics on the printing unions alone, the indices for printing unions in Germany and the United States fall below 1.0. The smaller coalmining unions in Germany and the major British coalmining unions are

[17] The index of organizational stability is calculated by adding the points for years in which membership declines and dividing by the sum of observations of yearly membership change. The lower the index, the more stable is union organization.

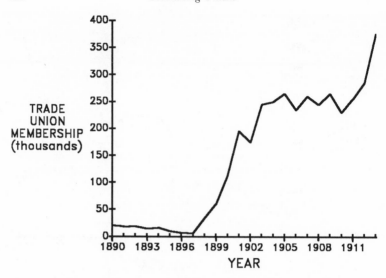

Figure 5.3 Membership of the United Mine Workers of America, 1890–1913
SOURCES: 1890–1896: Suffern, *The Coal Miner's Struggle for Industrial Status.* 1897–1913: Wolin, *The Growth of American Trade Unions, 1880–1923*, pp. 110–119.

more stable than the Alter Verband and the United Mine Workers of America, although they do not match the printing unions. The index for the German Christian coalminers' union, the Christlicher Gewerkverein, is 2.2 and that for the German Polish coalminers' union is 1.8. The Miners' Federation of Great Britain has an index of 1.9, the South Wales Miners' Federation, 1.7, and the Yorkshire Miners' Association, 1.3.

There are two theoretically interesting exceptions to this picture of organizational instability, the North-Eastern unions of Great Britain. The Northumberland Miners' Association has an index of 0.25 and the Durham Miner's Association has an index of zero. Incredibly, these unions suffered virtually no drops in membership between 1898 and 1910. Both unions escaped the sharp setbacks suffered by the Yorkshire Miners' Association and the Miners' Federation from 1908. In terms of membership stability they are closer to printing unions than to other coalmining unions. As we shall see later, this was reflected in their strategies for improving their members' working conditions.

The massive size of coalmining unions was conditioned by constraints on their strategy in the labor market. Unlike printing

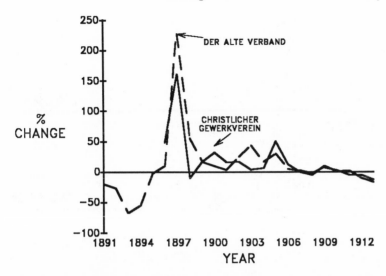

Figure 5.4 Annual Change in Membership of der Alte Verband and the Christlicher Gewerkverein, 1891–1913

unions, they were unable to take advantage of a specific job territory and defend this within the changing division of labor. Coalminers lacked traditions of apprenticeship and other guild controls on the supply of labor in their industry, and although their work was physically demanding, the skills it demanded could be readily learned on the job. Because they could not restrict the entry of labor into their occupation, coalminers had no reason to limit their recruitment to a particular labor market. Instead their unions pursued an open strategy, encompassing all those employed in the industry.

The geographical concentration of coalminers and their numerical weight made it possible for them to engage in politics as a practical strategy for improving their working conditions, hours, and pay. While smaller occupational groupings were faced with the prospect of building broad coalitions if they were to have some impact on national politics, coalmining unions could conceive of political pressure as just one more weapon in their own arsenal for improving their members' welfare. Coalmining unions were in the forefront of their respective movements in sending representatives to the legislature to voice their demands directly in national politics.

The normality of politics was reinforced because the miners'

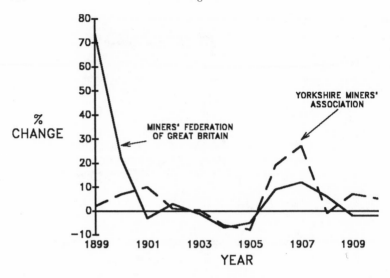

Figure 5.5 Annual Change in Membership of the Miners' Federation of Great Britain and the Yorkshire Miners' Association, 1899–1910

chief weapon in the labor market—the mass strike—could not be considered a purely economic activity. If they were to succeed in the labor market, coalmining unions had to pressure employers by force of numbers rather than through more subtle control of the labor supply, and this involved a clash of massive proportions between large-scale unions and powerful employers often backed by the state. Moreover, even in more tranquil times, economic decision making in the coalmining industry could rarely be divorced from issues of power and purposive manipulation. The boundaries between economic and political activity became increasingly blurred from the last decades of the nineteenth century, when industrial conflict in the industry could bring the economy as a whole to a standstill and governments scurrying directly into industrial relations. The coalmining industry departed considerably from economists' notions of pure competition in which neither buyers nor sellers control the terms at which goods are traded. The size of the industry, and the tendency towards oligopolistic control on the one side and large-scale union organization on the other, created transparent power relations in place of market anarchy. The effects of the Organizational Revolution both on industrial relations in the industry and on the organized behemoths it created meant that eco-

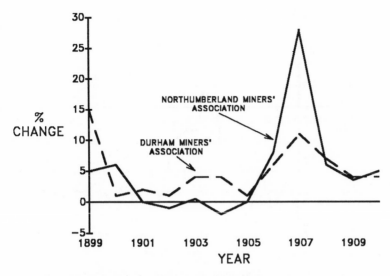

Figure 5.6 Annual Change in Membership of the Durham Miners' Association and the Northumberland Miners' Association, 1899–1910

nomic decision making in coalmining could never be so autonomous from political activity as in smaller or more peripheral industries.

The personal interdependence among miners in close-knit groups demanded by the mode of production underground gave coalminers a capacity for grass-roots organization.[18] Their identity as coalminers, which was based on the workplace, common dangers, and isolation from other workers, helped mold coalminers into occupational communities. But opposing these factors were the sharp growth and transiency of the work force, ethnic and cultural divisions, the huge size of the coalminers' organizational task, the determined opposition of large-scale employers, and the vulnerability of unions to large swings in the price and demand for coal. The relative weight of these factors varied from country to country and, within countries, from region to region and even from mine

[18] See, for example, Raymond Challinor and Brian Ripley, *The Miners' Association: A Trade Union in the Age of the Chartists* (London: Lawrence & Wishart, 1968), p. 242. The shared experience of danger has also been stressed as a factor making for solidarity, for example in Roger Dataller, *From a Pitman's Note Book* (London: Jonathan Cape, 1924), p. 158. On the miners' work group setting in the contemporary era see E. L. Trist et al., *Organizational Choice: Capabilities of Groups at the Coal Face under Changing Technologies* (London: Tavistock Publications, 1963).

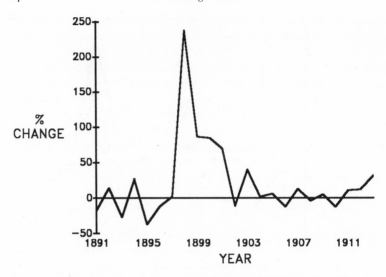

Figure 5.7 Annual Change in Membership of the United Mine Workers of America, 1891–1913

to mine. Because coalmining unions faced such difficult obstacles in bargaining effectively with employers, legislation of minimum standards for the work force as a whole often appeared a more practical option than reliance on collective bargaining. In many cases coalmining unions had less capacity for gaining and defending improvements in the labor market than for pressing their demands through the legislature.

The state is a cumbrous machine for trade union purposes. The process of achieving authoritative regulation of working conditions is convoluted, time-consuming, and, above all, uncertain. And legislation itself is an inflexible instrument of regulation. But, as Sidney and Beatrice Webb appreciated, legislation of working conditions, if it can be achieved, holds out for unions the advantages of "permanence and universality."[19] Once a law is gained, a union need expend only minimal effort in maintaining it and none in ensuring its application to competing but nonunionized workers.

Coalmining unions pursued a political strategy, but they rarely campaigned for the overthrow of capitalism or the abolition of wage labor. Most viewed both political and labor market activity as

[19] Sidney Webb and Beatrice Webb, *Industrial Democracy*, 2d ed. (London: Longmans, Green, 1920), 1: 255.

useful under the right conditions. They framed their legislative demands so as not to hinder their efforts to take immediate advantage of favorable inequalities in the supply and demand for labor. Thus the kind of legislation of working conditions they demanded stipulated the minimum parameters below which working conditions could not legally fall but above which they could rise freely. Minimum safety standards, maximum hours, minimum wages, as well as the elimination of cheap sources of competing child labor or immigrant labor were their chief legislative goals.

COALMINING UNIONS IN BRITAIN

The first coalmining unions in Britain were ephemeral organizations that sprang up in response to some immediate grievance and declined just as suddenly. Their methods were those that were closest to hand, the riot, directed against employers or food merchants, and the strike, usually backed by violence, or the threat of violence, to ward off blacklegs imported from mines in other localities.[20] Unlike the "freeborn" journeyman, with his sense of occupational status, expectation of advancement, and traditional privileges, the coalminer had no prospect of ever owning his means of production and no assumed recourse to law to defend traditional rights. Although the Combination Acts of 1800 to 1824 were used to suppress outbreaks of unionism in the mines, and were an obvious target for pressure-group activity, coalminers lacked the rudimentary organization to amass petitions and send delegates to testify in Parliament. However, once coalminers were given the opportunity to organize, they turned their efforts to politics. The history of the mining trade unions, as Raymond Challinor and Brian Ripley have pointed out, "probably more than any other section of the working class, has been one of intense political involvement."[21]

The first miners' union to have a measure of durability was the Miners' Association of Great Britain and Ireland, based largely in Northumberland and Durham. The coalfields of the North-East were worked mainly by indigenous workers having long-standing roots in their communities. Miners in Northumberland and Durham were well-placed to organize, although they had to do so in the

[20] See, for example, N. Edwards, *The Industrial Revolution in South Wales* (London: The Labour Publishing Company, 1924), pp. 86–100.
[21] Challinor and Ripley, *The Miners' Association*, p. 209.

face of powerful and recalcitrant employers who were backed by
the law and the army in suppressing strikes. Collective bargaining
was out of the question. The Miners' Association had to rely on
political pressure if it was to improve conditions of employment.
The inaugural meeting of the Miners' Association in 1842 was
called "for the purpose of taking into consideration the distress of
the coalminers and adopting a petition to Parliament."[22] The union
was involved in the general strike of 1842 and the "great strike" of
1844, but these took the form of rebellious uprisings rather than
calculated attempts to control working conditions, and both strikes
collapsed in the face of employer intransigence and military intervention.

The Miners' Association was the first union in Britain, and perhaps the world, to organize an extensive and coordinated strategy
of pressure-group activity. The principal goals of the union were
minimum safety standards, legislation restricting the labor of children and women, and legislation putting an end to the powers of
employers to enforce the bond, a system of yearly hiring that legally
bound the worker to his job. The union collected parliamentary petitions, organized marches, and retained an attorney, W. P. Roberts,
described by Friedrich Engels as the miners' "incomparable . . . Attorney General," who defended miners in court against penalties
incurred by breaking the bond and led the battle against provisions
of the Masters' and Servants' Bill giving employers sweeping rights
against workers.[23] The Miners' Association also attempted to gain
direct representation in Parliament when Roberts and one of its
leaders, William Dixon, stood for election in 1847. In this, as in
many of its other political activities, the union apparently had close
links with the Chartist movement, which reached its peak in these
years.[24]

The Miners' Association was swept away in the depression of the
late 1840s, but the union provided a model for succeeding unions,
in particular the Miners' Federation of Great Britain established in
Yorkshire, South Wales, and Scotland in 1888 and 1889. The major
exceptions were the unions that succeeded the Miners' Association

[22] Ibid., p. 210. On the association's influence on future trade unionism in coalmining see A. J. Taylor, "The Miners' Association of Great Britain and Ireland, 1842–48:
A Study in the Problem of Integration," *Economica* 22 (1955): 59–60.
[23] Friedrich Engels, *The Condition of the Working-Class in England in 1844* (London:
Allen & Unwin, 1892), pp. 253–254.
[24] Challinor and Ripley, *The Miners' Association*, chap. 15.

in the North-East in the 1860s, the Northumberland Miners' Mutual Confident Association and the Durham Miners' Association. These unions reached a mutual understanding with employers based on the sliding scale, which specified a fixed relationship between the level of wages and the price of coal. Employers recognized the unions and, in return, unions recognized the laws of the market as the determinant of the price of coal and labor.

The North-Eastern unions were stronger from the 1860s than any other mining unions in Britain. This was partly because the labor force was relatively stable. Although the number of workers employed in the North-Eastern coalmines increased more than fivefold between 1840 and 1900, this was substantially less than in the other major coal-producing regions, which had rates of increase that were between 50 and 100 percent greater.[25] The distinctiveness of the North-Eastern unions also appears to be related to the long traditions of exclusiveness among hewers and their domination of labor organization. Under the bord and pillar method, which was retained longer in the North-East than in any of the other major coal-producing areas, hewers were responsible only for filling the coal trucks. Other functions in the mine, including timbering, hauling, etc., were each carried out by separate groups of workers whose employment conditions were much inferior to hewers but who had the prospect of rising to the status of hewer when they gained sufficient experience. The North-Eastern hewers were willing to compromise their traditional demands for a "living wage" by accepting market constraints because those constraints did not threaten their bargaining role or their status in the division of labor. Their elite position in the mining hierarchy had unique roots, but it resembled that of the true labor aristocrats in the crafts.[26]

The strategy of the North-Eastern unions was closer to the business unionism of the highly effective printing unions than it was to the struggling mining unions of Scotland or Yorkshire, or to the earlier Miners' Association. As John Wilson, the secretary of the Durham Miners' Association, recorded in his 1907 history of the union, the leadership of the union demanded that "mutuality with employers should be reciprocated. They hoped that the members would not be rash nor doubtful, for those were dangerous and de-

[25] Benson, *British Coalminers in the Nineteenth Century*, p. 217.
[26] H. A. Turner, *Trade Union Growth, Structure and Policy* (London: Allen & Unwin, 1962), pp. 185–192; Mike Holbrook-Jones, *Supremacy and Subordination of Labour* (London: Heinemann, 1982), pp. 109–119.

structive to their interests. We must meet these situations like business men."[27]

The North-Eastern miners were the driving force behind a peak organization, the Miners' National Union, which was active in pushing for legislation of minimum safety standards, the amendment of the Master and Servant Act of 1867, and improvements in union legal rights. The North-Eastern mining unions also agitated in the early 1870s for manhood suffrage, and although their demands were not met, in 1874 they were able to send the secretary of the Northumberland Association, Thomas Burt, and the president of the Miners' National Union, Alexander McDonald, to Parliament.[28] The North-Eastern unions were thus the first in Britain to gain direct political representation in the House of Commons.

It is an interesting commentary on the political tendencies of coalmining unionism that the most market-oriented mining unions in Britain opened the way to labor political representation. The political opportunities offered by their strength of numbers and geographical concentration at the beginning of the age of mass democracy were too much to resist. But, at the same time, the narrow use these unions made of political representation reveals the scope for contrasting strategies among coalmining unions.

The North-Eastern unions saw political activity as a limited means of gaining improvements in their members' employment and working conditions. They took advantage of the opportunity to send representatives to Parliament, but once there these representatives took the whip of the Liberal party and focussed their efforts on safety standards rather than on wages or hours. The rationale for this was expressed by Burt at the 1889 Miners' National Conference when he stated that he was "perfectly sure they would get what they wanted much more speedily and effectively if they depended on themselves and their organizations than by means of the House of Commons. . . . Let the delegates go to their men and tell them to look to themselves rather than to Parliament."[29]

[27] John Wilson, *History of the Durham Miners* (London: J.H. Veitch, 1907), pp. 229–230; Gaston V. Rimlinger, "Labor Protest in British, American and German Coal Mining Prior to 1914" (Ph.D. diss., University of California, Berkeley, 1956), p. 100.

[28] Willian H. Maehl, Jr., "The Northeastern Miners' Struggle for the Franchise, 1872–74," *International Review of Social History* 20 (1975). On Friedrich Engels' reaction, see Raymond Challinor, *The Lancashire and Cheshire Miners* (Newcastle-on-Tyne: Graham, 1972), p. 147.

[29] Robert P. Arnot, *The Miners: A History of the Miners' Federation of Great Britain, 1889–1919* (London: Allen & Unwin, 1949), p. 137.

The strategy of the North-Eastern unions was disputed by less effective unions, such as the Yorkshire Miners' Association, the Scottish Miners' Federation, and the South Wales Miners' Federation, which were represented in the Miners' Federation of Great Britain. While the North-Eastern unions had gained a seven-hour shift for hewers by 1891, hewers in the remaining unions were still working from nine to as many as ten hours a day. This difference was partly due to the unique shift arrangement in the North-East that eased the hours of the hewers while increasing those of their younger helpers.[30] But underlying this was a sharp contrast in market power. As a German miner who visited Britain in 1892 observed, "No doubt Northumberland and Durham enjoy the shortest working day of any in Great Britain. It is much longer in Scotland, Ireland, and Wales, being in some pits as much as ten hours. The Miners' Unions in these three countries are very weak. The natives are indifferent, and look for help from the English, so that the working day may be fixed by law at eight hours from bank to bank, for it would be impossible for them to force the eight-hours day by a strike."[31] The same point was made in starker language by Robert Smillie, the president of the Scottish Miners' Federation: "If they got it [the eight-hour day] by organization, in dull times the owners would try to smash it, and therefore he would prefer . . . a legislative measure."[32]

This fundamental difference in strategy was to bring the Miners' Federation into collision with the "old" unions of Northumberland and Durham. The leaders of the Miners' Federation saw legislation as a vital means of gaining permanent improvements in conditions of employment. From the 1890s the demand for a legal eight-hour day became the dominating goal of the movement.

The battle among the mining unions was played out in ideological debate as well as in terms of conflicting group interest. The leaders of the North-Eastern unions had gained significant reforms with Liberal support and remained wedded to the philosophy of individualism, market competition, and laissez-faire. The sliding scale, the foundation of their strategy in the labor market, implicitly

---

[30] W. J. Ashley, *The Adjustment of Wages*, p. 81.

[31] E. Dückershoff, *How the English Workman Lives* (London: P.S. King, 1899), pp. 81–82. See also R. P. Arnot, *South Wales Miners: A History of the South Wales Miners' Federation, 1898–1914* (London: Allen & Unwin, 1967), pp. 127–128.

[32] *Proceedings of the Annual Conference of the Miners' Federation of Great Britain* (Birmingham, 1901), p. 22.

accepted the primacy of the market in setting the level of wages,
while their legislative proposals concerning safety, workers compensation, and the restriction of womens' and childrens' labor left
the working of the market essentially intact.

The Organizational Revolution that began in the final decades of
the nineteenth century undermined the miners' liberal doctrine. By
1901, 56 percent of the 944,000 workers employed in the mining
industry were unionized.[33] And with the establishment of the Miners' Federation a single industrial organization could claim more
than 300,000 members by the turn of the twentieth century. Employers, for their part, were organized into peak organizations that
had equally broad coverage.[34] As a consequence, industrial conflict
that formerly had regional consequences now could bring the national community into its orbit. Governments that had once maintained a posture of nonintervention, at least on substantive issues,
were now impelled to intervene to prevent widespread economic
dislocation.

This became increasingly clear after the great coal strike of 1893,
which involved 300,000 workers and a five-month cessation of production in the coalfields organized by the Miners' Federation. Eventually the prime minister, William Gladstone, despite his liberal
qualms, was pressured to intervene and provide government mediation, later institutionalized under the 1896 Conciliation Act. The
dramatic consequences of the growth of massive labor market organizations for the role of the state in the economy could neither
be ignored nor reversed. As B. J. McCormick has pointed out:
"Though Baldwin attempted in the twenties to take the State out of
industrial relations, it became exceedingly doubtful after 1893
whether the distribution of income could be left to negotiation between private parties: 1893 was the year in which the State became
a party to industrial matters and voluntary collective bargaining
started to decline."[35]

As labor market organization intensified, it became ever more
difficult to claim that market forces were the decisive arbiter of the
level of wages. Power relations involving organized labor and capital were replacing atomistic market competition as the chief determinant of wages. Especially in the coalfields that produced for domestic consumption, increases in wages could be passed on in prices

[33] Clegg et al., *A History of British Trade Unions since 1889*, vol. 1, table 6, p. 468.
[34] Jevons, *The British Coal Trade*, chap. 13.
[35] B. J. McCormick, *Industrial Relations in the Coal Industry* (London: Macmillan, 1979), p. 21.

without a drastic decline of demand. Why, it was asked, should wages follow prices when prices were themselves determined by wages.

Reasoning along these lines gave rational justification to prior ethical concerns. As Sam Woods, vice-president of the Miners' Federation, thundered: "Notwithstanding all the teaching of political economists, all the doctrines by way of supply and demand, we say there is a greater doctrine overriding all these, and that is the doctrine of humanity."[36] Translated into practical politics, the "doctrine of humanity" encompassed a variety of legislative demands for improving the miner's health, working conditions, hours, and wages. The central demand was for a government-enforced maximum working day of eight hours, which the federation achieved in 1908 despite the opposition of the North-Eastern unions. In 1912, after a bitter strike designed to put pressure on the government, the federation achieved a legislated "living wage."

It is not difficult to see how the desire to override the market in the interests of a moral economy—Woods' "doctrine of humanity"—led many workers to socialism. In the years after the First World War the mining unions were a bastion of the Labour party. They provided more than their share of labor parliamentary representatives, even considering the large proportion of coalminers in the labor force. But the turn towards socialism before 1914 was a slow and uneven process that had to overcome traditional commitments to the Liberal party and loyalty to an old guard of union leadership who retained liberal sympathies even after the majority of their membership had switched.

Support for socialism was strongest in regions where unionism was least effective. Before the turn of the century, as Page Arnot has noted:

> The number of miners who joined these socialist societies was but small, yet from these little meetings there began a stir throughout the ranks of the working class. Amongst the miners this feeling was most strongly found in just those counties which were least organized, or where the ill-success of existing methods had been most obviously expressed in diminution of the membership of the unions.[37]

[36] Arnot, *The Miners: A History of the Miners' Federation of Great Britain, 1889–1919*, p. 205.
[37] Ibid., p. 79.

Thus, socialism was especially strong in Scotland, where the level of union membership remained relatively low.[38] In South Wales, where unionism was also weak, the emergence of socialism was hindered by traditional nonconformist loyalty to the Liberal party.[39] But once the turn to socialism began, the pace was swift, and by 1914 the South Wales Federation of Miners was solidly socialist. As we might expect, miners in Durham and Northumberland were late in supporting Labour party candidates. Although independent Labour party branches were established in the 1890s, most miners retained strong loyalty to union leaders, most notably Thomas Burt, John Wilson, and Charles Fenwick, who continued to support the Liberal party.[40] The path for socialism was clear only in the second decade of the twentieth century, once this generation of leaders had either died or retired.

The increased emphasis on legislation of working conditions and the growth of socialism eventually led coalmining unions into class-wide alliances. Political success is governed by the art of coalition making, and this drove unions in Britain, as it did elsewhere, to aggregate their interests in broad national organizations. But many miners resisted the idea of supporting the Labour party, and the federation did not join until 1909. The justification for this was bluntly stated by Ben Pickard, the president of the Miners' Federation, in his opening address to the union's 1898 congress:

> How does it come about that these gentlemen go outside of their own trades to invite others to assist them in doing what they are either unable or unwilling to do for themselves? . . . I should like to ask why we as a Federation would be called upon to join an Association to find money, time or intellect to focus the weaknesses of other Trade Unionists to do what you are doing for yourselves, and have done for the last fourteen years.[41]

The conception of self-interest that motivated such sectionalism should not really surprise us. Geographical isolation, occupational

---

[38] R. P. Arnot, *A History of the Scottish Miners* (London: Allen & Unwin, 1955), pp. 65, 94–96.

[39] Roy Gregory, *The Miners and British Politics: 1906–1914*, pp. 119–143.

[40] Ibid., pp. 68–81; Robert S. Moore, *Pit-Men, Preachers and Politics* (Cambridge: Cambridge University Press, 1974), p. 40. On the role of Methodism in South Wales, see ibid., especially pp. 223–224.

[41] *Proceedings of the Annual Conference of the Miners' Federation of Great Britain* (Bristol, 1898).

distinctiveness, and exclusive traditions set coalminers apart from other workers at the same time that they helped mold coalminers into cohesive occupational communities. A deep-seated sense of independence and separateness led many coalminers to view class-wide alliance in narrowly pragmatic terms. Moreover, one ironic consequence of their extraordinary political opportunities and early successes is that many miners developed strong political loyalties to the Liberal party before the establishment of the Labour party.

COALMINING UNIONS IN GERMANY

The coalmining industry in Germany was closely regulated by the state in the first half of the nineteenth century. The coalmines in the Saar were actually run under state ownership, while those in the Ruhr and Silesia, which were privately owned, were subject to extensive state control of production, prices, and conditions of labor.[42] The labor force in the coalmines was organized in Knappschaften, guildlike miners' societies that were explicitly designed along corporatist lines. As in the urban guilds, workers' rights and duties were differentiated on a hierarchial basis. At the highest rung were miners who had full rights in the Knappschaften, including exemption from certain taxes and military service. These workers were a privileged stratum embedded in a paternalistic system that gave them job security and provided benefits in time of old age, injury, or sickness. At the next level were junior workers who had lesser benefits but had the future expectation of full membership in the Knappschaft, while at the lowest level were temporary workers, usually from neighboring agricultural areas, who were employed by the day as the demand for coal allowed.[43]

We hear little of coalminers as a political grouping in the first half of the nineteenth century. Coalminers do not appear at all in the

[42] W. O. Henderson, *The Rise of German Industrial Power, 1834–1914* (London: Temple Smith, 1975), pp. 54–59; Hans-Dieter Krampe, *Der Staatseinfluss auf den Ruhrkohlenbergbau in der Zeit von 1800 bis 1865* (Köln: Rheinish-westfälisches Wirtschaftsarchiv, 1961).

[43] Wolfgang Köllmann, "Vom Knappen zum Bergarbeiter: *Die Entstehung der Bergarbeiterschaft an der Ruhr,* in W. Först, *Ruhrgebiet und neues Land* (Köln: Grote, 1968), pp. 49–56; J. Lignau, *Das System sozialer Hilfeleistungen* (Köln, 1965), pp. 42–63; G. V. Rimlinger, "Labor Protest in British, American and German Coal Mining Prior to 1914," pp. 220–232; H. Karwell, "Die Entwicklung und Reform des deutschen Knappschaftswesens" (inaugural-dissertation, Universität Jena, 1907).

detailed listing of strikes drawn up by Elisabeth Todt and Hans Radandt for the period prior to 1848.[44] They stood aloof during the
1848 Revolution and are described by Klaus Tenfelde, in his study
of the Ruhr miners, as "little-German (kleindeutschpreussisch), mo-
narchial, conservative, and loyal to the system."[45]

Only when their corporate system of employment disintegrated
under liberal reforms between 1850 and 1865 did coalminers begin
to act in concert to defend their working conditions. When they did
so, they followed the early combinations of craft workers by appealing to the state to reconstitute the traditional paternalistic order. The leader of the Catholic Christlicher Gewerkverein, Heinrich Imbusch, observed in his history of the union that the
coalminers "were so accustomed to the tutelage and wardship of the
state that . . . for years it would not even occur to them to look after
themselves."[46]

Up to 1889 the chief focus of union activity was the petition, de-
livered to the kaiser or Bergbehörden (mine officiate), which asked,
or more literally "begged," for state intervention to ease harsh
working conditions. When strikes took place they were generally
spontaneous uprisings rather than calculated attempts to pressure
employers. A noteworthy feature of industrial conflict in the Ruhr
coalmines is that unions tended to follow workers rather than lead
them. The strikes of 1889 and 1905, which were the largest that
Germany had seen until that time, began as grass-roots rebellions
over which union leadership had little control.

The major coalmining unions were rarely in a position to bargain
effectively with employers in the labor market. The coal industrialists were among the best organized in any sector of the economy.
Their peak organization, the Bergbau Verein, was established as
early as 1858 and encompassed all the major coalmining employers.
In 1908, largely in response to calls for stronger organization after
the 1905 strike, the Zechen-Verband was created to administer an
employers' strike fund and coordinate blacklisting of workers who

[44] Elisabeth Todt and Hans Radandt, *Zur Frühgeschichte der deutschen Gewerkschaftsbewegung, 1800–1849* (Berlin/DDR: Die Freie Gewerkschaft, 1950), pp. 68–78.

[45] Klaus Tenfelde, *Sozialgeschichte der Bergarbeiterschaft an der Ruhr im 19.Jahrhundert*
(Bonn-Bad Godesberg: Neue Gesellschaft, 1978), p. 158.

[46] Heinrich Imbusch, *Arbeitsverhältnis und Arbeiterorganisationen im deutschen Bergbau*
(Berlin: Verlag des Gewerkvereins christlicher Bergarbeiter, 1908), p. 164; Gastan V.
Rimlinger, "The Legitimation of Protest: A Comparative Study in Labor History,"
Comparative Studies in Society and History 2, no. 3 (April 1960).

changed jobs without sufficient notice or who participated in strikes.[47] Although union membership grew in the decades around the turn of the twentieth century, the Organizational Revolution was more evident on the side of employers. In these years there was a powerful trend towards the concentration of ownership of the mines. Whereas in 1885 only seven companies owned more than one mine, by 1910 just nine firms produced about two-thirds of the total coal output in the Ruhr.[48] Coalmining employers were determined to cling on to the doctrine of *Herr im Haus*, the claim that they should have absolute authority over the labor process. Employers totally rejected union offers to negotiate during the 1889 and 1905 strikes on the grounds that workers should be employed on the basis of individual contracts with individual employers. It was not until the end of the First World War that employers in coalmining accepted the principle that unions could be regarded as legitimate representatives of workers.

If the barriers to effective bargaining in the labor market were formidable, the miners themselves had considerable resources in their occupation and the workplace for expressing their grievances collectively. The sense of solidarity among miners was strong. Hewers worked in small groups, called Kameradschaften, and had a large measure of autonomy over their pace and style of work. Until the years just before the First World War the typical method of mining was stall and pillar, in which men would work in widely scattered teams. The characteristic features of the miners' occupation and work—the ever-present dangers of mining, exceptionally harsh conditions, group self-reliance, and feelings of separateness from other workers—strengthened occupational community and provided a basis for collective mobilization.

The size of the labor force increased immensely in the half century before the First World War. But amid this dynamic growth were important continuities that reinforced the miners' collective identity. As Barrington Moore has stressed, coalminers could draw on their past experience to develop standards against which they could judge their present conditions.[49] The persistence of tradi-

[47] Elaine Glovka Spencer, "Employer Response to Unionism: Ruhr Coal Industrialists before 1914," *Journal of Modern History* 48, no. 3 (September 1976); Hickey, *Workers in Imperial Germany*, pp. 214–215.

[48] Hickey, *Workers in Imperial Germany*, p. 15.

[49] Barrington Moore, Jr., *Injustice: The Social Bases of Obedience and Revolt* (New York: M.E. Sharpe, 1978), pp. 233–257.

tional institutions, in particular the Knappschaften, giving the miner a semblance of economic security, and the Berggesetz that still provided some legal protection for the miner, served both to instill in miners a sense of sharing the same history and to sensitize them to the drastic decline of paternalism that had taken place since the liberal reforms of the 1850s and 1860s.

However, the consolidation and unity of employers contrasted sharply with the position of labor. The dominant influence on the shape of union organization was the deep cleavage between the socialist movement and the Catholic/Center movement. Both the socialist Alter Verband and the Catholic-dominated Christlicher Gewerkverein formally excluded party-political matters from their proceedings in an attempt to extend their appeal to the labor force as a whole, and on more than one occasion they discussed the possibility of merging.[50] But attempts to overcome dual unionism failed in the face of the traditional enmity of the two movements and the close personal ties of leaders in each union to their respective political parties, the Social Democratic party and the Catholic Center party. Whereas coalmining unions in Britain and the United States were formed as autonomous organizations, coalmining unions in Germany were established by political parties to serve expressly political purposes. Ideological conflict between the socialist and Catholic movements made cooperation, even on nonpolitical issues, problematic.

The smaller Catholic union continually feared that the socialists were out to destroy it, while the socialists saw the Catholic union as a fifth column—as essentially sympathetic to the existing capitalist system. In contrast to the situation in Britain, where coalmining unions were divided on strategic issues, the conflict between Catholics and socialists was a deep-seated cultural and ideological one. Just as important, conflicts in Britain were among unions entrenched in different regions, whereas in Germany the conflict was so intense that it could not be bounded by separate geographical spheres of control. The unity of labor was further weakened by the

[50] Max Jürgen Koch, *Die Bergarbeiterbewegung im Ruhrgebiet zur Zeit Wilhelm II, 1889–1914* (Düsseldorf: Drost-Verlag, 1954), pp. 57–58 and chap. 3; Köllmann, "Vom Knappen zum Bergarbeiter," pp. 64–65, 76–84. The official name of *Der Alte Verband* was *Verband zur Wahrung and Föderung der bergmännischen Interessen im Rheinland und Westfalen*; the official name of the *Christlicher Gewerkverein* was *Gewerkverein Christlicher Bergarbeiter für den Oberbergamtsbezirk Dortmund*. On party-political neutrality in earlier unions see Otto Hue, *Die Bergarbeiter* (Stuttgart: J.H.W. Dietz, 1913), 2: 745, 749.

influx of large numbers of Polish workers into the coalmines in the early 1900s—and the emergence of a specifically Polish union, the Polnische Berufsvereinigung der Bergarbeiter, committed to Polish national autonomy.[51] To complete the picture of disunity, I should mention the existence of a small fourth union, the Gewerkverein der Bergarbeiter (Hirsch-Dunker), which supported the middle-class Progressive party.

Such polarization was much more injurious for the unions it affected than for the parties that sustained it. The logic of power is decisively different for trade unions and political parties. An ideologically motivated party may draw votes by defining its constituency in restrictive terms, by appealing to a specific social class or religious grouping. A union can never afford to do that. The extension of political division into the labor force always injures trade unionism, for the effectiveness of a union in the labor market depends on its ability to bring all workers into its ranks so as to monopolize the relevant supply of labor.

Divisions within the work force, coupled with the strength and intransigence of employers, made it impossible for coalmining unions to pursue an effective strategy of business unionism. Industrial conflict in the Ruhr took place on a massive scale, but this revealed the economic weakness of workers as much as their strength. In each of the three major strikes—1889, 1905 and 1912—unions were unable to coordinate workers' resistance or mount a united front for more than a short time. The strikes of 1889 and 1905 saw miners drift back to work before unions officially called an end to the strike, and the 1912 strike failed mainly because it never gained the support of the Christlicher Gewerkverein.[52]

The Ruhr coalminers provide us with a case in which party domination of unions and politicized union strategy were mutually reinforcing. The close ties that union leaders had to political parties predisposed them to seek political solutions to labor market problems. As Gaston Rimlinger has argued, the dependence of German

[51] Christoph Klessmann, *Polnische Bergarbeiter im Ruhrgebiet, 1870–1945* (Göttingen: Vandenhöck und Ruprecht, 1978); Richard C. Murphy, "The Polish Trade Union in the Ruhr Coal Field: Labor Organization and Ethnicity in Wilhelmian Germany," *Central European History* 2, no. 4 (1978).

[52] Hickey, *Workers in Imperial Germany*, chap. 5; Hans Mommsen, "Soziale Kämpfe im Ruhrbergbau nach der Jahrhundertwende," in Mommsen and Ulrich Borsdorf, eds., *Glück auf, Kameraden! Die Bergarbeiter und ihre Organisationen in Deutschland* (Köln: Bund-Verlag, 1979), pp. 259–260.

miners on state paternalism was later replicated in their dependence on outside party leadership.[53] At the same time, union-party connections fragmented and weakened unions in the labor market and reduced the effectiveness of a labor market strategy for improving workers' welfare.

The strikes that took place before the First World War were directed to the political authorities as much as to employers. The largest strikes, including those of 1889 and 1905, were settled by the intervention of the state rather than by compromise between unions and employers. Having little chance of wresting improvements directly from employers, the coalmining unions framed their demands in terms easily translatable to legislation: the eight-hour day, prohibition of women's and children's labor, improvements in safety, prohibition of Sunday and overtime work, standardized methods of weighing the coal produced, and the establishment of arbitration boards.[54]

In this concern with state regulation of their working conditions the unions were pursuing a strategy that had begun with the petitions in the 1870s and 1880s. From the 1890s, however, the motion passed at union conferences was replacing the petition. In addition, the unions were gradually becoming involved in the administration of the growing web of coalmining regulations. One of the principal demands of the 1905 strike was worker participation in the administration of state welfare benefits for miners, and from this time union cooption into the public sphere steadily broadened.[55]

COALMINING UNIONS IN THE UNITED STATES

Like their early counterparts in Britain and Germany, the first coalmining unions in America were unstable organizations. They

[53] Rimlinger, "The Legitimation of Protest," p. 340.

[54] *Correspondenzblatt der Generalkommission der Gewerkschaften Deutschlands*, 7 January 1895, vol. 5, no. 1, p. 1; Dieter Baudnis and Helga Nussbaum, *Wirtschaft und Staat in Deutschland Ende des 19. Jahrhunderts bis 1918/19* (Berlin/DDR: Topos, 1978), pp. 165–167; Köllmann, "Vom Knappen zum Bergarbeiter," pp. 73–75; Gerhard Griep, *Zur Geschichte der deutschen Gewerkschaftsbewegung, 1890–1914* (Berlin: Tribune, 1960), pp. 122–124; Klaus Tenfelde, "Gewalt und Konfliktregelung in den Arbeitskämpfen der Ruhrbergleute bis 1918," in Friedrich Engel-Janosi et al., eds., *Gewalt und Gewaltlosigkeit* (München: Oldenbourg, 1977), pp. 208–209.

[55] Baudnis and Nussbaum, *Wirtschaft und Staat in Deutschland Ende des 19. Jahrhunderts bis 1918/19*, pp. 169–171; Köllmann, "Vom Knappen zum Bergarbeiter," pp. 86–94.

had strong roots in some mining communities, but at the regional
and interregional level they were fragile, for they were subject to
the centrifugal pressures of local particularism and ethnic diversity.
Moreover, many unions had to cope with the determined opposition of regional employers' associations, some backed by the giant
railroad combinations, that were determined to suppress any organization that reduced their competitiveness.[56]
   Coalmining unionism was a story of persistent spurts and repeated disintegration in the years before the United Mine Workers
of America was established in 1890. The early unions—Bates
Union, the Amalgamated Miners' Association, the Miners' National
Association, the Workingmen's Benevolent Association, and National Trade Assembly 135 of the Knights of Labor—were weak
and had little chance of exerting the kind of steady pressure in the
labor market necessary to gain and defend advances in employment conditions. To the extent that they were active in the labor
market they emphasized their role as regulators of competition and
prices in cooperation with employers.[57] These unions rejected the
model of "pure and simple" unionism developed by the exclusive
craft unions. Instead they took an active part in politics, searching
for viable third-party channels for asserting working-class interests.
Many of the leaders of these unions were Britons who brought to
the New World a tradition of political activism derived from their

[56] Much less has been written on employers' organizations in coalmining than on
coalmining unions. But see, for example, E. Jones, *The Anthracite Coal Combination in
the United States* (Cambridge, Mass.: Harvard University Press, 1914); Joseph M. Gowaskie, "From Conflict to Cooperation: John Mitchell and Bitumous Coal Operators,
1898–1908," *Historian* 38 (1976); William Graebner, "Great Expectations: The Search
for Order in Bitumous Coal, 1890–1917," *Business History Review* 48 (1974).

[57] On early coalmining unions in the United States see Harold W. Aurand, *From the
Molly Maguires to the United Mine Workers of America* (Philadelphia: Temple University
Press, 1971); H. W. Aurand, "The Workingmen's Benevolent Association," *Labor His-
tory* 7 (1966); Katherine A. Harvey, "The Knights of Labor in the Maryland Coal
Fields," *Labor History* 10 (1969); David Montgomery, *Beyond Equality: Labor and the
Radical Republicans, 1862–1872* (New York: Knopf, 1967), especially chap. 4; Rimlin-
ger, "Labor Protest in British, American and German Coal Mining Prior to 1914,"
chaps. 5 and 6; Norman J. Ware, *The Labor Movement in the United States, 1860–1895*
(New York and London: D. Appleton and Company, 1929), pp. 209–221; W. J.
Walsh, "The United Mine Workers of America as an Economic and Social Force in
the Anthracite Territory" (Ph.D. diss., Catholic University of America, 1931), chaps.
1–3; Edward A. Wieck, *The American Miners' Association* (New York: Russell Sage
Foundation, 1940), especially chap. 13.

experiences in British unions and working-class movements such as Chartism.[58]

The major coal-producing area before the intensive exploitation of soft bitumous coal in the Midwest towards the end of the nineteenth century was eastern Pennsylvania. The Pennsylvania anthracite fields were split into three distinct geoeconomic regions, the Luzerne basin in the north, and the Schuylkill and Lehigh basins in the south, and these set the geographical boundaries of the early anthracite unions.[59] In the 1860s attempts were made to unify these organizations, and a loosely federated alliance, the Workingmen's Benevolent Association, was established in 1868. But local particularism remained and was encouraged by the bargaining power given to workers in one region if they remained at work when workers in the other restricted coal production by going on strike.[60]

This was particulary damaging for the Workingmens' Benevolent Association because its chief strategy in the labor market was the industrywide strike, aimed to restrict production throughout the anthracite industry and so regulate the price of coal and increase wages. Until its demise in 1875 the WBA was also deeply involved in politics. The year before its establishment, miners had pressed for the enactment of an eight-hour law in the state of Pennsylvania.[61] A law was passed, but it included a provision making eight hours a legal working day only in cases where there was no private contract to the contrary, and employers immediately made such a contract a condition of employment. From its inception the WBA campaigned for more direct eight-hour legislation, and this led it to join the Labor Reform party, a broad coalition of working-class organizations centered on the demand for monetary and land reform, the establishment of worker-owned cooperatives, and the

[58] The links between the early British and American coalmining unions are stressed by C. K. Yearley, *Britons in American Labor* (Baltimore: The Johns Hopkins University Press, 1957), pp. 123–141; Amy Zahl Gottlieb, "The Influence of British Trade Unionists on the Regulations of the Mining Industry in Illinois, 1872," *Labor History* 19 (1978).

[59] Good accounts of the geography of coalmining in America are Aurand, *From the Molly Maguires to the United Mine Workers of America*, pt. 1; Ashley, *The Adjustment of Wages*, pp. 87–95; Arthur E. Suffern, *Conciliation and Arbitration in the Coal Industry of America* (Boston: Houghton Mifflin Company, 1915).

[60] Aurand, *From the Molly Maguires to the United Mine Workers of America*, chap. 8.

[61] Chris Evans, *History of the United Mine Workers of America* (Indianapolis: Hollenbeck Company, 1920), 1: 17.

eight-hour day.[62] Like other early American coalmining unions, the WBA also campaigned for legislation of a broad range of working conditions, including safety hazards, semimonthly wage payments, standards for grading and weighing coal, and the restriction of women's and children's labor.

The greatest challenge confronting unions in the coalmines was ethnic diversity. This was not a specifically American phenomenon; there were tensions between Welsh and English miners in South Wales and between Germans and Poles in the Ruhr. But it was in America that ethnic diversity took its most extreme form. The first workers in the American coalmines were English, Scots, Welsh, Irish, and Germans, and from the last two decades of the nineteenth century these were followed by immigrants from central and southern Europe: Poles, Russians, Lithuanians, Slovaks, and Italians. Tensions within the first wave of immigrants, especially between the Irish and the English, were sometimes sharp, but these faded into relative insignificance with the arrival of the second wave of immigrants, the "Slavs," who were different on religious, cultural, and linguistic, as well as ethnic, grounds. In 1890 this grouping accounted for 26 percent of the labor force in coalmining, rising to 46 percent in 1900.[63]

Cultural tensions were exacerbated by ethnically based distinctions in working conditions and occupational status. In Britain and Germany the division of labor in the coalmines was often very hierarchical, but the potentially fractionalizing effects of this were mitigated because ascent, and eventual descent, in the mining hierarchy was determined more by age than by ethnicity. The young helper, sorting or carting coal, could expect that in time he would reap the benefits, in status and income, that were enjoyed by hewers at the coal face. But in America age mobility was reduced by ethnic barriers that were mobilized initially against Welsh and Irish workers and later used against Italians and Slavs. Instead of binding the coalmining work force together through the distribution of reward by age, hierarchy in the American setting buttressed the cultural animosities that existed between ethnic groups outside the workplace. Whereas the newer groups of workers complained bitterly about their inferior status and life chances, they themselves

[62] John G. Rayback, *A History of American Labor* (New York: Macmillan, 1959), pp. 25–26.
[63] Peter Roberts, *Anthracite Coal Communities* (New York: Macmillan, 1901), p. 21.

were viewed by established groups as a source of excess labor that weakened their bargaining position.[64]

Ethnic divisions undoubtedly delayed the establishment of effective unionism in the American coal industry. When a resilient union, the United Mine Workers of America, was formed in 1890, it had its membership base in the central competitive coalfields of Illinois and western Pennsylvania, coalfields that contained the largest concentrations of British workers who had moved westward as central and southern European workers arrived in the East.[65] The Pennsylvania anthracite coalfields were much more heterogeneous, and until the turn of the century organizational efforts were restricted by deep-seated prejudices on the part of second generation miners against the new immigrants. Cultural animosities were all the stronger because central and southern European workers were Catholic, while earlier immigrants were mostly Protestant. Although many of the Pennsylvanian mining towns were isolated, there was little cultural intermixing within them. Slavs were regarded by Anglo-Irish miners as little more than barbarians who lacked the rudimentary standards of injustice necessary for supporting unions. These views were generally echoed by visiting social science observers.[66] It was not until a series of strikes in the late 1890s and early 1900s, culminating in the massive strike of 1902, that union organizers, led by John Mitchell, came to regard the intense group loyalty of the new immigrants as a resource that could provide the basis of unionism.

The institutional history of the UMWA before 1918 was marked by factional struggles between socialists, who maintained their stronghold in the largest union local, Illinois District 12, and the more moderate national leadership.[67] The socialists never captured the administration of the UMWA, nor did they succeed in winning a socialist platform for the union. But from the early 1900s to be-

[64] See Michael A. Barendse, *Social Expectations and Perception: The Case of the Slavic Anthracite Workers* (University Park: Pennsylvania State University Press, 1981), chaps. 3 and 4; Rimlinger, "Labor Protest in British, American and German Coal Mining Prior to 1914," p. 190.
[65] See A. C. Everling, "Tactics over Strategy in the United Mine Workers of America: Internal Politics and the Question of the Nationalization of the Mines, 1908–1923," (Ph.D. diss., Pennsylvania State University, 1976), pp. 12–13.
[66] See Barendse, *Social Expectations and Perception*, pp. 30–33.
[67] John H. M. Laslett, *Labor and the Left* (New York: Basic Books, 1970), pp. 205–206.

yond the end of the First World War they exerted a significant left-ward pressure.

The socialists themselves were a heterogeneous group, ranging from moderate reformists, such as Frank Hayes, who had a brief tenure as president of the union from 1917 to 1920, to left-wing radicals, among them Adolf Germer, who was an active union official in Illinois and leader of the Socialist party. These wings of the socialist movement clashed on the question of whether the union should support the Socialist party or should form a union-based party along the lines of the British Labour party. They also differed on the issue of whether the union should demand the socialization of all the means of production or focus its activity more narrowly on the coalmining industry. But, as Everling Clark has emphasized in his study of the internal politics of the UMWA, socialists of all hues agreed on the general premise that "the functioning of the union could not be separated from politics and workers' political concerns could not be represented by parties which were dominated by the employers."[68]

Socialist influence was resisted by the dominant faction in the union. With the exception of Frank Hayes, successive UMWA presidents from John Rae to John Mitchell and John Lewis emphasized the benefits to be gained by a voluntarist approach to collective bargaining. This view was expressed in the 1888 Preamble to the Constitution of the National Progressive Union, the precursor of the UMWA, which stated that " . . . upon matters of wages and obnoxious rules that oppress and rob us, we should not look to legislative bodies for protection. It would be unmanly for us as miners to ask either national or State legislatures to exercise a paternal surveillance over us and the difficulties which we ourselves can supervise and control."[69]

But such advice was never meant to exclude attempts to gain legislation of working conditions. The same preamble called for "stringent laws providing for employers' liability; the prohibition of child labor, the examination and appointment of competent persons for mine inspectors and for fire bosses in mines where gas is generated; a uniform system of weighing coal before screening, and for the crushing of that swindling machine, the 'truck system,' together with the practice on the part of employers of importing cheap labor

[68] Everling, "Tactics over Strategy in the United Mine Workers of America," p. 4.
[69] Evans, *History of the United Mine Workers of America*, 1: 403.

to their mines."[70] When the United Mine Workers of America was established in 1890, it devoted six of its eleven planks to explicit demands for legislation and a further two planks to demands for the end of the truck system and improved safety, demands that usually involved legislation.[71] Even under the leadership of the dominant conservative faction of the UMWA, the proposed scope for legislation was far wider than for most other unions affiliated with the American Federation of Labor.

Like the AFL itself, the United Mine Workers pursued a policy of acting within the existing two-party system, rewarding friends and punishing enemies. But while the AFL was quite content to support any candidate for political office who was a friend of labor, the UMWA attempted to elect miners themselves to office, a policy that was, as John Laslett notes, "considerably more radical than the general position of the AFL."[72] The commitment of the United Mine Workers to increasing its influence within the major two parties was a conditional strategy. John Mitchell, the president of the UMWA during the union's critical period of struggle and growth between 1898 and 1908, made this quite clear in his book on union principles.

> In declaring against a third labor party, however, I wish it to be understood that this refers only to the immediate policy of the unions. One cannot foresee what the future of the dominant parties in the United States will be, and if it should come to pass that the two great American political parties opposed labor legislation, as they now favor it, it would be the imperative duty of unionists to form a third party in order to secure some measure of reform.[73]

The most successful attempt to gain broad ascent within the UMWA for a third-party strategy followed the swell of support for the Peoples' party during the economic depression of the early 1890s. The UMWA convention of 1894 adopted Thomas J. Morgan's political program, which called for, among other things, government control of the railroads, telegraphs, and mines.[74] The

[70] Ibid.

[71] Ibid., 2: 18–19.

[72] Laslett, *Labor and the Left*, p. 199.

[73] John Mitchell, *Organized Labor* (Philadelphia: American Book and Bible House, 1903), pp. 207–208.

[74] Laslett, *Labor and the Left*, p. 200.

United Mine Workers' Journal campaigned vigorously for the Peoples' party, asserting that "independent political action is . . . more important than all trade union matters combined."[75] The demand to form a third party, along the lines of the British Labour party, resurfaced after 1900 but never again gained majority support within the union. However, the experience of the First World War radicalized large sections of the UMWA membership, and in 1919 a resolution at the UMWA Convention instructing the officers of the union to call a conference of unions and other workers' and farmers' organizations to set up a national labor party was adopted unanimously.[76]

The turn of events after 1920—the reassertion of the conservative wing in the UMWA with the accession of John L. Lewis to the presidency, general disappointment with the performance of the initial postwar labor party movements, and the split within the Left over the issue of communism—served to undermine the radical movement within the union.[77] However, the position of the UMWA as the foremost union proponent of political activity was reestablished a decade later in its support of the Confederation of Industrial Organizations in its battle with the American Federation of Labor.

CONCLUSION

Looking back over the experience of coalmining unions in Britain, Germany, and the United States, three factors appear to be especially important in explaining why these unions pursued a political strategy.

First of all, the organizational character of coalminer's unions predisposed them to political pressure as a means of improving their members' conditions. Unlike groups of skilled craftsmen who could form exclusive combinations based on control of the labor supply in a particular occupation, miners were compelled to form highly inclusive unions if they were to have any chance of controlling their conditions of employment. Coalminers were not able to

---

[75] *United Mine Workers' Journal*, 1 March 1894, p. 2; quoted in Michael H. Nash, "Conflict and Accommodation: Some Aspects of the Political Behavior of America's Coal Miners and Steel Workers, 1890–1920" (Ph.D. diss., State University of New York at Binghamton, 1975), p. 64.

[76] Laslett, *Labor and the Left*, p. 223.

[77] Ibid., pp. 225–229.

impose their terms on employers by building and sustaining barriers around their job territory and denying employers the freedom
to hire new workers. This was the printers' strategy. Instead, they
had to try to impose their will on employers by using industrial/
political muscle. Both strategies are based on countering the sys-
temic vulnerability of labor under capitalism by organizing workers
as completely as possible. But whereas the printers tried to achieve
some control over their working lives within the market by maintaining a monopoly of the supply of their labor, coalminers tried to
negate the market entirely by demanding legislation of employment conditions or by taking on employers head to head and forcing concessions through strikes or the threat of them.

The character of the mining industry was a second factor favoring intensive political activity. The sheer size of the industry, alongside the necessity for an inclusive organizational strategy, meant
that coalmining unions would be giants among labor, encompassing
hundreds of thousands of workers by the first decade of the twentieth century. Coalmining unions had the numerical weight and financial resources to take advantage of whatever political opportunities were offered for pressure politics and political representation. In addition, the geographical concentration of the mining
industry meant that coalminers were often in a majority in particular political constituencies.

The character of the mining industry also favored a political
strategy through its effects on industrial conflict. As union organization became national in scope from the last decade of the nineteenth century, strikes could bring the entire industry to a standstill. The strategic location of coalmining in the national economy
gave strikes an overtly political character as governments inter-
vened either to repress the strikers or bring about a settlement. In
no other industry were the political consequences of economic conflict so transparent.

Third, even when they were entrenched among the work force,
coalmining unions were rarely strong enough to wrest improvements from employers. Coalminers had a remarkable capacity for
collective mobilization but faced immense problems in bargaining
effectively with employers. Given this combination of collective
strength and economic impotence, political activity often appeared
a more practical avenue than bargaining in the labor market.

Unlike the majority of workers, coalminers had social resources
in the workplace that gave them the capacity to express their griev-

ances collectively. The dangers they faced, their constant interdependence, and their group autonomy in the mine contributed to an immensely strong sense of collective identity. Their unique traditions, reinforced by geographic isolation, gave coalminers a keen sense that they were different from other workers. These social resources gave them a collective capacity for strategy, a capacity to be heard and to back up their grievances in an ongoing, institutionalized fashion. But in the period before the First World War coalminers tended to be extremely transient and ethnically heterogeneous. They were often faced by employers who were more united than they were and better equipped to engage in industrial conflict.

In explaining the strategies of coalmining unions I have had to generalize about the working lives of the people who comprised them. How cohesive were their occupational communities? How did the organization of work impede or strengthen their sense of collective identity? How hierarchical was the division of labor, and to what extent did hierarchy in the workplace coincide with ethnic divisions? The answers that I have offered to these questions are preliminary in the absence of additional sustained efforts to bring our knowledge of individual unions and localities into broader comparative focus. However, the point remains that we must engage these kinds of questions to understand the political orientations of the unions coalminers formed. The study of how individuals and groups worked and lived is intimately related to the institutional development of trade unionism. My guiding supposition has been that these two fields are closely intertwined through their links with occupational community. As a dependent variable, occupational community is profoundly influenced by the organization of work, the ongoing division of labor, and the social resources of workers. As an independent variable, occupational community helps determine the capacity of groups of workers to create unions to gain decent treatment and exert some collective control over their working lives. From this standpoint the new social history and the more traditional concern with the institutional history of trade unionism are complementary rather than exclusive approaches. In this and the previous chapter I have sought to combine elements of each approach to better understand the political orientations of printing and coalmining unions.

My focus here has been to explain aspects of working-class political activity that escape national characterization. Individual unions, such as those formed by printers or coalminers, share fundamental commonalities of political orientation across societies as different as the United States, Britain, and Germany. To explain such commonalities we must dig beneath nationwide variables and analyze the situation of the worker in the labor market, the workplace, and occupational community. Types of union political orientation depend on the strategies that are available to unions both in the labor market and in politics, and these are rooted in the economic and social resources of workers in their working lives, the kinds of occupational communities they formed, and the capacity of unions to adapt to changes in the division of labor. These are factors that vary more across occupations and industries than they do across societies.

At the same time, union political activity is influenced by national factors. Unions within a given society share a legal environment that establishes—or denies—the legitimacy of their organizations and their various activities. Opportunities for union political activity are also constrained by whether a labor or socialist party exists, the level of its support, and the character of union/party links. In each of these respects we find a solid basis for making national comparisons and arriving at a view of union political activity that is distinctly national in focus. In the following chapter I examine a central question involving an aggregate conception of working-class politics—the issue of American Exceptionalism—and explore the ways in which my approach to union political activity bears on more familiar issues of national political development.

CHAPTER 6

AMERICAN EXCEPTIONALISM IN
COMPARATIVE PERSPECTIVE

When we take a long view of the development of union political orientation it is possible to see fundamental similarities as well as differences across unions in Western societies. The Organizational Revolution, beginning in the most economically developed societies in the decades around the turn of the twentieth century, saw a vast expansion of the role of the state in the labor market and the power of labor market organizations in the political arena. Over the last century unions in all Western societies have extended and deepened their involvement in politics and have come to regard that involvement as a normal extension of their concern with workers' welfare.

To understand this shared development alongside variations in union political orientation requires a flexible methodology involving comparison at more than one level. In this book I have made a case for breaking out of the mold of limiting cross-national comparison of working-class political activity to the comparison of whole societies. However, national differences among labor movements remain an important topic of inquiry, and some central puzzles persist.

During the Organizational Revolution, national differences were reemphasized in the institutional forms that mediated union participation in politics. In particular, union-party relations varied decisively. The strongest case for a national perspective derives from the observation that the United States is unique among Western democracies in not having a labor or socialist party. Since the 1930s the AFL-CIO has been closely linked to the Democratic party, but this party/union relationship is considerably weaker than in other Western democracies. Unlike their counterparts in other Western societies, American unions have no party-political arm, nor are they integrated into a wider labor movement that is directly represented in party-politics.

The absence of a strongly entrenched labor or socialist party is especially important because it has probably reinforced the distinctive weakness of class consciousness in America. No one can be sure what American unionism would have looked like in the First World War or beyond if a viable labor party had been established, but the experience of other Western societies suggests that the difference might have been great. The causality linking the growth of left-wing political parties to the development of working-class consciousness appears to run in both directions. Working-class political representation was part of a learning process that both strengthened—and was strengthened by—working-class political consciousness. Socialist and labor parties in Western Europe were not merely political instruments to express preconceived interests; they shaped and institutionalized class consciousness in a mutually causative learning process.[1]

In this concluding chapter I take up the question of the absence of a labor party in the United States. The question involves national comparison, but I do not believe that it can be answered by focussing exclusively on nationwide variables. To explain why American unions failed to support a labor party demands that we analyze the character of unions in America and the strategies they pursued—both in politics and the labor market. Here there is no escaping the diversity of union orientation, particularly within the dominant union movement, the American Federation of Labor. Some unions, in particular open unions like the United Mine Workers of America, provided substantial support for a labor party, while some unions, such as the International Typographical Union, consistently opposed the idea. To what extent were these contrasting political orientations typical of unions in the AFL, and what were the consequences of differing patterns of unionism for national politics?

RECONCEPTUALIZING AMERICAN EXCEPTIONALISM

The issue of American Exceptionalism is an extraordinarily difficult one to come to grips with not because there are few plausible explanations but because there are so many. Observers of American labor have offered a rich variety of economic, social, political, and cultural factors that plausibly explain the weakness of socialism in America and, by inference, the absence of a labor party. Hy-

[1] James E. Cronin, *Labour and Society in Britain, 1918–1979* (London: Batsford, 1984), provides a perceptive analysis of the relationship between the working class and the Labour party.

potheses that have been formulated in this literature have stressed the role of stratification and the absence of an entrenched class system; the strength of American capitalism and the relative wealth of the country; the American Constitution and the flexibility of American parties; social and economic mobility; the economic and psychological impact of the frontier; the absence of feudalism and the pervasiveness of liberalism and bourgeois culture; traditions of equality, individualism, and antistatism; the absence of a revolutionary intelligentsia; ethnic and racial conflict; immigration; Catholicism; slavery; and state repression.[2] The literature in the field is so replete with probable causes that we may be justified in thinking that we have hit upon a bogeyman of systematic social explanation—a nonoccurrence that is vastly overdetermined. The diffuse character of the phenomenon to be explained and the fact that we are explaining why something failed to materialize, rather than why it did, may easily lead to vague explanations that are posed in highly abstract terms and that are overgeared for the task at hand.[3]

However, the question I am concerned with here—"Why no labor party?"—is narrower than that of "Why no socialism?" and it might not be misplaced to hope that it could be answered more precisely. After all, a number of unions campaigned hard for the creation of a labor party, and they were supported by sizeable minorities in the AFL as a whole. On a number of occasions between 1885 and 1916 the issue of independent political representation dominated debate among American labor unions, and if the outcome of those debates appears overdetermined from the standpoint of the present day, it was not in the eyes of many contemporaries.

The absence of a labor party is a particularly distinctive feature of American political development in comparison with that of Britain and other Anglo-American societies. In none of these societies were socialist parties well established before the First World War.

[2] For an overview of the literature see John H. M. Laslett and Seymour Martin Lipset, eds., *Failure of a Dream? Essays in the History of American Socialism* (New York: Anchor Press, 1974); Seymour Martin Lipset, "Why No Socialism in the United States?" in Seweryn Bialer and Sophia Sluzar, eds., *Sources of Contemporary Radicalism* (Boulder, Colo.: Westview Press, 1977); Seymour Martin Lipset, "Socialism in America," in Paul Kurtz, ed., *Sidney Hook: Philosopher of Democracy and Humanism* (Buffalo, N.Y.: Prometheus Books, 1983); Gwendolyn Mink, *Old Labor and New Immigrants in American Political Development* (Ithaca, N.Y.: Cornell University Press, 1986), chap. 1.

[3] A similar point is made by Theodore J. Lowi, "Why Is There No Socialism in the United States?" *Social Science and Modern Society* 22, no. 2 (January/February 1985).

Eugene Debs, who ran as the presidential candidate of the American Socialist party in 1912, received 6 percent of the national vote, a share exceeding that received by any other socialist party in an English-speaking democracy before 1914. In other Anglo-American societies the chief expression of labor in politics was a party supported by the dominant union movement. Although socialists helped establish these parties, they were not viewed as socialist in orientation. Unlike the situation in the United States, where the working-class party was Marxist, in other Anglo-American societies the major working-class parties were relatively unideological. Henry Pelling has remarked that before the end of the First World War the British Labour party had virtually no policies that were in advance of the Liberal party.[4] Although socialism was strong among some unions in western Canada, particularly among the miners of British Columbia, the dominant strain among unions was laborism, a progressive movement that had a clear affinity with the left wing of the Liberal party led by Wilfred Laurier. Likewise, the Australian Labor party was almost oblivious to socialism as an ideology. It began as a class-conscious party in a narrow and defensive sense only—as a means of pursuing immediate working-class interests on a rather limited front, mainly by demanding a more favorable legal climate for unions and a limited framework of state-provided economic benefits (many of which were already proposed by progressive liberals). Socialism eventually succeeded in these societies not because committed socialist parties managed to gain mass support but because socialism became influential within established labor parties.

Depending on our frame of reference, then, it is possible to view American political development as exceptional in two distinct ways. First, by comparison with Germany and the societies of continental Europe, the United States is exceptional because of the failure of the Socialist party to gain a mass following. Even at its strongest, in the years immediately preceding the First World War, the party never threatened to displace one of the two major parties. Second, by comparison with Great Britain and other Anglo-American societies, the United States is exceptional because of the failure to create and sustain a labor party that had the backing of organized labor.

[4] Henry Pelling, *The Origins of the Labour Party, 1880–1900* (Oxford: Clarendon Press, 1965), p. 38.

This distinction is a fundamental one and it clarifies the divergent ways in which American Exceptionalism can be conceptualized. In this chapter I shall focus on the sources of the second aspect of American Exceptionalism.

Three factors appear to be particularly important here. The first is the composition of American unionism during the critical quarter century prior to the First World War. What kinds of unions made up the American Federation of Labor and what difference did this make for the political policies of the organization? These questions relate individual unions and macro politics and provide an opportunity to explore the ways in which a disaggregated approach to working-class political activity helps explains national outcomes. At the same time union decision making was shaped by its national political context. The structure of political constraints embedded within the political system made some forms of institutional activity practical and others appear almost utopian. Finally, the orientation of socialists to the labor party question, and towards the AFL itself, helped shape the political strategies of American unions. In no other Anglo-American society was there so great a rift between the dominant working-class party and the major union movement.

ATTEMPTS TO ESTABLISH A LABOR PARTY IN THE UNITED STATES

The contrast between Britain, in which a viable labor party was created with union support in 1900, and the United States, which lacked a labor party, is sharp in retrospect. But at times in the past it appeared to contemporaries as if the United States led the way, and British unionists could learn from the American example. In 1886 unions affiliated with the AFL and Knights of Labor, along with various radical groups, established united labor parties which succeeded in electing several local tickets in eastern and midwestern cities.[5] These early political successes for labor were reported in Britain as models for British union development. On returning from their visit to the United States in 1886, Eleanor and Edward Aveling wrote that "the example of the American working man will be followed before long on the European side of the Atlantic. An

[5] Morris Hillquit, *History of Socialism in the United States* (New York: Funk and Wagnalls, 1910), pp. 247–248.

English, or, if you will, a British Labour party will be formed."[6] *Reynold's Newspaper*, the British working-class organ, admonished the TUC to model its newly formed labor Electoral Association on the United Labor party. As it turned out, however, support for the United Labor party was diminished by a series of disputes between Henry George, the figurehead of the party, and socialists who accused George of accommodationism and by the willingness of the major parties to enact a series of labor laws that met many of the unions' most immediate demands.

In the early 1890s the most severe economic depression of the nineteenth century made many American unionists sensitive to the potential benefits of broad-based independent political activity with other hard-pressed groups. In these years a number of socialists and union leaders attempted to build a bridge between their own aspirations for a labor party and the sharp rise of agrarian radicalism among poorer farmers and sharecroppers, particularly in the south and west, as expressed in the populist Farmers' Alliance. In February 1892 delegates from several AFL unions, including the Mineworkers and Machinists, met in St. Louis with representatives from farmers' organizations and the Knights of Labor to express their support for the People's party launched the year before. The movement appealed most strongly to small farmers and artisans who felt threatened by economic changes over which they had no control. Its chief support among organized workers was from shoe workers, metal miners, and machinists, each of whom, as Michael Rogin points out, "faced a similar threat, as the rapid introduction of machinery undermined their autonomy, reduced their income, and devalued their skills."[7]

Although Samuel Gompers was critical of union support for populism on the grounds that it detracted from their immediate concerns in the labor market, the 1892 AFL Convention in Philadelphia adopted two planks of the Populist platform, government ownership of the telegraph and telephone systems and the popular

[6] Henry Pelling, *America and the British Left* (London: Adam and Charles Black, 1956), p. 63.

[7] Michael Rogin, "Radicalism and the Agrarian Tradition: Comment," in John Laslett and Seymour Martin Lipset, eds., *Failure of a Dream? Essays in the History of American Socialism* (New York: Anchor Press, 1974), p. 149. See also Theodore Saloutos, "Radicalism and the Agrarian Tradition," in the same volume; Philip Foner, *History of the Labor Movement in the United States*, 2d ed. (New York: International Publishers, 1975), vol. 2 chap. 21.

initiative and referendum. More broadly, the convention instructed the executive council "to use their best endeavors to carry on a vigorous campaign of education . . . in order to widen the scope of usefulness of the trade union in the direction of political action."[8]

At its next convention the AFL came close to establishing a labor party along the lines of the Labour Representation Committee in Britain. An eleven-point program was adopted, calling for a series of state measures, including compulsory education; a legal eight-hour day; abolition of sweating; municipal ownership of street cars, gas, and electric plants; nationalization of telegraphs, telephones, railroads, and mines; the referendum; and, most controversial of all, the "collective ownership by the people of all means of production and distribution" (plank ten). The preamble to the program urged American unionists to follow the example of British unionists, who "by the light of experience and the logic of progress [have] adopted the principle of independent political action."[9] The program was to be referred back to the membership of individual unions who would instruct their delegates how to vote at the next convention. Although the convention narrowly voted against referring the program back with their "favorable recommendations," a more neutral motion containing the program was passed by a vote of 2,244 to 67.[10]

In the following months the eleven planks found support in many unions. Only the Bakers' Union rejected them as a whole, while the International Typographical Union was one of only two unions to reject plank ten. Despite this procedure, the results of the 1894 convention in Denver were ambiguous. Instead of voting on the program as a whole, the preamble and individual planks were taken one by one. With the exception of the preamble, which was rejected, and plank ten, which was amended to the abolition of the monopoly system of landholding, all remaining planks were adopted. However, when the platform was voted on as a whole, it was defeated by 735 votes to 1,173. At this convention Samuel Gompers, who orchestrated the fight against independent political action from the chair, was defeated by John McBride of the United

[8] *Report of Proceedings of the Twelfth Annual Convention of the American Federation of Labor* (Philadelphia, 1892), p. 43.

[9] See Philip Taft, *The A.F. of L. in the Time of Gompers* (New York: Harper, 1957), p. 72.

[10] American Federation of Labor, *A Verbatim Report of the Discussion on the Political Programme, 1894* (New York: The Freytag Press, 1985), p. 63.

Mine Workers, who had argued in favor of a labor party. McBride, along with other socialists, claimed that the program remained almost intact because the convention adopted ten of the eleven original planks, while Gompers stressed the failure of the platform as a whole to gain majority support.

Over the next several years the impetus towards independent labor representation weakened. The Labor-Populist movement dispersed into its constituent elements, and the failure of the political program to win wholehearted AFL approval turned some leading socialists away from the organization. Thomas J. Morgan, the Chicago machinist who introduced the political program, left the AFL in 1895 on the grounds that most union leaders were incorrigibly conservative and because he believed that the AFL would, in any case, be superceded as labor became more revolutionary.[11] At the 1895 AFL Convention the pure and simple conception of unionism was dominant. Gompers was reelected AFL president, a position he went on to hold for the rest of his life, and an extreme statement of voluntarism was passed which declared that "party politics whether they be democratic, republican, socialistic, prohibition, or any other, should have no place in the convention of the A.F. of L." Only 158 delegates dissented.[12]

In the "Golden Era" of growing socialist strength from 1902 to 1912 there was fluctuating support within the AFL for independent labor representation. At the 1902 convention a resolution, introduced by Max Hayes, requiring the AFL to "advise the working people to organize their economic and political power to secure for labor the full equivalent of its toil and the overthrowal of the wage system and the establishment of an industrial cooperative democracy" was narrowly defeated by a vote of 4,897 to 4,171, with 309 abstaining.[13] At the next convention, however, socialist resolutions along similar lines were decisively rejected.

Over the next few years the AFL policy of rewarding its friends and punishing its enemies led it to more explicit support of the Democratic party as President Taft and the Republican party ignored labor demands for protection from injunctions. At a special meeting in 1906 representatives from fifty-one AFL unions drew

[11] Foner, *History of the Labor Movement in the United States*, 2: 293.

[12] *Report of Proceedings of the Fifteenth Annual Convention of the American Federation of Labor* (New York,1895), p. 100.

[13] *Report of Proceedings of the Twenty-Second Annual Convention of the American Federation of Labor* (New Orleans, 1902), p. 183.

up a bill of grievances and established a national organization to focus the AFL's legislative activity. The name of the organization— the Labor Representation Committee—was the original name of the British Labour party, but the resemblance was only partial. Like their British counterparts, American unions were now engaged in intensive political activity. The ever more transparent linkages between politics and the labor market and the continued use of court injunctions against unions had seen to that. But the AFL participated in election campaigns as a pressure group and still refused to take any steps towards an independent party.

The failure of this new concentration of effort to break Republican control of the House of Representatives in the 1906 congressional elections or limit the use of injunctions raised hopes that the AFL would be more sympathetic to the creation of a labor party. In the wake of the Supreme Court's 1908 decision on the Danbury Hatters' Case, which made the Sherman Act applicable to unions, even moderates began to consider drastic remedies. John B. Lennon, treasurer of the AFL and a stalwart of conservatism, threatened that "if the wage-workers in this country become thoroughly convinced that there is no policy to pursue except that of independent politics, they will pursue it with a vim and determination and effectiveness that has never been dreamed of by the workers of any country in the world."[14] Over the next decade the demand for independent labor representation came up directly or indirectly at several AFL conventions. Without ever marshalling a majority of AFL delegates behind the idea, supporters of a labor party were entrenched in some of the largest unions, including the United Mine Workers, the Brewery Workmen, and the Ladies Garment Workers, and regularly polled up to one-third of the votes at AFL conventions.

However, support for a new independent political role for unions did not increase over the years as it did in Britain in the years around the turn of the twentieth century. This is all the more noteworthy because it cannot be ascribed to the relative weakness of socialism in these years. Electoral support for the Socialist party of America was not much weaker than that for the British Labour party before the First World War. The peak for the Socialist party was 6.0 percent for Debs in the 1912 presidential election, while the

---

[14] The *American Federationist* (1908); quoted in William M. Dick, *Labor and Socialism in America: The Gompers Era* (Port Washington, N.Y.: Kennikat Press, 1972), p. 120.

prewar peak for the Labour party was 7.6 percent in January 1910. Moreover, the American Socialist party was one of the most radical left-wing parties to be found in any Western society; the Labour party one of the most moderate. Thus general explanations of socialist weakness do not, ipso facto, suffice to explain the absence of an American labor party.

PATTERNS OF UNIONISM

The question of American exceptionalism involves national comparisons. After all, to say that some phenomenon is unique is to compare and contrast it with other phenomena. But national comparison does not have to be exclusively national in focus. Our understanding of the sources of national differences or similarities may be greatly enriched by looking at patterns that exist at lower levels of analysis.

Although a labor party was never established, the idea of independent political representation was supported by significant minorities within the AFL. How can we explain both the persistence of support for a labor party and its rejection by a majority of AFL unions? Is it possible to see patterns of support and opposition at the level of individual unions that help us explain outcomes in national policy?

Summarizing the analysis of printing and coalmining unions in the preceding chapters, Table 6.1 outlines two types of union strategy: closed unionism, approximated by the printers, and open unionism, approximated by the coalminers. These types are theoretical constructions, composed of elements abstracted from reality that form logically coherent clusters. They encapsulate the argument I have elaborated linking the labor market strategies of unions with their political orientations.

From its establishment in 1886 to the 1920s, the AFL was dominated by relatively closed unions to an extent that was unparalleled in any other major union movement. These unions were, above all, committed to the sectional defense of their members' job territory. This strategy infused their political doctrines and those of the AFL. On the one hand, closed unions struggled against employers to adapt their job control to changes in the division of labor. If they could not resist technological change, they sought to encompass the new tasks created by technology within their job territory. On the other hand, they strove to defend their exclusive job territory

TABLE 6.1
Closed Unionism and Open Unionism

	Closed Unionism	Open Unionism
Composition	*Craft* and other skilled workers in a particular *occupation*	*All grades* of workers, unskilled as well as skilled, in a particular *industry*
Labor market strategy	*Restrictionist*: Ability to control the supply of labor in a given job territory	*Solidary*: Inability to control supply of labor. Attempt to pressure employers by force of numbers and militant tactics
Membership strategy	*Exclusive*: Defense of apprenticeship regulations and other barriers to entry in relevant labor market(s)	*Inclusive*: Expansionist effort to encompass all who work for given employers
Political resources	Relatively *small membership thinly spread* across country	Relatively *large membership geographically concentrated* depending on location of industry
Political orientation	*Weakly politicized*: Political activity viewed as marginal to regulation of working conditions	*Highly politicized*: Focus on gaining improvements in working conditions through legislation

against the incursion of other groups of workers. Closed unions could be militant in the defense of their members' interests, but their militancy was directed to preserving their special position in the division of labor rather than reforming the basis of the wage system.

Closed unions in the AFL, represented most forcefully by the International Typographical Union and the Cigar Makers' International Union, viewed political activity as a secondary strategy to be undertaken only under exceptional circumstances. To the extent that these unions campaigned for legislation of working conditions it was to complement rather than replace their efforts in the labor market. From their perspective proposals to establish a labor party detracted from the immediate tasks of consolidating union organization and pressuring employers in the labor market. These unions had little regard for arguments in favor of a third-party policy based on the desirability of working-class solidarity or far-reaching political change. Their opposition to those who pressed for a more active political strategy and their overriding confidence that they could achieve their primary goals in the labor market gave these unions a syndicalist tinge. Many socialists viewed them as irrational because they combined militancy and voluntarism, working-class consciousness and sectionalism, yet these ambiguities were a response to the opportunities and constraints that faced these unions in the labor market.

When closed unions edged further into politics from the early 1900s, they did so in self-defense. They were impelled into politics to fend off mounting threats from the courts, to counter the political mobilization of employers in the open shop drive, and to restrict immigration. The obvious advantages of joint action on these issues led unions, even in the AFL, to expand their national political organization. In this respect developments in the United States testify to the strength of underlying commonalities in western societies in this period. By the second decade of the twentieth century unions in the United States, as well as in Britain and Germany, were deeply involved in national politics. But closed craft unions in the AFL continued to view their political activity in narrow, instrumental terms and to reject the view that they needed to build up an independent third party.

The core support for socialism and an independent labor party came from open unions composed of all grades of workers, skilled and unskilled, who were employed in a particular industry. Before the First World War there were five major industrial unions affiliated with the AFL—the United Mine Workers, the Brewery Workmen, the Amalgamated Clothing Workers, the Western Federation of Miners, and the Ladies Garment Workers—and these unions provided a disproportionately large share of delegate votes in favor of independent political activity within the AFL.[15] Appendix A de-

---

[15] John H. M. Laslett, *Labor and the Left* (New York: Basic Books, 1970), describes the sources of radicalism in the United Mine Workers, the Brewery Workmen, the Western Federation of Miners, and the Ladies Garment Workers.

tails union voting on four key political resolutions—in favor of independent political representation (1894); proposing political organization to secure for labor "the full equivalent of its toil" (1902); condemning the National Civic Federation and labor's connection with it (1911); and opposing the view that political regulation of hours is impractical and undesirable (1915). Together, the five unions listed above accounted for 49.1 percent, 54.1 percent, 77.4 percent, and 59.5 percent, respectively, of left-wing votes on these issues. This support was quite out of proportion to their numerical weight within the AFL as a whole; the membership of these industrial unions never amounted to more than one-fourth of the total membership of the AFL.

The political orientation of these unions reflected their labor market strategy and organizational structure. In contrast to the majority of AFL unions, these unions were expansionist and inclusive. The workers they encompassed had no means of restricting the supply of labor into their job territory; indeed they had no exclusive job territory to defend. Because they could not exert steady pressure on employers by controlling the supply of labor into their members' occupations, they were forced back on other kinds of leverage, including mass strikes, boycotts, demonstrations—and political pressure. What they could not achieve through the subtle exclusionary tactics used by closed craft unions, they had to make up for by organizing all the workers in a particular industry and using their broad-based solidarity and force of numbers to put maximum pressure on employers.[16]

This strategy was reinforced by the political opportunities that their organizational structure offered them. While the membership of craft unions was usually spread thinly over the country along occupational lines, that of industrial unions tended to be more concentrated, for it mirrored the distribution of particular industries. The sheer size and geographical concentration of industrial unions frequently made it possible for them to dominate particular political constituencies and offered the possibility of gaining direct political representation.

The causal links between union structure and political orientation ran in both directions in cases where leaders with political programs created unions in accord with their principles of labor soli-

[16] See H. A. Turner, *Trade Union Growth, Structure and Policy* (London: George Allen & Unwin, 1962), pt. 5, chap. 1.

darity. Socialists, particularly from Germany, had long favored the principle of inclusive unionism, and where they were influential in the creation of unions in the New World these unions tended to be organized along industrial lines. Thus, the turn to an industrywide structure on the part of the Brewery Workmen in 1887, the year after it was founded, was largely due to the influence of German socialists in the union. Similarly, the International Ladies Garment Workers' Union was formed in 1900 mainly by socialist Jewish intellectuals from Russia and eastern Europe. Industrywide organization reflected their own prescriptions about the best structure for militant labor organization as well as the challenge of organizing women in the sweatshops. In both of these cases, union organizers were acutely aware of the consequences of different kinds of union structure and shaped unions in accordance with their political convictions.

The five industrial unions were flanked by craft unions impelled into radical politics by their weakness in the labor market. Various groups of artisans, the largest of which were boot and shoe workers, lasters, machinists, and carpenters, found their skills, job control, and traditional work practices drastically eroded by economic forces beyond their control. The radicalism of these workers was a response to the failure of pure and simple unionism to secure their niche in the division of labor in the face of decisive economic change.

In the last quarter of the nineteenth century boot and shoe workers were threatened on several fronts simultaneously. The introduction of machines that could be operated by unskilled workers to stitch and weld at many times the pace of the skilled journeyman, the emergence of national markets and competition in the industry, and the influx of cheap immigrant labor served to undermine the traditional economic independence, status, and way of life of the boot and shoe craftsmen. In their desperation these artisans first searched for a way to maintain their craft by organizing their own production and later turned to De Leonite socialism. The Boot and Shoe Workers' International Union voted at the 1894 AFL Convention to retain the most radical proposal in the political program, plank ten, calling for the collective ownership of all means of production and distribution.[17] A preamble along these lines was ac-

[17] *Report of Proceedings of the Fourteenth Annual Convention of the American Federation of Labor* (Denver, 1894), p. 39. Interestingly, James Tobin, the president of the Boot

tually incorporated into the Boot and Shoe Workers' constitution. Once conditions in the industry became more stable, the orientation of the union changed. By the early 1900s the industry had made the transition to the factory system and the Boot and Shoe Workers' Union adopted the methods of business unionism. As the strategy of pure and simple unionism was found to provide some prospect of economic security and advancement under capitalism, the search for broad class alliances to press radical change diminished.[18]

A fundamentally similar, though less extreme, set of developments served to sensitize machinists to the benefits of independent political activity and broad class coalition. From the 1890s the machinists' craft was transformed by the introduction of large-scale machinery, rapid specialization of work tasks, and the growth of large machine shops. Traditional skills were not completely displaced, and these years did not see any precipitous decline in wage levels as in the craft side of the boot and shoe industry, but the machinist's autonomy in the workplace and his sense of pride as an all-round craftsman were thoroughly undermined. From 1904 the machinists were the target of a furious open shop drive, led by U.S. Steel, which further undercut support for pure and simple unionism. These developments split the International Association of Machinists between an old guard led by President James O'Connell and a new and growing group of reformist socialists who campaigned for an independent labor party. In 1911 socialists succeeded in capturing the presidency of the union, and over the next decade they challenged voluntarism on several fronts, attacking the involvement of AFL leaders in the National Civic Federation, supporting efforts to nationalize the railroads, which employed many machinists, and pressing for a national labor party.[19]

The two kinds of union that provided the core support for class-based politics—open unions of unskilled and skilled workers and

and Shoe Workers' Union, and at that time a left-wing socialist, opposed the adoption of the amended political program at the 1894 AFL Convention. A vote in favor of the adoption of the political program, which is usually taken as an indicator of the strength of socialism in the AFL at this time, was in fact a vote in favor of a compromise because plank ten had been dropped. Tobin presumably was not content to settle for anything but the original version of the political program.

[18] See Laslett, *Labor and the Left*, chap. 3.

[19] See David Montgomery, *Workers' Control in America* (Cambridge: Cambridge University Press, 1979), chap. 3; Laslett, *Labor and the Left*, chap. 5.

unions of craft workers in retreat—formed a minority within the AFL. Precise figures can be misleading because most unions combined elements of each of the types elaborated here: most craft unions included some unskilled workers, and some unions, such as the carpenters and the machinists, became increasingly open in response to the changing division of labor. The boundaries of union recruitment were shifting, not static. But even counted generously, such unions accounted for no more than one-third of total AFL membership before the First World War.

The importance of closed unionism for American Exceptionalism can be gauged from a comparative perspective. The spontaneous emergence of closed unions, based in cohesive occupational communities, is a phenomenon that is common to all market societies. Closed unions appear to have been the first to be institutionalized in most—perhaps all—Western societies. Where they were given the political space to develop, they tended to dominate the early growth of unionism. Closed craft unions were particularly well entrenched in Britain and other English-speaking societies as well as in the United States. But in no other society was the grip of craft unions on the union movement as strong or as durable as in the United States from the last decade of the nineteenth century.

Britain is a particularly revealing case for comparison with the United States. In both countries unions were deeply rooted before the rise of mass working-class parties, and craft unions were dominant within early unionism. In Britain the New Model Unions, which arose from the 1850s and which marked the institutionalization of British unionism, were created to defend exclusive job territories that had survived the ongoing division of labor, or, as in the case of engineering and spinning, were created in the process of mechanization in the old crafts. However, the preponderance of such unions was never as great as in the United States. Alongside them there were large open unions of coalminers and weavers, and from the time of the upheaval of New Unionism in 1888/1889 they were joined by a number of open unions composed of dockers, gas workers, and diverse groups of unskilled workers. By my calculations these unions made up 38.5 percent of the TUC's affiliated membership by the turn of the century, and by 1913 their share had risen to 55 percent.[20]

[20] The percentages are based on data provided in the *Report of Proceedings of the Thirty-Second Annual Conference of the Trades Union Congress* (Plymouth, 1899), and the

The party-political sympathies of these open unions were influenced by their historical connections to the major parties. The Textile Workers continued to lean towards the Conservative party until the early 1900s, while elements of the Miners' Federation retained strong Liberal sympathies after affiliation with the Labour party in 1909. But even when these unions did not support the Labour party, they were committed to union political representation and revealed to other unions what could be achieved given sufficient determination and resources.

Socialist sympathies ran deepest among the new unions created in 1889/1890. Such unions played a role well beyond their proportion in the union movement as a whole in supporting the Labour Representation Committee in its early years. Several of the largest unions that affiliated with the fledgling LRC when it was established in 1900–1901 were industrial or general unions. These included the United Builders' Labourers, the National Union of Dock Labourers, the Dock, Wharf, Riverside, General Labourers' Union, the National Union of Gasworkers and General Labourers, alongside the older Amalgamated Railway Servants. Together, these and other smaller unions representing semiskilled and unskilled workers accounted for 47 percent of the total union membership affiliated with the LRC when it was first established.[21] Over the next two years, before the lessons of the Taff Vale court case had boosted the cause of labor representation, the ranks of the LRC were swelled by other large open unions, including the United Builders' Labourers, the National Amalgamated Union of Labour, and, largest of all, the United Textile Factory Workers' Association.[22]

Report of Proceedings of the Forty-Sixth Annual Conference of the Trades Union Congress (Manchester, 1913). For 1899 the following are included as open unions (membership rounded to the nearest hundred): Dock Labourers (12,000); Dock, Wharf, Riverside, and General Labourers (10,000); Gas Workers and General Labourers (45,000); Labour, National Amalgamated Union (21,600); Miners' Federation (213,000); Navvies, Bricklayers, Labourers (5,000); Railway Servants (54,000); Weavers (73,600). The following are included as open unions in 1913: Dock Labourers (32,000); Dock, Wharf, Riverside, and General Workers (37,000); Sailors and Firemen (60,000); Gasworkers and General Labourers (82,100); Gasworkers, Brickmakers, and General Labourers (7,600); Labour, National Amalgamated Union (51,000); Miners' Federation (600,000); Railwaymen (132,000); Weavers (182,800); Postmen (42,600).

[21] A list of affiliated unions is provided in the *Report of the First Annual Conference of the Labour Representation Committee* (Manchester, February 1901).

[22] *Report of the Second Annual Conference of the Labour Representation Committee* (Birmingham, February 1902); *Report of the Third Annual Conference of the Labour Representation Committee* (Newcastle-on-Tyne, February 1903). The role of the Independent

The reasons for the failure of American unions to mobilize less-skilled workers, and the corresponding weakness of open unionism, are rooted in the particular circumstances under which the AFL arose and in broader social and cultural factors long associated with American Exceptionalism.

The AFL was established in 1886 mainly to defend craft unions against one of the most open union organizations that has ever existed, the Knights of Labor. The Knights sought to encompass all workers without regard for their industry or occupation, and this brought it into direct conflict with craft unions protecting specific job territories. While the Knights favored the mixed assembly, made up of all kinds of workers in a particular locality, the craft unions were based strictly on occupational lines. The conflict, eventually decided in favor of the AFL, confirmed the notion that closed craft unionism was the only effective solution to the organization of labor.[23] Industrial unions were tolerated by the AFL establishment, but they were viewed as exceptions that proved the rule. General unions, such as those that arose in Britain after 1889, were deemed to be totally unsuitable to the American context. One of the lessons that came out of the founding period of the AFL—and which subsequently was raised to a brittle orthodoxy—was that effective organization demanded exclusive jurisdiction based on occupational boundaries.

This impetus towards closed craft unionism was strengthened by some fundamental characteristics of the labor force and its development in the decades around the turn of the twentieth century. Mass immigration in these years brought diverse groups of workers to America who had little experience of labor organization and who were more oriented to ethnic than class affiliations. The inrush of new immigrants confirmed the determination of many established skilled workers that their best policy was to defend job territories against incursion rather than build more inclusive organizations. In

---

Labour party and the grounds for conversion to support for the LRC are discussed in David Howell, *British Workers and the Independent Labour Party, 1888–1906* (Manchester: Manchester University Press, 1983), pt. 1, and Pelling, *The Origins of the Labour Party, 1880–1900*, pp. 195–201.

[23] The conflict is analyzed in Lloyd Ulman, *The Rise of the National Trade Union* (Cambridge, Mass.: Harvard University Press, 1955), pp. 348–377; Taft, *The A.F. of L. in the Time of Gompers*, chap. 2; Foner, *History of the Labor Movement in the United States*, 2: 78–80.

a number of instances the strategy of closed unionism was defended on explicitly racist grounds.[24]

The decades around the turn of the twentieth century saw a tremendous growth in immigration, particularly among workers who were potential union members. The labor force in the United States was the most heterogeneous in the world, made up of groups of workers having vastly differing religious and cultural traditions. In these years immigrants made up 13 to 15 percent of the total population, but the proportion was much higher among male manual workers. As Table 6.2 shows, native-born whites were outnumbered by immigrants and blacks in both mineral extraction and manufacturing, the sectors of the economy that provided the focus of union recruitment. The data presented in this table includes all those occupied, not merely wage workers. When one considers that immi-

TABLE 6.2
Immigrants in Industry, 1910

	Native White-Native Parentage	Native White-Foreign or Mixed Parentage	Foreign-Born White	Black Asian	Totals
All occupations	47.0%	18.4%	20.5%	14.1%	100%
Mineral extraction	31.8	13.6	48.0	6.6	100
Manufacturing	39.3	22.6	31.9	6.2	100
Transportation	45.1	18.5	26.3	10.3	100

SOURCE: Data based on U.S. Bureau of the Census, *Immigrants and Their Children*, p. 274.

[24] Racism was deeply rooted at the highest levels of the AFL. In a pamphlet attacking Chinese immigrants, Samuel Gompers and Herman Gutstadt quoted approvingly from a study that purported to show "that the habits and mode of life among Asiatics here are not much above 'those of the rats of the waterfront.'" A section entitled "Have Asiatics any Morals?" expressed the view that "sixty years' contact with the Chinese, twenty-five years' experience with the Japanese and two or three years' acquaintance with Hindus should be sufficient to convince any ordinarily intelligent person that they have no standard of morals by which a Caucasian may judge them." See Samuel Gompers and Herman Gutstadt, *Meat vs. Rice: American Manhood against Asiatic Coolieism: Which Shall Survive?* (San Francisco: American Federation of Labor, 1902).

grants and blacks were weakly represented among white collar and supervisory staff in these industries, the proportion of manual workers who were immigrant or black must have been higher than these figures indicate.[25] Moreover, immigrants were concentrated in the twenty-to-forty-year age group, the age group that usually provided most first-time union members. In relation to their proportion in the population as a whole immigrants were overrepresented in this age group by 46 percent in 1880 and by 70 percent in 1910.[26]

The challenge of unionizing such workers was made more difficult by the changing patterns of immigration in this period. Unlike previous waves of immigration, those around the turn of the century were mainly composed of peasants from southern and eastern Europe who had virtually no experience of unions and whose culture emphasized hierarchy and submissiveness in the face of authority. The orientation of new immigrants to work tended to be highly instrumental, and because the economic rewards offered in the New World were generally far higher than in the Old, they could find economic betterment and opportunity where others experienced relative or absolute deprivation.[27] Immigrants tended also to have exceptionally low rates of job stability and high rates of geographical mobility. Many regarded their stay in the United States as temporary: about one-third of those who immigrated to America in the period 1880 to 1920 returned to their home country. Both on account of their culture and expectations, most immigrants lacked collective standards that could provide a basis for the expression of grievances. From the perspective elaborated by Barrington Moore in his study of the social conditions of revolt, such workers could not draw on collective past experience to develop standards of injustice through which they might condemn the present.[28]

[25] A census of immigrants in seven states (Massachusetts, New York, Pennsylvania, Michigan, Minnesota, and Wisconsin) found that less than one percent of those whose mother tongue was Polish, and only 0.1 percent of those whose mother tongue was Slovak, had risen to the position of manager or foreman in the manufacturing industries. See U.S. Bureau of the Census, *Immigrants and Their Children: 1920*, Census Monographs 7 (Washington D.C.: Department of Commerce, 1927), p. 286.

[26] Computed from *Historical Statistics of the United States* (Washington D.C.: Bureau of the Census, 1975), series A91–104.

[27] Michael Harrington, *Socialism* (New York: Saturday Review Press, 1972), p. 132.

[28] Barrington Moore, Jr., *Injustice: the Social Bases of Obedience and Revolt* (New York: M.E. Sharpe, 1978). See also David Brody, *Workers in Industrial America* (New York:

The heterogeneity of American labor was a recurring, dynamic process rather than an initial condition as successive waves of immigrants, each different in language and culture, reached the United States and began the gradual process of absorbtion into the labor market. The chief loci of identification and loyalty were along ethnic lines that cut across class or occupation.[29] Occupational community, which, as we have seen, was so important in sustaining unions, was often eclipsed by ethnic identifications that divided the work force. Although they were by no means as impossible to organize as many AFL union leaders maintained, the new immigrants presented a challenge to unionism even greater than that of Irish and English workers in, say, Liverpool, or Polish and German workers in Silesia. To the extent that the new immigrants created organizations, these were usually benevolent societies, affiliated with national ethnic associations, providing insurance benefits, job contacts, and an array of other services. Virtually every ethnic group had its own association, made up of numerous regional and local societies that were set up in the footsteps of ethnic migration throughout the country. In New York alone there were more than five hundred such societies by 1914.[30]

The effects of ethnic diversity for unionization and class cohesion are nicely brought out in John Cumbler's study of two contrasting eastern industrial cities, Lynn and Fall River.[31] Workers in Lynn formed a cohesive community with a militant tradition of trade unionism. The housing patterns and diverse social institutions that expressed this community were sustained through the long decline of the city's shoe industry in the late nineteenth and early twentieth centuries. In Lynn the relatively small and steady stream of new immigrants was integrated into existing working-class institutions. The sense of working-class community in Fall River, by contrast, was shattered under the pressure of a flood of immigration from the 1890s. The Portuguese and Poles who poured into Fall River

---

Oxford University Press, 1980), pp. 15–21. The chief exceptions to the generalization about ethnicity and low potential for radical politics were, of course, Jews and Finns.

[29] See Ira Katznelson, "Considerations on Social Democracy in the United States," *Comparative Politics* 11, no. 1 (October 1978); Ira Katznelson, *City Trenches: Urban Politics and the Patterning of Class in the United States* (New York: Pantheon Books, 1981); and Mike Davis, "Why the U.S. Working Class is Different," *New Left Review* 123 (1980).

[30] James R. Green, *The World of the Worker* (New York: Hill and Wang, 1980), p. 28.

[31] John T. Cumbler, *Working-Class Community in Industrial America* (Westport, Conn.: Greenwood Press, 1979).

were excluded by entrenched English, Irish, and French Canadian workers and were dispersed into disparate ethnic communities.

Workers who formed the strongest occupational communities were usually found in the crafts. These workers were early immigrants, predominantly from the British Isles and Germany, who brought their skills with them to America. One of the chief purposes of unionization for these groups was precisely to defend their job territories from an influx of new immigrant labor. The mass immigration from the last decades of the nineteenth century not only presented a huge and intractable organizational task for those who wished to establish open unions, it also threatened existing craft unions and intensified the craft defensiveness of unionized workers.

Because the new immigrants were excluded from closed craft unions they were forced back on ethnic strategies of cooperation and survival. Thus ethnic divisions within labor both reinforced and were reinforced by the exclusive policies of established AFL unions. The gulf between unionized and nonunionized workers was deepened because it coincided with racial and cultural differences, differences that were exacerbated by nativism and racism on the part of the AFL establishment. Furthermore, as Gwendolyn Mink emphasizes, the AFL's attempts to halt immigration by political means extended its labor market sectionalism into the political arena.[32] Instead of encompassing the new immigrants in a class-based fashion, the AFL was led by its narrow labor market concerns to promote the exclusive demands of unionized workers against nonunionized immigrants.

To be convincing, the argument that the AFL's political orientation was influenced by the unique character of immigration needs to be combined with analysis of the responses of individual unions. Here, as elsewhere, there are variations among unions that escape national characterization. The United Mine Workers of America was faced by large numbers of new immigrants working in the mines, yet, as I detailed in Chapter Five, the union pursued a political strategy and provided significant support for independent political representation. Few industries were more permeated by im-

---

[32] Mink, *Old Labor and New Immigrants*, p. 49. See also A. T. Lane, "American Trade Unions, Mass Immigration and the Literacy Test: 1900–1917," *Labor History* 25, no. 1 (Winter 1984).

migrants than coalmining, but the UMWA was more politically radical in this period than secure craft unions.

An ethnically diverse labor force doubtless made it more difficult to create open unions like the UMWA that were based on an inclusionary organizational strategy encompassing all workers within an entire industry. But the effects of ethnic diversity were not cast in stone. Conditions in the workplace, relations with employers, and experience of industrial conflict could counter the fractionalizing consequences of ethnic diversity. From the early 1900s the United Mine Workers engaged in a fierce membership drive against employer opposition that was successful in organizing more than one hundred thousand Polish and East European workers in the anthracite mines of Pennsylvania, workers who were previously believed to be totally beyond the reach of labor organization. Intense mutual dependence within the mine, shared horror of large-scale industrial disasters, and the bitter experience of government and employer repression created a sense of occupational community that could overcome deep-seated ethnic hostilities.

Although coalminers succeeded in establishing durable unionization, it was the kind of unionism typified by the printers that dominated the AFL. This preponderance of closed unionism helped shape the political orientation of the AFL, weakening the case of those within it who wanted to follow the lead of British unionists and create an independent working-class political party.

THE AMERICAN POLITICAL SYSTEM

No country has seen a greater number of parties contest elections than the United States, yet nowhere over the last century have third parties been so weak. Since the Civil War the number of parties that have contested local, state, and national elections have to be counted in the hundreds, yet only eleven times over the last hundred years have third parties gained more than 5 percent of the total vote in a presidential election, and no party has managed to accomplish even this feat more than once.[33] Given the duopoly of the Democratic party and the Republican party, it is not unreasonable to view the unwillingness of most union leaders to set up a

[33] See Walter Dean Burnham, "The United States," in Richard Rose, ed., *Electoral Behavior: A Comparative Handbook* (New York: Free Press, 1974), table 3.

labor party as an adjustment to the logic of two-party competition in the American political system.

In the United States, as in Britain, the electoral system is based on the plurality, or "winner take all," principle, in which new parties stand to gain nothing if they come second in a constituency. In such a system a third party is faced with a stark choice between political principles and political outcomes because its electoral participation will normally draw votes away from the party that is ideologically closest to it. To the extent that a third party is successful in garnering votes, it threatens to open the door to its political adversaries.

The affect of this is particularly acute in the United States because it is virtually alone in having an electoral system for its executive that effectively encompasses the whole country as a single constituency through the electoral college.[34] Because the office of the executive cannot be shared, it is difficult to exploit regional concentrations of support as a base for later advances. In parliamentary systems, by contrast, labor parties developed an electoral strategy of focussing on select constituencies where they had extraordinary strength, and this partially offset the disproportional consequences of their plurality electoral systems. In the three general elections that the British Labour party fought before the First World War, it managed to receive roughly its proportional share of seats in the House of Commons: twenty-nine seats (4.3 percent of the total) in 1906 with 4.8 percent of the national vote; forty seats (6.0 percent) in January 1910 with 7 percent of the vote; and forty-two seats (6.3 percent) in December 1910 with 6.4 percent of the vote. In the United States the electoral system undercuts this strategy. Both the Socialist party in the first two decades of the twentieth century and the Farmer-Labor party of 1924 came up empty-handed in national elections even though their share of the national vote was similar to that of the British Labour party.

The effects of the presidential electoral system were countered to some extent by the division of the republic into separate governments, each of which had considerable autonomy. In this respect the barriers to third-party success in Britain were more formidable than in the United States. Because Britain has a unitary constitution, with a sovereign Parliament, the Labour party had to battle in

[34] France now also has a nationally elected president, although third parties have the advantage of a two-tiered electoral system involving a run-off election.

the national political arena from its inception. The only executive power worth having was at the national center of the political system. In the United States individual states were crucial arenas, and it was possible to exercise executive power in several political units short of the presidency. The Socialist party managed to elect some one thousand two hundred representatives to city and state office before the First World War and controlled the mayoralty or municipal county in over thirty cities.

In most other respects the American political system posed far more difficult obstacles for a labor party than did the British political system. The American constitution has created flexible, ideologically diffuse parties that have consistently undercut third parties by incorporating parts of their programs and encapsulating their constituencies. Political parties in the Western European mold, combining party-centered selection of candidates, party discipline, a high degree of institutionalization, and a concern with the formulation of political programs, do not exist in America. In the United States, congressmen are uniquely able to represent the varied interests of their constituents without having to subordinate their political stance to national party platforms. Primaries have reinforced this by providing multiple opportunities for entry into each party and for the expression of diverse political viewpoints within the two-party system.

These considerations have been made all the more compelling by the sheer size and geographical, ethnic, and social diversity of the population. As James MacGregor Burns notes, a "great variety of sections and groups and classes and opinions [are] stitched into the fabric of society and thus into the majority's coalition. . . . Moreover, the majority party—and the opposition that hopes to supplant it—must be competitive; if either one forsakes victory in order to stick to principle, as the Federalists did after the turn of the century, it threatens the whole mechanism of majority rule. Majoritarian strategy assumes that in the end politicians will rise above principle in order to win an election."[35]

The logic of electoral competition and party coalition building detracted from the potential benefits of a third-party strategy and made more viable the policy of trying to influence the major parties

[35] James MacGregor Burns, *The Deadlock of Democracy* (London: Calder and Boyar, 1965), pp. 40–41; quoted in Seymour Martin Lipset, "Why No Socialism in the United States?" pp.129–131.

by "rewarding friends" and "punishing enemies." The AFL's pressure-group policy emerged in a learning process begun in the lessons of the failure of Henry George and the Populists in 1884 and
completed in the successful campaign to unseat President Cleveland as the 1896 Democratic presidential nominee in favor of William Jennings Bryan. Bryan's platform included both antiinjunc-
tion and antiimmigration planks specifically directed to gain the
support of organized labor. After 1896 Democratic efforts to woo
the AFL intensified, as did the AFL's need for respite from the legal
offensive mounted by the courts. Eventually, with Woodrow Wilson's administration and the Clayton Act (1914), which exempted
unions from antitrust legislation, the AFL could point to results as
a justification of its policy. In addition, the Wilson administration
enacted several prolabor measures, including workmen's compensation, child labor legislation, a progressive income tax, legislation
regulating the working conditions of seamen, and appointed William B. Wilson, an official of the UMW, as first secretary of labor.
As a result, unions that favored the establishment of a labor party
were drawn into the orbit of two-party competition in support of
the Democratic party. In 1916 most socialist union officials followed
the AFL's policy of supporting prolabor candidates when there was
a clear choice between the parties. As the Machinists monthly journal noted in October 1916, "The time may come in this country
when organized labor will have a party of its own, but until then
labor will lend its sympathy to those in sympathy with its aims and
objectives."[36]

Given the highly decentralized and fragmented character of the
American political system, it was difficult for socialists to convince
labor that the state could be transformed into a more potent source
of improvement than collective bargaining. In England, Sidney and
Beatrice Webb had argued that national legislation of working conditions had inherent advantages over collective bargaining. In the
first place, it was permanent, for once it was achieved it was difficult
to reverse, and, second, legislation was universal in the sense that it
extended to all workers, whether unionized or not.[37] However,
these grounds for a more activist party-political strategy were weak

[36] Quoted in John H. M. Laslett, "Socialism and American Trade Unionism," in
Laslett and Seymour Martin Lipset, eds., *Failure of a Dream? Essays in the History of
American Socialism* (New York: Anchor Press, 1974), p. 218.

[37] Sidney Webb and Beatrice Webb, *Industrial Democracy* (London: Longmans,
Green, 1920), 1: 255.

in America. Any national legislation achieved by unions still had to traverse the courts and be implemented in individual states, many of which had constitutional limitations on the power of the government to interfere with private property. Pure and simple unionists argued that independent political activity was impractical given the fractionalization of government in the United States. Adolf Strasser emphasized this during the early fight over a labor party at the 1894 AFL Convention in Denver.

> There is one fact that cannot be overlooked. You cannot pass a general eight hour day without changing the constitution of the United States and the constitution of every State in the Union. . . . I hold we cannot propose to wait with the eight hour movement until we can secure it by law. I am opposed to wasting our time declaring for legislation being enacted for a time possibly, after we are dead. I want to see something we can secure while we are alive.[38]

The early gift of the ballot to white workers in America contributed to the absence of a revolutionary tradition linking the demand for economic equality to basic political rights. As Lenin stressed in 1907, socialism in America was weakened by "the absence of any at all big, nation-wide *democratic* tasks facing the proletariat."[39] The combination of early suffrage with the cultural heterogeneity of la-

---

[38] *A Verbatim Report of the Discussion on the Political Program at the Denver Convention of the American Federation of Labor, December 14, 15, 1894* (New York: The Freytag Press, 1895), pp. 19–20. State autonomy was also viewed as an obstacle by Morris Hillquit: "The main socialist program, as well as the most important immediate reforms advocated by the socialists, can be realized only on a national scale. In every other country it is always some concrete demand addrest to the national legislature, the parliament, which united the masses of the population into one solid reform or revolutionary movement. In the United States, where the powers and the scope of the national government are exceedingly limited, and the most vital industrial and social problems of the country are left to be dealt with by the 46 different and independent legislatures of our States, general social reform movements have to traverse a much more difficult road" (*History of Socialism in the United States*, pp. 360–361). A similar point was raised by T. J. Tracey, who represented the AFL at the 1899 TUC Congress. He argued that one of the most important differences between Britain and the United States was that "instead of having one Imperial Government to appeal to for relief, there were forty-five States to be won over to their side, each requiring separate and distinct propaganda work." *Report of Proceedings of the Thirty-Second Trades Union Congress*, 1899, p. 63.

[39] V. I. Lenin, *On Britain* (Moscow: Foreign Languages Publishing House, n.d.), p. 51.

bor created a patchwork of conflicting party-political allegiances. Party loyalties were already formed by the 1890s when the AFL was debating whether to form a labor party. Native-stock, Protestant, and English-speaking immigrant workers were predominantly Republican, while Irish, Catholic, and east and south European workers were predominantly Democratic.[40] Opponents of independent political activity continually pointed out that union activities united workers and politics divided workers. To the extent that effective unionism was a valued goal, so the argument went, independent politics should be divorced from union activity. As Walter Mac-Arthur, a leading unionist from the West Coast, argued in the 1894 convention debate on the political program:

> I am in favor of political action. What bothers me is how to do it. I am satisfied that we cannot do it as trade unionists and preserve the efficiency of the trades union. It is all very well to cite our British brethren on the subject, but the illustrations are irrelevant, immaterial. . . . In San Francisco we have all nationalities in our unions, men who will stand together to a unit on wages and conditions generally in every craft, but if you mix politics, even a suspicion of them, the specter of disintegration arises right there and stays there.[41]

By the time socialists and others were pressing for the establishment of a labor party, workers and many union locals were already integrated into local political machines that were strongest precisely where unions had the most members, in the larger cities and particularly in New York and Chicago. Tammany Hall in New York,

[40] The consequences of the internal stratification of the American working class for socialist support are discussed in Mike Davis, "Why the U.S. Working Class is Different."

[41] *A Verbatim Report of the Discussion on the Political Program at the Denver Convention of the American Federation of Labor, December 14, 15, 1894*, p. 6. Speeches by AFL delegates at TUC congresses and by TUC delegates at AFL conventions provide an interesting commentary on differences of perception in the two countries. In a speech before the 1902 TUC Congress, P. Dolan, an AFL delegate from the miners, pointed out that "there was one thing, however, in which America had to give Great Britain best—that was with regard to the Parliamentary representation of Labour. So far, they had totally failed in that direction. They possessed the franchise fully enough, but did not use it in the right way. The Democrats and Republicans adhered to their parties as closely as to their religion. . . . Many of us think it just as easy to get the most bigoted Roman Catholic and Protestant to kneel down at the same altar to pray as to get the workers to vote together." See the *Report of Proceedings of the Thirty-Fifth Annual Trades Union Congress*, 1902, p. 61.

and its functional equivalents elsewhere, provided patronage, favors, and political access that cut across ethnic or class lines. In a succinct analysis of the functions of voluntarism Michael Rogin points out that this was one of the outstanding virtues of the doctrine: "voluntarism required no commitment on political issues that might upset a local alliance. To local unionists a national policy of nonpartisanship meant that they could be Democratic in Democratic cities and Republican in Republican cities."[42]

Envisioning a labor party dedicated to the pursuit of working-class representation was made more difficult in the years around the turn of the twentieth century by the relative numerical weakness of industrial workers. The agricultural labor force exceeded that employed in industry as late as 1910, with 31.4 percent of the labor force compared to 30.3 percent in manufacturing, construction, and mining.[43] More importantly, unionists realized that to succeed a labor party would have to form some alliance with agrarians, yet their interests did not mesh well. Agriculture was conducted mainly by independent family farmers whose concerns centered on farm prices and debt rather than conditions of employment. In contrast to the development of the frontier in other Anglo-American societies, in particular Canada and Australia, the American frontier was settled in the image of the Jeffersonian yeoman farmer rather than the large-scale enterprise employing a landless proletariat.

Differences between the fundamental concerns of farmers and industrial workers undermined the Peoples' party, the one institutionalized attempt in these years to encompass both groups in a third force. The farmers' demand for free and unlimited coinage of silver, which became the chief plank of the Peoples' party, had little meaning for industrial workers. The increase in farm prices that would result would hardly benefit city dwellers. Both farmers and industrial workers were pressed down by the economic depres-

[42] Michael Rogin, "Voluntarism: The Political Functions of an Antipolitical Doctrine," *Industrial and Labor Relations Review* 15 (1961/1962): 535. In the words of John B. Lennon of the Tailors, "We have in this country conditions that do not exist in Great Britain. We have the 'spoil' system which is something almost unknown in Great Britain and on account of it we cannot afford to try at this time to start a political party as an adjunct with their unions." See *A Verbatim Report of the Discussion on the Political Program at the Denver Convention of the American Federation of Labor, December 14, 15, 1894*, p. 8.

[43] *Historical Statistics of the United States*, Labor Force and Employment by Industry, D167–181.

sion of the late 1880s and early 1890s, and both were concerned to reassert popular control over increasingly large-scale capitalist society, but the political means they proposed were different. Samuel Gompers was opposed to the Peoples' party because he wished to focus workers' energies on the labor market strategy of business unionism. In an article published in 1892 he pointed out that the Populist movement was made up of "*employing* farmers without any regard to the interests of the *employed* farmers of the country districts or the mechanics and laborers of the industrial centers," and concluded that the Peoples' party could not be considered a "Labor party."[44]

These features of the American political system and society greatly reduced the potential benefits of independent party-political activity for American labor leaders. But the existence of major obstacles to third-party success does not explain why union leaders did attempt to surmount them. If we assume that labor leaders wished to maximize their political influence within the political process, then their decision not to create a labor party appears rational in the light of the opportunities and constraints that faced them. But an analysis of the American political system cannot shed light on the political aspirations of labor. Why did labor leaders reject basic demands for the universal political regulation of minimum wages and maximum hours that might have galvanized support for a labor party despite political obstacles? Why did most labor leaders view politics in a minimalist fashion, as the pursuit of narrow union interests, instead of campaigning for inclusive, classwide, political regulation of the labor market? To answer these questions we must return to the kinds of unions that workers formed and the strategies they pursued in the labor market. The political arguments advanced here are forceful because most unions within the AFL were attuned to the logic of political influence rather than fundamental demands for economic legislation. They wished to gain a favorable political context for collective bargaining, not gain political regulation of the labor market. In short, their demands were amenable to pressure politics exercised through the major parties, and they re-

[44] Quoted in Foner, *History of the Labor Movement in the United States*, 2: 306. David Brody emphasizes the role of "farm-conscious agrarianism" alongside job-conscious unionism in explaining the failure of radical politics in the 1920s. See David Brody, "On the Failure of U.S. Radical Politics: A Farmer-Labor Analysis," *Industrial Relations and Labor Review* 22, no. 2 (Spring 1983).

sisted the notion of creating a labor party for its own sake, as an expression of working-class solidarity.

It is in conjunction with other variables described in this chapter that American political structure affected party-political outcomes. The obstacles that the American political system placed in the way of an independent labor party loomed larger because the impetuses for forming such a party were weaker than in Anglo-American democracies. In America, perhaps more than in any other Western society, the establishment of a labor party was viewed in instrumental terms, in the light of its expected political costs and payoffs.

SOCIALIST STRATEGY

Could socialists themselves have improved the chances of establishing a labor party with AFL support? This is a complex hypothetical question, and the difficulties of coming to grips with it should not be minimized. Even with the immense advantage of hindsight, how can we know the consequences of alternative causes of action in a complex and evolving situation? However, there is some agreement among writers of diverse ideological persuasions that socialist policies of dual unionism—of supporting union movements in competition with the AFL—weakened the Socialist party and negated the possibility of creating a viable labor party. This view is put forward by those including Daniel Bell and Laurence Moore who emphasize the dogmatic, sectarian, and factional character of the American socialist movement.[45] But it is also held by some writers who share the socialists' condemnation of AFL policies yet believe that socialists should have worked to change those policies from within rather than abandon the AFL to create their own unions. Ira Kipnis, who argues that the decline of socialist strength after 1912 was due mainly to socialist opportunism and collaborationism, also maintains that the refusal of left-wing socialists "to work within the A.F. of L., their dual unionism and their neglect of political activity all served to isolate them from the rank and file of

[45] See Daniel Bell, *Marxian Socialism in the United States* (Princeton, N.J.: Princeton University Press, 1967); R. Laurence Moore, *European Socialists and the American Promised Land* (New York: Oxford University Press, 1970). Moore, for example, points out forcefully that "De Leon and his followers in the Socialist Labor Party engaged in an almost perverse attempt to cut themselves off from the American electorate" (p. 207).

American labor."[46] Likewise, Philip Foner attacks the voluntarist
policies of the established leadership of the AFL yet also criticizes
the De Leonites "for precipitating a conflict with the AF of L leadership which ended with their isolation from the main body of the
American labor movement."[47]

Leaders of the AFL were alienated by socialist demands for ideological purity, their deemphasis of unions as a means of working-
class improvement, and, most of all, by the support given by leading socialists, particularly Daniel De Leon and Eugene Debs, for
dual union movements.

The first open rupture between socialists and the future leadership of the AFL, Adolph Strasser and Samuel Gompers, arose in
1882 when the Cigar Makers' International Union endorsed a Republican, Edward Grosse, in return for his sponsorship of a bill to
outlaw sweatshop manufacture of cigars in tenement houses. Socialist members of the union objected vehemently on the grounds
that supporting parties other than the Socialist Labor party led
workers to think that collaboration with the establishment could
bring gains. In his autobiography Gompers remarked acidly that
socialists "preferred to see evils continue rather than see remedies
from any other agencies than those prescribed by Socialism."[48]

The dispute intensified when a socialist slate led by Samuel
Schimkovitz was victorious in the elections for Local 144 in New
York, the results of which were promptly thrown out by Strasser on
the grounds that Schimkovitz was an employer and thus ineligible
for union membership or office. Gompers never forgave the socialist faction when it seceded to form the Cigarmakers' Progressive
Union, imitating the International's seal and issuing union cards
supposedly entitling its members to the older union's benefits.[49]

Antisocialist feelings within the AFL were exacerbated by several
clashes between AFL leaders and the Socialist Labor party from the
late 1880s. In 1888 Gompers rejected an application by the N.Y.

---

[46] Ira Kipnis, *The American Socialist Movement, 1897–1912* (New York: Columbia
University Press, 1952), p. 424.

[47] Philip S. Foner, "Socialism and American Trade Unionism: Comment," in John
H. M. Laslett and Seymour Martin Lipset, eds., *Failure of a Dream? Essays in the History
of American Socialism* (New York: Anchor Press, 1974), p. 235.

[48] Samuel Gompers, *Seventy Years of Life and Labor* (New York: E.P. Dutton, 1925),
p. 191.

[49] See Dick, *Labor and Socialism in America*, pp. 20–21; Gompers, *Seventy Years of Life
and Labor*, pp. 200–202; Harold C. Livesay, *Samuel Gompers and Organized Labor in
America* (Boston: Little, Brown, 1978), pp. 69–71.

Central Labor Federation for a charter from the AFL on the grounds that the N.Y. section of the SLP was affiliated with the body, and as a political party the SLP had no right to be represented in a trade union organization. De Leon and his followers refused to divorce the SLP from the N.Y. Central Labor Federation, even though Gompers made it clear that he had no objection to admitting the federation if the socialists joined as individual members of their trade unions. Gompers' position was supported by many socialists outside New York. Thomas J. Morgan, leader of the Chicago socialists and later proponent of the eleven-point program, wrote to the New York branches of the SLP urging compliance with Gompers' conditions. In 1891 Gompers wrote to Friedrich Engels on the matter, noting that "I do so because as I have said I have respect for your judgement, and as a student of your writings and those of Marx and others in the same line I would not have your judgement formed upon the base of erroneous information."[50] Engels never wrote back, evidently meaning to talk in person with Gompers when he came to Brussels for the International Labor Congress. But in his correspondence Engels made plain that his sympathy on the issue was with Gompers. As he wrote to Hermann Schlüter, "His Federation is, as far as I know, an association of trade-unions and nothing but trade-unions. Hence they have the *formal right* to reject anyone coming in as the representative of a labor organization that is *not* a trade-union, or to reject delegates of an association to which such organizations are admitted."[51] Later in the same letter Engels asked, "Where do you find a recruiting ground if not in the trade unions?" De Leon, however, continued his battle with the AFL, denouncing the leadership as "labor fakers," "agents of the capitalists inside the trade unions," and advising socialists to leave the organization. In December 1895 De Leon took the further step of creating the Socialist Trade and Labor Alliance in overt competition with the AFL.

Many socialists, including Morris Hillquit and Victor Berger, disapproved of DeLeon's tactics, favoring instead a strategy of working within the AFL. They were supported by several unionists, including Max Hayes, an official of the International Typographical Union, who were determined to straddle the AFL and the Socialist

---

[50] Quoted in Foner, *History of the Labor Movement in the United States*, 2: 284–285.

[51] Karl Marx and Friedrich Engels, *Letters to Americans* (New York: International Publishers, 1953), pp. 233–234.

Labor party. In 1899 the Socialist Labor party split, largely on the issue of policy towards the unions, and the Socialist party of America, established in 1901, went on record against dual unionism in several of its conventions. But socialists who wished to bore the AFL from within were continually attacked by large minorities within the Socialist Labor party who saw the AFL as a traitorous and irredeemable organization. Few issues were more contentious at Socialist party conventions. As John Spargo told the Trade Union Resolutions Committee in 1904, the year before the establishment of the IWW, "You have drawn up resolutions which are bound to be the source and center of a fight that is going to shake this convention to its very basis."[52] The ensuing debate was an uproarious affair that lasted two days and dominated the convention. The resolution that was eventually adopted followed the orthodox Marxian line of the International Socialist Congress in maintaining that "trade and labor unions are a necessity in the struggle to aid in emancipating the working class" and that "neither political nor other differences of opinion justify the divisions of forces of labor in the industrial movement. The interests of the working class make it imperative that the labor organizations equip their members for the great work of the abolition of wage slavery by educating them in Socialist Principles."[53] That this resolution was attacked much more from the Left than from the Right reveals much about the tenor of the American Socialist party. The radical wing of the party, which could count on the support of about one-third of the conference delegates, demanded more forceful condemnation of the AFL and the cessation of efforts to reform it from within.[54]

The notion of a labor party in the mold of the British Labour party found little support within the Socialist party. Most moderates still hoped to bring the AFL into line behind the Socialist party. Morris Hillquit and Adolf Germer opposed the creation of a labor party on the grounds that it would detract from the Socialist party and would almost certainly be insufficiently radical.[55] Victor Berger, the leading municipal socialist in the party, said that he did not want official AFL support for the Socialist party because his expe-

[52] *Proceedings, National Convention of the Socialist Party* (Chicago, 1904), p. 174.
[53] Ibid., p. 206.
[54] Fifty-one of the 147 delegates voted against the resolution. See ibid., p. 214.
[55] See Laslett, "Socialism and American Trade Unionism," p. 213.

rience in Milwaukee had shown him that socialists did better in elections when they were not endorsed by the unions.[56]

The leading light of the Socialist party, and its presidential candidate from 1900 to 1916, Eugene Debs, was on the radical wing, particularly on questions relating to unions and the AFL. Although he usually avoided intraparty fights, he argued strongly against a labor party in a letter to William English Walling that he allowed to be published in the *International Socialist Review*: "I have been watching the situation closely and especially the tendencies to reaction to which we are so unalterably opposed. The Socialist party has already CATERED FAR TOO MUCH to the American Federation of Labor, and there is no doubt that A HALT WILL HAVE TO BE CALLED."[57] Debs believed that the AFL was so hopelessly wedded to narrow craft unionism that it was useless to try to reform it. Instead he supported a variety of dual union movements, from the American Labor Union and the Western Federation of Miners to the Industrial Workers of the World.

Debs' antipathy to the AFL was matched by Gompers' opposition to socialists who wished to create a more inclusive and politicized union movement. Socialist attacks strengthened Gompers' belief that there was an irreconcilable conflict between the principles of trade unionism and those of socialism. Gompers made this absolutely plain in his confrontation with Morris Hillquit before the U.S. Commission on Industrial Relations in May 1914. Both men were given the opportunity to cross-examine the other, and the transcription provides a fascinating insight into the tensions between socialists and the AFL in these years. Hillquit argued that there were substantial commonalities between the Socialist party and the AFL and that the AFL would be well served if it supported the Socialist party in the political arena. Gompers rejected Hillquit's offer of alliance on the grounds that socialists had repeatedly at-

[56] Dick, *Labor and Socialism in America*, p. 62.

[57] Quoted in David A. Shannon, *The Socialist Party of America* (New York: Macmillan, 1955), p. 67. See also Nick Salvatore, *Eugene V. Debs: Citizen and Socialist* (Urbana Ill.: University of Illinois Press, 1982), chap. 7. When it came to the AFL, Debs' invective rivalled De Leon's. As Debs argued in a speech to the IWW representatives in Chicago in November 1905: "At the very threshold of this discussion I aver that the old form of trade unionism no longer meets the demands of the working class. I aver that the old trade union has not only fulfilled its mission and is maintained, not in the interests of the workers who support it, but in the interests of the capitalist class who exploit the workers who support it." *Writings and Speeches of Eugene V. Debs* (New York: Hermitage Press, 1948), p. 171.

tacked the AFL in the past and, worse, had supported rival union movements. To substantiate his point, Gompers quoted from Eugene Debs no less than six times. In reply to Hillquit's protestations that Debs spoke only for himself and not for the Socialist party, Gompers struck home: "Do you regard that as the individual expression of opinion, when a man thrice the candidate of a political party, urges that a movement be inaugurated to dissolve the only general federation of organized workmen that ever existed for a period of time, such as the A.F. of L.?"[58]

The strategies of American socialists with respect to the unions and their political representation contrast sharply with that of socialists in Britain. As in the United States, British socialists were fractionalized, but neither of the two leading groupings, the Social Democratic Federation (1881) nor the Independent Labor party (1893), supported dual unionism.

The Social Democratic Federation was, as Engels described it, "an orthodox sect" that transformed Marxism into "rigid dogma."[59] But fortunately for those who wished to create a labor party, the SDF did not pay much attention to the unions. Its dogmatic and sectarian leader, H. M. Hyndman, argued that unions were merely a transitional phenomenon and would be superceded by the socialist party. To the extent that the SDF was concerned with unions it was to convince them to turn their energies to socialist politics. Individual members of the SDF, including Will Thorne, John Burns, and Tom Mann, played leading roles in the new unionism of 1888 and 1889, but the federation maintained its remarkable official policy of disinterest in union affairs. Rather than recognize that the new unionism meant a significant extension of organization to unskilled workers, the SDF manifesto to the unions took the view that the movement merely represented "a lowering of the flag, a departure

---

[58] Morris Hillquit, Samuel Gompers, and Max Hayes, *The Double Edge of Labor's Sword* (New York: Arno, 1971), p. 47. This debate set the scene for some famous hairsplitting when Gompers interrupted Hillquit to assert that "we go farther than you. You have an end; we have not." This was good theater and has become a part of the lore of the American labor movement. But taken out of context this exchange gives a misleading idea of the whole debate. Gompers is usually credited with having silenced Hillquit with this remark, but those who read on hear Gompers refusing to elaborate on his comparison of the aims of the AFL and the Socialist party because "I don't know that it is necessary that I should make the comparison" (pp. 124–126).

[59] Engels to F.A. Sorge, 10 November 1894; quoted in Henry Collins, "The Marxism of the Social Democratic Federation," in Asa Briggs and John Saville, eds., *Essays in Labour History, 1886–1923* (London: Macmillan, 1971), p. 48.

from active propaganda, and a waste of energy."[60] By the time the SDF began to rethink this policy in 1897, its best-known unionists were no longer in the party.

This left the field virtually wide open to the Independent Labour party, and this body pursued an energetic and pragmatic set of policies to gain union support. From its inception, the leaders of the ILP realized that if they were going to succeed they would have to appeal broadly to the benefits of an institutionalized working-class political presence, even if this meant diluting the ideological purity of the party. At the second annual conference of the party in 1894 a proposal to bind all members to vote exclusively for candidates supporting ILP principles was defeated. The party welcomed non-socialists who were prepared to press working-class interests by party-political means. Ideological purity was secondary to gaining the broadest possible base of working-class support. Even so, the ILP was doggedly opposed by unionists who had long identified with Gladstone and the Liberal party. At the TUC Congress in 1895, the "old guard" succeeded in excluding trades councils, in which socialists were strongly represented, from the TUC. But far from turning away from that body, socialists redoubled their efforts to gain influence in affiliated unions.[61]

Socialists in America were closer ideologically to those in Germany—and even here some scholars have argued that American socialists were the more radical. Whether or not this is the case, the context in which American socialists acted made their strategies particularly sectarian. Whereas German socialists played a vital role in creating the Free Union movement, American socialists from the late 1880s had to respond to the establishment of an independent union movement along economistic craft lines. German socialists saw unions as means through which workers would be educated into socialism. The leadership of socialists within the labor movement was assumed, and was only modified later, from the mid-1890s, as unions grew in strength and self-confidence. American

[60] Ibid., p. 55. On the SDF's union policy see David Kynaston, *King Labor: The British Working Class, 1850–1914* (London: Allen & Unwin, 1976), pp. 121–123; H. A. Clegg, Alan Fox, and A. F. Thompson, *A History of British Trade Unions since 1889* (Oxford: Clarendon Press, 1964), 1: 291.

[61] See Howell, *British Workers and the Independent Labour Party, 1888–1906*, pp. 124–128, 355–357; Pelling, *The Origins of the Labour Party, 1880–1900*, pp. 205–210, 219–221; and Keith Burgess, *The Challenge of Labour: Shaping British Society, 1850–1930* (New York: St. Martin's Press, 1980), pp. 98–103.

socialists, by contrast, had to struggle to exert any influence at all within the unions. Doctrinal purity had a very different meaning and vastly different consequences in the United States because the context in which socialists acted was one of union autonomy, not union dependence as in Germany.

CONCLUSION

How can we explain the absence of a labor party in the United States? One basic line of analysis focusses on the American political system. Central features of the American Constitution, including the separation of powers, the electoral system, and federalism made it very difficult for unionists to conceive of a labor party as a practical political proposition. Each of these features of the American political system helped to sustain a party system dominated by two broad, extremely flexible, coalitions. The benefits of an independent party-political strategy appeared uncertain, while the potential costs of abandoning existing channels of influence within the major parties were clear and predictable. Those who pressed for the creation of an independent labor party were put in the uncomfortable position of having to argue that the principle of labor political autonomy should take precedence over the immediate benefits that could be gained by allying unions with the major party that best expressed labor's interests. In other words, the possibility of a third-party strategy was squeezed from two directions. On the one side, there were obvious barriers to third-party effectiveness; on the other, there was the lure of influencing those extremely porous political coalitions that, in the American context, served as political parties.

These factors are especially powerful when seen in conjunction with the early extension of suffrage for white males and the remarkable heterogeneity of labor. The United States was the only Western society in which workers could participate in the political system before the institutionalization of unions and socialist political parties. The dominant parties mobilized workers not on the basis of class but as members of distinct ethnic and religious groups. If a labor party were to be created it would have the enormous task of overcoming these prior loyalties and prejudices. Unions that had striven to build a sense of unity among their members on economic grounds were fearful of being torn apart by the task of creating an exclusive political loyalty. Deep-seated divisions within the work force led many union leaders to conceive of their mission in highly restrictive terms.

But to say that the barriers were high does not explain why unionists did not try to surmount them. After all, a labor party might have been established as an act of principle even if the immediate material benefits were seen to be small. We would expect to find the strongest proponents of independent working-class representation in the Socialist party. In Germany socialists created unions with the express desire to bind them closely within a coherent political movement. In Britain unions were created before the rise of socialist parties, but most socialists still wished to establish an independent working-class political party with union backing, even if they could not guarantee that they would dominate it. In the United States, by contrast, socialists never gave their wholehearted support to the cause of independent labor representation. They were split between those who tried to bore the AFL from within and diverse groupings who promoted dual unions because they thought that the AFL was irredeemable. Many influential socialists, including both Daniel De Leon and Eugene Debs, were in favor of a union-supported political party only if it was explicitly socialist. For most American socialists the cause of independent working-class political representation was not worth pursuing if it was achieved at the expense of socialist demands for abolition of the system of wage labor. Given this set of priorities it is not surprising that demands for an American labor party took place in the context of an increasingly acrimonious debate between leading socialists and the established leadership of the AFL. In no other English-speaking democracy was the ideological distance between the leading socialist party and the dominant union movement so great.

This distance was a function of the orientations of unionists as well as the strategy of socialists. The AFL was unique among Western union federations in its composition. No other union federation in the Western world was so dominated by closed craft unions. This type of union—formed by exclusive groups of workers based in small, close-knit, occupational communities—maintained a remarkable grip on the national union movement. The political orientation of the AFL, shaped by the business unionism of closed unions, was challenged by larger, open unions from the beginning of the twentieth century, but it was never displaced. In these years the AFL became more politicized, but its political goals were circumscribed by the narrow concerns of its union constituents.

The absence of an American labor party focusses our attention on the existence of sharp national contrasts among Western societies. What I have tried to do here is show that a systematic understanding of the political orientations of individual unions helps explain those contrasts. The experiences of workers in the workplace, their occupational communities, and the strategies they pursued to defend or improve the conditions under which they worked deeply influenced the political orientations of their unions. Working-class politics is rooted both in the labor market and in the state. An explanation of American Exceptionalism—and union political development in general—must, therefore, come to grips with patterns of unionism alongside national political factors.

UNION SUPPORT FOR RADICAL POLITICAL
MEASURES AT AFL CONVENTIONS

1894: Independent Political Activity*

Union	Delegates in Favor: Total Delegates	Convention Votes**
Mine workers	3:4	258
Garment workers	1:1	100
Brewery workers	2:2	60
Painters and decorators	2:3	54
Lasters	2:2	50
Boot and shoe workers	1:1	41
Railway employees	1:1	40
Longshoremen	1:1	25
Horse shoers	1:1	20
Hotel and restaurant employees	1:1	20
Seamen	1:2	20
Brass workers	1:1	10
Carriage and wagon workers	1:1	8
Pattern makers	1:1	8
Machinists	1:1	5

* The vote was on whether to strike out the preamble to the political program. The preamble was as follows: "Whereas, The Trade Unionists of Great Britain, have by the light of experience and the logic of progress, adopted the principle of independent labor politics as an auxiliary to their economic action; and Whereas, Such action has resulted in the most gratifying success; and Whereas, Such independent labor politics are based upon the following programme" [here the Ten Points followed]. The vote was 1,345 votes in favor of striking out the preamble and 861 against. *Report of Proceedings of the Thirteenth Convention of the American Federation of Labor* (Chicago, 1893), p. 36.

** Representatives of trades assemblies and labor councils are not listed here or in subsequent tables.

1902: Organizing Labor's Economic and Political Power*

Union	Delegates in Favor: Total Delegates	Convention Votes
Mine workers	7:7	1855
Carpenters and joiners	5:6	666
Brewery workers	4:4	291
Steam fitters and steam fitters' helpers	3:3	128
Garment workers	2:4	121
Iron, steel, and tin workers	1:1	100
Typographical workers	1:4	98
Railroad telegraphers	3:3	80
Electrical workers	2:3	77
Clothing makers	2:2	60
Metal workers, united	1:1	43
Brick, tile, and terra cotta workers	1:1	41
Printing pressmen	1:3	39
Railway employers	1:3	32
Musicians	1:3	32
Carriage and wagon workers	1:1	31
Piano and organ workers	1:2	29
Horse shoers	1:1	28
Car workers	1:1	24
Pattern makers	1:1	23
Stage employees	1:2	22
Leather workers	1:2	21
Ladies garment workers	1:1	21
Cloth hat and cap makers	1:1	20
Steam and hot water fitters and helpers	1:1	15
Upholsterers	1:1	13
Blast furnace workers and smelters	1:1	10

* The resolution was as follows: "That the twenty-second annual convention of the American Federation of Labor advise the working people to organize their economic and political power to secure for labor the full equivalent of its toil." The vote was 4,171 votes in favor, 4,897 against, with 309 abstaining. *Report of Proceedings of the Twenty-Second Annual Convention of the American Federation of Labor* (New Orleans, 1902), p. 179.

1911: Condemning the National Civic Federation and Labor's Connection with It*

Union	Delegates in Favor: Total Delegates	Convention Votes
Mine workers	7:7	2504
Ladies garment workers	5:5	525
Miners, western federation	4:4	513
Brewery workers	3:5	270
Machinists	2:5	268
Cigarmakers	2:4	218
Typographical workers	1:5	104
Tailors	2:3	80
Railway car men	1:4	67
Boot and shoe workers	1:5	65
Car workers	1:2	23
Iron, steel, and tin workers	1:2	22
Cloth hat and cap makers	1:1	22

* The vote was on three similar resolutions, the first of which stated "that this Convention condemn the Civic Federation, Citizens' Alliance, Chamber of Commerce, and all kindred bodies as hostile to the interests of organized labor and call upon all members of organized labor to sever their connection with such bodies." The vote was 11,851 votes accepting the Committee on Resolutions' report rejecting the resolutions, 4,924 against, with 465 abstaining. *Report of Proceedings of the Thirty-First Annual Convention of the American Federation of Labor* (Atlanta, 1911), p. 217.

1915: A Legislated Eight-Hour Day*

Union	Delegates in Favor: Total Delegates	Convention Votes
Mine workers	8:8	3116
Machinists	5:5	719
Brewery workmen	5:5	520
Molders	5:5	500
Railway car men	3:3	293
Plasterers	4:4	183
Stage employees	4:4	180
Metal workers	4:4	178
Miners, western federation	4:4	167
Bridge and structural iron workers	3:3	100
Metal polishers, buffers, platers, brass and silver workers	3:3	100
Cigarmakers	1:5	79
Barbers	1:5	68
Printing pressmen	1:4	56
Railway clerks	1:1	50
Quarry workers	1:1	36
Railway postal clerks	1:1	20
Stove mounters	1:1	11
Slate and tile roofers	1:1	6

* The vote was on a Committee of Resolutions' substitute for resolutions favoring a legislated eight-hour work day. The substitute ran as follows: "The American Federation of Labor, as in the past, again declares that the question of the regulation of wages and the hours of labor should be undertaken through trade-union activity, and not to be made subjects of laws through legislative enactment, excepting insofar as such regulations affect or govern the employment of women and minors, health and morals; and employment by federal, state or municipal government." The vote was 8,500 in favor, 6,396 against, with 4,061 abstaining. *Report of Proceedings of the Thirty-Fifth Annual Convention of the American Federation of Labor* (San Francisco, 1915), pp. 503-504.

BIBLIOGRAPHY

PRIMARY SOURCES

Abstracts of Labour Statistics: United Kingdom Census Reports, 1880–1928.

American Federation of Labor. *A Verbatim Report of the Discussion on the Political Programme at the Denver Convention of the American Federation of Labor, December 14, 15, 1894*. New York: The Freytag Press, 1895.

British Labour Struggles: Contemporary Pamphlets, 1727–1850. 32 vols. New York: Amo Press, 1972.

Commons, John R., Ulrich B. Phillips, Eugene A. Gilmore, Helen L. Sumner, and John B. Andrews. *A Documentary History of American Industrial Society*. 10 vols. Ohio, 1910.

Comparative Occupation Statistics for the United States, 1870–1940. Sixteenth Census of the United States.

Correspondenzblatt der Generalkommission der Gewerkschaften Deutschlands, 1892–1919.

Geschichte der deutschen Arbeiterbewegung. Vols. 1–3. Berlin: Dietz Verlag, 1966.

Hoffmann, W. G. *Das Wachstum der deutschen Wirtschaft seit der Mitte des 19.Jahrhunderts*. Berlin: Springer Verlag, 1915.

Labor Statistics Bureau: Handbook of Labor Statistics. Washington, D. C., 1972.

Minutes of Conference of the Miners' National Association: Glasgow, 1873; Newcastle-upon-Tyne, 1874; Saltburn, 1875; Manchester, 1878; Manchester, 1886; Manchester, 1887; Edinburgh, 1887.

Minutes of Conference of the Miners' National Union, Durham, 1891.

Mitchell, B. R., and P. Deane. *Abstract of British Historical Statistics*. Cambridge: Cambridge University Press, 1971.

Proceedings of the Annual Conference of the Miners' Federation of Great Britain: Birmingham, 1890; Birmingham, 1891; Stoke-on-Trent, 1892; Birmingham, 1893; Leicester, 1894; Birmingham, 1895; Leicester, 1897; Bristol, 1898; Edinburgh, 1899; Cardiff, 1899; Saltburn, 1900; Birmingham, 1901; Southport, 1902; Glasgow, 1903; Bristol, 1904; Blackpool, 1905; Swansea, 1906; Southport, 1907; Scarborough, 1913; Nottingham, 1915; Buxton, 1916; Glasgow, 1917; Southport, 1918.

Proceedings, National Convention of the Socialist Party: Chicago, 1904.

Proceedings of the Delegate Meeting of the Typographical Association, Manchester, 1881.

Protokoll der Generalversammlung des Verbändes der deutschen Buchdrucker: Dresden, 1905; Köln, 1908; Hannover, 1911; Danzig, 1913.

Report of Proceedings of the Annual Conference of the Trades Union Congress: Plymouth, 1899; Manchester, 1913.

Report of Proceedings of the Convention of the American Federation of Labor: Philadelphia, 1892; Chicago, 1893; Denver, 1894; New York, 1895; New Orleans, 1902; Atlanta, 1911; San Francisco, 1915.

Report of Proceedings of the Meeting of Delegates from the Provincial Typographical Association and Mileage Relief Association: Manchester, 1861; Manchester, 1872; Birmingham, 1877.

Report of the Annual Conference of the Labour Representation Committee: Manchester, 1901; Birmingham, 1902; Newcastle-on-Tyne, 1903.

Report of the Quinquennial Delegate Meeting of the Typographical Association: Liverpool, 1898; Birmingham, 1903; London, 1908; Northampton, 1913.

Reports of Proceedings of Conventions of the International Typographical Association: Atlanta, 1890; Boston, 1891; Philadephia, 1892; Chicago, 1893; Louisville, 1894; Colorado Springs, 1896; Syracuse, 1898; Detroit, 1899; Milwaukee, 1900; Birmingham, 1901; Cincinnati, 1902; Washington D.C., 1903; St. Louis, 1904; Toronto, 1905; Colorado Springs, 1906; Hot Springs, 1907; Boston, 1908; St. Joseph, 1909; Minneapolis, 1910; San Francisco, 1911; Cleveland, 1912.

U.S. Bureau of the Census. *Historical Statistics of the United States*. Washington, D.C.: Bureau of the Census, 1975.

——. *Immigrants and Their Children: 1920*. Census Monographs 7. Washington, D.C.: Department of Commerce, 1927.

——. "Comparative Occupation Statistics for the United States 1870 to 1940." *Sixteenth Census of the United States*. Washington, D.C.: U.S. Department of Commerce, 1943.

——. *Forty-Fourth Statistical Abstract of the United States*. Washington, D.C.: U.S. Department of Commerce, 1922.

SECONDARY SOURCES

Abraham, K. *Der Strukturwandel im Handwerk in der ersten Hälfte des 19. Jahrhunderts*. Köln: S.N., 1955.

Akin, William E. "Arbitration and Labor Conflict: The Middle Class Panacea, 1886–1900." *Historian* 29 (1966/1967).

Allen, G. C. *British Industries and Their Organization.* London: Longmans, 1970.

Allen, V. L. *The Sociology of Industrial Relations.* London: Longman, 1971.

————. *Trade Unions and the Government.* London: Longmans, 1960.

Aminzade, Ronald. "Capitalist Industrialization and Patterns of Industrial Protest: A Comparative Urban Study of Nineteenth-Century France." *American Sociological Review* 49 (August 1984).

Amsden, J., and S. Brier. "Coal Miners on Strike." *Journal of Interdisciplinary History* 7, no. 4 (1977).

Anderson, J. E. *Politics and the Economy.* Boston: Little, Brown, 1966.

Arnot, Robert P. *A History of the Scottish Miners.* London: Allen & Unwin, 1955.

————. *The Miners: A History of the Miners' Federation of Great Britain, 1889–1919.* London: Allen & Unwin, 1949.

————. *South Wales Miners: A History of the South Wales Miners' Federation, 1898–1914.* London: Allen & Unwin, 1967.

Asher, Robert. "Union Nativism and Immigrant Response." *Labor History* 23, no. 3 (1982).

Ashley, W. J. *The Adjustment of Wages: A Study of the Coal and Iron Industries of Great Britain and America.* London: Longmans, Green & Company, 1903.

Ashton, T. S. *An Economic History of England: The Eighteenth Century.* London: Methuen, 1966.

Aurand, Harold W. *From the Molly Maguires to the United Mine Workers of America.* Philadelphia: Temple University Press, 1971.

————. "The Workingmen's Benevolent Association." *Labor History* 7 (1966).

Avis, F. C. *The Early Printers' Chapel in England.* London: Avis, 1971.

Bain, George Sayers, and F. Elsheikh. *Union Growth and the Business Cycle.* Oxford: Basil Blackwell, 1976.

Bain, George Sayers, and Robert Price. *Profiles of Union Growth.* Oxford: Basil Blackwell, 1980.

Baker, Elizabeth F. *Printers and Technology.* New York: Columbia University Press, 1957.

Balser, Frolinda. *Sozial-Democratie 1848/49–1863: Die erste deutsche Arbeiterorganisation "Allgemeine Arbeiterverbrüderung" nach der Revolution.* Stuttgart: E. Klett, 1962.

Barendse, Michael A. *Social Expectations and Perception: The Case of*

the Slavic Anthracite Workers. University Park: Pennsylvania
State University Press, 1981.

Barnett, George E. "Collective Bargaining in the Typographical
Union." In Jacob H. Hollander and George E. Barnett, eds.,
Studies in American Trade Unionism, pp. 167–181. New York:
H. Holt & Company, 1905.

——. *Machinery and Labor.* Cambridge, Mass.: Harvard University
Press, 1926.

——. "The Printers: A Study in Trade Unionism." *American Economic Association Quarterly*, 1909.

Baudis, Dieter, and Helga Nussbaum. *Wirtschaft und Staat in
Deutschland am Ende des 19.Jahrhunderts bis 1918/19.* Berlin/
DDR: Topos, 1978.

Beer, Samuel H. *British Politics in the Collectivist Age.* New York: Vintage Books, 1969.

——. *Modern British Politics.* New York: Norton, 1982.

Beier, Gerhard. *Schwarze Kunst und Klassenkampf.* Vol. 1. Frankfurt
am Main: Europaische Verlaganstalt, 1966.

Bell, Daniel. *Marxian Socialism in the United States.* Princeton, N.J.:
Princeton University Press, 1967.

Bendix, Reinhard. *Nation Building and Citizenship.* Berkeley: University of California Press, 1969.

Benson, John. *British Coalminers in the Nineteenth Century: A Social
History.* New York: Holmes and Meier, 1980.

——. "Coalmining." In Cris Wrigley, ed., *A History of British Industrial Relations, 1875–1914.* Sussex: Harvester Press, 1982.

Bergman, J. *Das Berliner Handwerk in den Frühphasen der Industrialisierung.* Berlin: Colloquium Verlag, 1973.

Berman, Edward. *Labor Disputes and the President of the United States.*
New York: Columbia University Press, 1924.

Bernstein, Eduard, ed. *Dokumente des Sozialismus.* Vol. 1. Berlin: Sozialistische Monatshefte, 1902.

Bernstein, Leonard. "The Working People of Philadelphia from
Colonial Times to the General Strike of 1835." *Pennsylvania
Magazine of History and Biography.* 94 (1950).

Berthoff, Rowland T. "The Social Order of the Anthracite Region,
1825–1902." *Pennsylvania Magazine of History and Biography* 89
(July 1965).

Beyer, F. C. *Die volkswirtschaftliche und sozialpolitische Bedeutung der
Einführung der Setzmaschine im Buchdruckgewerbe.* Karlsruhe:
B.G. Braun, 1910.

Blank, Steven. *Industry and Government in Britain: The Federation of British Industries in Politics, 1945–1965.* Lexington: Lexington Books, 1973.

Bonnell, Victoria E. "Radical Politics and Organized Labor in Pre-Revolutionary Moscow, 1905–1914." *Journal of Social History* 12 (Winter 1978).

Born, Karl. "Der soziale und wirtschaftliche Strukturwandel am Ende des 19.Jahrhunderts." *Vierteljahrschrift für Sozial– und Wirtschaftsgeschichte* 50 (1963).

———. *Staat und Sozialpolitik seit Bismarcks Sturtz, 1890–1914.* Weisbaden: F. Steiner, 1957.

———. *Von der Reichsgründung bis zum Ersten Weltkrieg.* Stuttgart: Deutscher Taschenbuch Verlag, 1970.

Boulding, Kenneth. *The Organizational Revolution.* New York: Harper, 1962.

Brentano, Lujo. "Entwicklung and Geist der Englischen Arbeiterorganisationen." *Archiv für Sozialwissenschaft und Sozialpolitik* 8 (1895).

Brepohl, W. *Industrievolk im Wandel von der agraren zur industriellen Daseinsform dargestellt am Ruhrgebiet.* Tübingen: Mohr, 1957.

Bridges, Amy. *A City in the Republic: Antebellum New York and the Origins of Machine Politics.* Cambridge: Cambridge University Press, 1984.

Briggs, Asa, and John Saville, eds. *Essays in Labour History, 1886–1923.* London: Macmillan, 1971.

Brody, David. "On the Failure of U.S. Radical Politics: A Farmer-Labor Analysis." *Industrial Relations and Labor Review* 22, no. 2 (Spring 1983).

———. *Workers in Industrial America.* New York: Oxford University Press, 1980.

Brown, Keith, D. *Labour and Unemployment, 1900–1914.* (Newton Abbot: David and Charles, 1971).

Bruce, M. *The Coming of the Welfare State.* London: Batsford, 1968.

Bry, Gerhard. *Wages in Germany, 1971–1945.* Princeton, N.J.: Princeton University Press, 1960.

Bryant, K. L., Jr. "Labor in Politics: The Oklahoma State Federation of Labor during the Age of Reform." *Labor History* 11 (1970).

Burgess, Keith. *The Challenge of Labour: Shaping British Society, 1850–1930.* New York: St. Martin's Press, 1980.

———. *The Origins of British Industrial Relations.* London: Croom Helm, 1975.

Burnham, Walter Dean. "The United States." In Richard Rose, ed., *Electoral Behavior: A Comparative Handbook.* New York: Free Press, 1974.

Burns, James MacGregor. *The Deadlock of Democracy.* London: Calder and Boyar, 1965.

Burt, Thomas. *An Autobiography.* London: Fisher Unwin, 1924.

Bythell, Duncan. *The Handloom Weavers.* Cambridge: Cambridge University Press, 1969.

Calhoun, Craig. "Community: Toward a Variable Conceptualization for Comparative Research." *Social History* 5, no. 1 (1980).

——. *The Question of Class Struggle.* Chicago: University of Chicago Press, 1982.

——. "The Radicalism of Tradition: Community Strength or Venerable Disguise and Borrowed Language." *American Journal of Sociology* 88, no. 5 (March 1983).

Cannon, I. C. "Ideology and Occupational Community: A Study of Compositors." *Sociology* 1, no. 2 (1967).

Carroll, M. R. *Labor and Politics.* Boston: Houghton Mifflin, 1923.

Cassau, Theodore. *Die Gewerkschaftsbewegung, Ihre Soziologie und Ihr Kampf.* Berlin, 1920.

Challinor, Raymond. *The Lancashire and Cheshire Miners.* Newcastle-on-Tyne: Graham, 1972.

——, and Brian Ripley. *The Miners' Association: A Trade Union in the Age of the Chartists.* London: Lawrence & Wishart, 1968.

Chamberlain, Neil W., and J. W. Kuhn. *Collective Bargaining.* 2d ed. New York: McGraw-Hill, 1965.

Chandler, Alfred D. *The Visible Hand: The Managerial Revolution in American Business.* Cambridge, Mass.: Belknap Press, 1977.

Checkland, S. G. *The Rise of Industrial Society, 1815–1885.* London: Longmans, 1964.

Child, John. *Industrial Relations in the British Printing Industry.* London: Allen & Unwin, 1967.

Church, R. *Economic and Social Change in a Midland Town.* London: A. M. Kelley, 1966.

Clapham, J.H.A. *An Economic History of Modern Britain.* Vol. 3. Cambridge: Cambridge University Press, 1938.

Clegg, Hugh. *The System of Industrial Relations in Britain.* Oxford: Rowman and Littlefield, 1972.

——, Alan Fox, and A. F. Thompson. *A History of British Trade Unions since 1889.* Vol. 1. Oxford: Clarendon Press, 1964.

Cochran, T. C., and W. Miller. *The Age of Enterprise.* New York: Harper, 1961.

Cohen, S. *Labor in the United States.* 3d ed. Columbus, Ohio: C.E. Merrill Publishing Company, 1970.

Coldrick, A. P., and Philip Jones. *The International Directory of the Trade Union Movement.* New York: Facts on File, 1979.

Cole, G.D.H. *Attempts at General Union, 1818–1834.* London: Allen & Unwin, 1953.

———. "Some Notes on British Trade Unionism in the Third Quarter of the Nineteenth Century." *International Review for Social History* 2 (1937).

———. *The History of Labor in the United States.* Vols. 1–3. New York: Macmillan Company, 1926.

Commons, John R. "Labor and Municipal Politics." In John R. Commons, *Labor and Administration.* New York: Macmillan, 1913.

Costas, Ilse. *Auswirkungen der Konzentration des Kapitals auf die Arbeiterklasse in Deutschland, 1880–1914.* Frankfurt: Campus Verlag, 1981.

Court, W.H.B. *A Concise Economic History of Britain.* Cambridge: Cambridge University Press, 1967.

Crew, David. *Town in the Ruhr: A Social History of Bochum, 1860–1914.* New York: Columbia University Press, 1979.

Cronin, James E. "Labor Insurgency and Class Formation: Comparative Perspectives on the Crisis of 1917–1920 in Europe." In James E. Cronin and Carmen Siriani, eds., *Work, Community, and Power: The Experience of Labor in Europe and America, 1900–1925.* Philadelphia: Temple University Press, 1983.

———. *Labour and Society in Britain, 1918–1979.* London: Batsford, 1984.

———. "Strikes and the Struggle for Union Organization: Britain and Europe." In Wolfgang J. Mommsen and Hans-Gerhard Husung, eds., *The Development of Trade Unionism in Great Britain and Germany, 1880–1914.* London: George Allen & Unwin, 1985.

———. "Strikes 1870–1914." In Chris Wrigley, ed., *A History of British Industrial Relations, 1875–1914.* Amherst: University of Massachusetts Press, 1982.

Cumbler, John T. *Working-Class Community in Industrial America.* Westport, Conn.: Greenwood Press, 1979.

Dahrendorf, Ralf. *Society and Democracy in Germany.* New York: Anchor books, 1969.

Dataller, Roger. *From a Pitman's Note Book.* London: Jonathan Cape, 1924.

Davidson, Roger. *Whitehall and the Labour Problem in Late-Victorian and Edwardian Britain.* London: Croom Helm, 1985.

Davis, Mike. "Why the U.S. Working Class is Different." *New Left Review* 123 (1980).

Dawson, Andrew. "The Parameters of Craft Consciousness: The Social Outlook of the Skilled Worker, 1890–1920." In Dirk Hoerder, ed., *American Labor and Immigrant History, 1877–1920.* Urbana, Ill.: Univeristy of Illinois Press, 1983.

Debs, Eugene V. *Writings and Speeches of Eugene V. Debs.* New York: Hermitage Press, 1948.

Deckers, H. *Betrieblicher oder Überbetrieblicher Tarifvertrag.* Münster: Aschendorffsche Verlagsbuchhandlung, 1960.

Deppe, Frank, Georg Fülberth, and Jürgen Harrer, eds. *Geschichte der deutschen Gewerkschaftsbewegung.* Köln: Pahl Rugenstein, 1977.

Deutscher, Isaac. "Russia." In Walter Galenson, *Comparative Labor Movements.* New York: Prentice Hall, 1952.

Dick, William M. *Labor and Socialism in America: The Gompers Era.* Port Washington, N.Y.: Kennikat Press, 1972.

Dobb, Maurice. *Studies in the Development of Capitalism.* New York: International Publishers, 1947.

Dubofsky, Melvyn. "Abortive Reform: The Wilson Administration and Organized Labor, 1913–1920." In James E. Cronin and Carmen Sirianni, eds., *Work, Community, and Power: The Experience of Labor in Europe and America, 1900–1925.* Philadelphia: Temple University Press, 1983.

———. *We Shall Be All: A History of the Industrial Workers of the World.* Chicago: Quadrangle Books, 1969.

Dückershoff, E. *How the English Workman Lives.* London: P.S. King, 1899.

Durkheim, Emile. *The Division of Labor in Society.* New York: Macmillan, 1933.

———. *Suicide: A Study in Sociology.* Glencoe, Ill.: Free Press, 1951.

Eckstein, Harry. "Case Study and Theory in Political Science." In Fred I. Greenstein and Nelson W. Polsby, eds., *Handbook of Political Science,* vol. 7. Reading: Addison-Wesley, 1975.

Edwards, N. *The Industrial Revolution in South Wales*. London: The Labour Publishing Company, 1924.

Eickhof, Norbert. *Eine Theorie der Gewerkschaftsentwicklung*. Tübingen: J.C.B. Mohr, 1973.

Emy, H. V. *Liberals, Radicals, and Social Politics, 1892–1914*. Cambridge: Cambridge University Press, 1973.

Engelhardt, Ulrich. "Gewerkschaftliches Organisationsverhalten in der ersten Industrialisierungsphase." In Werner Conze and Ulrich Engelhardt, eds., *Arbeiter im Industrialisierungsprozess: Herkunft, Lage und Verhalten*. Stuttgart: Klett-Cotta, 1979.

———. *"Nur Vereinigt sind wir stark": Die Anfänge der deutschen Gewerkschaftsbewegung, 1862/3 bis 1869/70*. Stuttgart: Klett-Cotta, 1977.

Engels, Friedrich. *The Condition of the Working-Class in England in 1844*. London: Allen & Unwin, 1892.

Evans, Chris. *History of the United Mine Workers of America*. Vol. 1. Indianapolis: Hollenbeck Company, 1920.

Everling, A. C. "Tactics over Strategy in the United Mine Workers of America: Internal Politics and the Question of the Nationalization of the Mines, 1908–1923." Ph.D. dissertation, Pennsylvania State University, 1976.

Faulkner, Harold U. *American Economic History*. New York: Harper, 1960.

———. *The Decline of Laissez-Faire, 1897–1917*. New York: Rinehart, 1951.

Feldman, Gerald D. *Army, Industry, and Labor in Germany, 1914–1918*. Princeton, N.J.: Princeton University Press, 1966.

Fink, Gary M. "The Rejection of Voluntarism." *Industrial and Labor Relations Review* 26 (1972/1973).

Fink, Leon. *Workingmen's Democracy*. Urbana: University of Illinois Press, 1983.

Fischer, Wolfram. "Bergbau, Industrie und Handwerk, 1850–1914." In H. Aubin and W. Zorn, eds., *Handbuch der deutschen Wirtschafts und Sozialgeschichte*, 2: 532–533. Stuttgart: Ernst Klett, 1976.

———. "Das Handwerk in den Frühphasen der Industrialisierung." In his *Wirtschaft und Gesellschaft im Zeitalter der Industrialisierung*. Göttingen: Vandenhöck & Ruprecht, 1972.

———. "Innerbetrieblicher and sozialer Status der frühen Fabrikarbeiterschaft." In W. Fischer and G. Bajor, eds., *Die Soziale Frage*. Stuttgart: Köhler, 1967.

Flanders, Allan. *Trade Unions.* London: Hutchinson, 1968.

——, and Alan Fox. "Collective Bargaining: From Donovan to Durkheim." In Allan Flanders, *Management and Unions.* London: Faber, 1970.

Flora, Peter, and Arnold J. Heidenheimer. *The Development of Welfare States in Europe and America.* New Brunswick, N.J.: Transaction Books, 1981.

Foner, Philip. *History of the Labor Movement in the United States.* Vols. 1–6. 2d ed. New York: International Publishers, 1975.

Förster, Alfred. *Die Gewerkschaftspolitik der deutschen Sozialdemokratie während des Sozialistengesetzes.* Berlin/DDR: Verlag Tribune, 1971.

Foth, J. H. *Trade Associations.* New York: The Ronald Press Company, 1930.

Fraser, W. Hamish. *Trade Unions and Society: The Struggle for Acceptance, 1850–1880.* London: Allen & Unwin, 1974.

Fricke, Dieter. *Die deutsche Arbeiterbewegung, 1869–1914.* Berlin: Dietz Verlag, 1976.

Friedman, Alan L. *Industry and Labor.* London: Macmillan, 1977.

Friedman, Gerald. "Politics and Unions." Ph.D. dissertation, Harvard University, 1986.

Gable, R. W. "Birth of an Employers' Association." *Business History Review* 33, no. 4 (1959).

Galenson, Walter. *The Danish System of Labor Relations.* Cambridge, Mass.: Harvard University Press, 1952.

——. *Labor in Norway.* Cambridge, Mass.: Harvard University Press, 1949.

Geary, Dick. *European Labour Protest, 1848–1939.* London: Croom Helm, 1981.

George, Alexander L. "Case Studies and Theory Development: The Method of Structured, Focussed Comparison." In Paul G. Lauren, ed., *Diplomatic History: New Approaches.* New York: Free Press, 1979.

George, M. D. "The Combination Laws." *Economic History Review* 6 (1935/1936).

——. "The Combination Laws Reconsidered." *Economic Journal* 1 (1926/1929).

Gerstenberg, A. *Die neuere Entwicklung des deutschen Buchdruckgewerbes.* Jena: G. Fischer, 1892.

Gillespie, S. *A Hundred Years of Progress: The Record of the Scottish*

Typographical Association, 1853 to 1952. Glasgow: R. Maclehose, 1953.

Gladen, Albin. *Geschichte der Sozialpolitik in Deutschland.* Weisbaden: F. Steiner, 1974.

Goldstein, Robert J. *Political Repression in Nineteenth-Century Europe.* London: Croom Helm, 1983.

Golembiewski, R. T. "Small Groups and Large Organizations." In James G. March, ed., *Handbook of Organizations.* Chicago: University of Chicago Press, 1965.

Gollan, Robin. "Nationalism, the Labour Movement and the Commonwealth, 1880–1900." In Gordon Greenwood, ed., *Australia: A Social and Political History.* Sydney: Angus and Robertson, 1974.

——. *Radical and Working-Class Politics: A Study of Eastern Australia, 1850–1910.* Melbourne: Melbourne University Press, 1960.

Gompers, Samuel. *Seventy Years of Life and Labor.* New York: E.P. Dutton, 1925.

——, and Herman Gutstadt. *Meat vs. Rice: American Manhood against Asiatic Coolieism: Which Shall Survive?* San Francisco: American Federation of Labor, 1902.

Gospel, Howard F., and Craig R. Littler, eds. *Managerial Strategies and Industrial Relations.* London: Heinemann Books, 1983.

Gottlieb, Amy Zahl. "The Influence of British Trade Unionists on the Regulations of the Mining Industry in Illinois, 1872." *Labor History.* 19 (1978).

Gowaskie, Joseph M. "From Conflict to Cooperation: John Mitchell and Bitumous Coal Operators, 1898–1908." *Historian* 38 (1976).

Graebner, William. "Great Expectations: The Search for Order in Bitumous Coal, 1890–1917." *Business History Review* 48 (1974).

Green, James R. *The World of the Worker.* New York: Hill and Wang, 1980.

Green, Marguerite. *The National Civic Federation and the American Labor Movement, 1900–1925.* Washington, D.C.: Catholic University of America Press, 1956.

Gregory, C. "Government Regulation or Control of Union Activities." In W. Haber, ed., *Labor in a Changing America.* New York: Basic Books, 1966.

Gregory, Roy. *The Miners and British Politics: 1906–1914.* Oxford: Oxford University Press, 1968.

Griep, Gerhard. *Zur Geschichte der deutschen Gewerkschaftsbewegung, 1890–1914.* Berlin: Tribune, 1960.

Groh, Dieter. "Intensification of Work and Industrial Conflict in Germany, 1896–1914." *Politics and Society* 8, nos. 3–4 (1978).

Gulick, Charles A. *Austria from Habsburg to Hitler*, vol. 1, *Labor's Workshop of Democracy.* Berkeley: University of California Press, 1948.

Gusfield, Joseph. *Community: A Critical Response.* New York: Harper, 1975.

Gutman, Herbert. *Work, Culture, and Society in Industrializing America.* New York: Vintage Books, 1977.

Guttsman, W. L. *The German Social Democratic Party, 1875–1933.* London: Allen & Unwin, 1981.

Hamerow, Theodore S. *Restoration, Revolution, Reaction: Economics and Politics in Germany, 1815–1871.* Princeton, N.J.: Princeton University Press, 1958.

Hammond, J. L., and B. Hammond. *The Town Labourer.* London: Longmans, Green, 1925.

Hanagan, Michael P. *The Logic of Solidarity: Artisans and Industrial Workers in Three French Towns, 1871–1914.* Urbana: University of Illinois Press, 1980.

———, and Charles Stephenson. "The Skilled Worker and Working-Class Protest." *Social Science History* 4, no. 1 (February 1980).

Hannah, Leslie. *The Rise of the Corporate Economy.* Baltimore: The Johns Hopkins University Press, 1976.

Harpham, Edward J. "Federalism, Keynesianism, and the Transformation of the Unemployment Insurance System in the United States." In Douglas E. Ashford and E. W. Kelley, eds., *Nationalizing Social Security in Europe and America.* Greenwich: JAI Press, 1986.

Harrington, Michael. *Socialism.* New York: Saturday Review Press, 1972.

Hartz, Louis. *The Liberal Tradition in America.* New York: Harcourt, Brace, 1955.

Harvey, Katherine A. "The Knights of Labor in the Maryland Coal Fields." *Labor History* 10 (1969).

Haumann, Hieko, ed. *Arbeiteralltag in Stadt und Land: Neue Wege der Geschichtsschreibung.* Berlin: Argument Verlag, 1982.

Hay, J. R. *The Origins of the Liberal Welfare Reforms, 1906–1914.* London: Macmillan, 1975.

Heclo, Hugh. *Modern Social Politics in Britain and Sweden.* New Haven, Conn.: Yale University Press, 1974.

Heinrich Kaufhold, Karl. "Handwerk und Industrie, 1800–1850." In Hermann Aubin and Wolfgang Zorn, eds., *Handbuch der deutschen Wirtschafts– und Sozialgeschichte.* Vol. 2. Stuttgart: Klett-Cotta, 1976.

Helfland, Barry F. "Labor and the Courts: The Common-Law Doctrine of Criminal Conspiracy and Its Application in the Buck's Stove Case." *Labor History* 18 (1977).

Henderson, W. O. *The Rise of German Industrial Power, 1834–1914.* London: Temple Smith, 1975.

Hickey, Stephen. "The Shaping of the German Labour Movement: Miners in the Ruhr." In Richard J. Evans, ed., *Society and Politics in Wilhelmine Germany.* London: Croom Helm, 1978.

———. *Workers in Imperial Germany: The Miners of the Ruhr.* Oxford: Clarendon Press, 1985.

Hilbert, F. W. "Employers' Associations in the United States." In Jacob B. Hollander and George Barnett, *Studies in American Unionism.* New York: Holt & Company, 1905.

Hilferding, Rudolf. *Das Finanzkapital.* 1910. Reprint ed., Berlin: Dietz, 1955.

Hillquit, Morris. *History of Socialism in the United States.* New York: Funk and Wagnalls, 1910.

———, Samuel Gompers, and Max Hayes. *The Double Edge of Labor's Sword.* New York: Arno, 1971.

Hinton, James. *The First Shop Stewards' Movement.* London: Allen & Unwin, 1973.

———. *Labour and Socialism: A History of the British Labour Movement, 1867–1974.* Amherst: University of Massachusetts Press, 1983.

———. "The Rise of a Mass Labour Movement: Growth and Limits." In Chris Wrigley, ed., *A History of British Industrial Relations, 1875–1914.* Amherst: University of Massachusetts Press, 1982.

Hirsch, Susan E. *Roots of the American Working Class: Industrialization of Crafts in Newark, 1800–1860.* Philadelphia: University of Pennsylvania Press, 1978.

Hirsch-Weber, Wolfgang. *Gewerkschaften in der Politik.* Köln: Westdeutscher Verlag, 1959.

Hobsbawm, Eric J. *Industry and Empire.* London: Weidenfeld and Nicolson, 1968.

———. *Labouring Men.* London: Weidenfeld & Nicolson, 1964.

———, and Joan W. Scott. "Political Shoemakers." In E. J. Hobsbawm, *Worlds of Labour*. London: Weidenfeld and Nicolson, 1984.

Hoffman, W. G. *Das Wachstum der deutschen Wirtschaft seit der Mitte des 19.Jahrhunderts*. Berlin: Springer Verlag, 1915.

Holbrook-Jones, Mike. *Supremacy and Subordination of Labour*. London: Heinemann, 1982.

Holton, Robert J. *British Syndicalism, 1900–1914*. London: Pluto Press, 1976.

Howe, Eric. *The British Federation of Master Printers, 1900–1950*. London: British Federation of Master Printers, 1950.

———, and H. E. Waite. *The London Society of Compositors*. London: Cassell, 1948.

Howell, David. *British Workers and the Independent Labour Party, 1888–1906*. Manchester: Manchester University Press, 1983.

Hue, Otto. *Die Bergarbeiter*. Vol. 2. Stuttgart: J.H.W. Dietz, 1913.

Hughes, J.R.T. *The Governmental Habit: Economic Controls from Colonial Times to the Present*. New York: Basic Books, 1977.

Hurwitz, S. J. *State Intervention in Britain: A Study of Economic Control and Social Response*. New York: Columbia University Press, 1949.

Imbusch, Heinrich. *Arbeitsverhältnis und Arbeiterorganisationen im deutschen Bergbau*. Berlin: Verlag des Gewerkvereins christlicher Bergarbeiter, 1908.

Industrial Trade Associations: Activities and Organization, Political and Economic Planning. London, 1957.

International Typographical Union. *A Study of the History of the International Typographical Union, 1852–1963*. Colorado Springs: Executive Council, ITU, 1964.

Jackson, Robert Max. *The Formation of Craft Labor Markets*. Orlando: Academic Press, 1984.

Janke, Carl. *Der Vierte Stand*. Freiberg: Herder, 1955.

Jevons, H. S. *The British Coal Trade*. London: Kegan Paul, 1915.

Johnson, Chalmers. *Revolutionary Change*. Boston: Little, Brown, 1966.

Jones, E. *The Anthracite Coal Combination in the United States*. Cambridge, Mass.: Harvard University Press, 1914.

Karson, Marc. *American Labor Unions and Politics, 1900–1918*. Carbondale: Southern Illinois University Press, 1958.

Karwell, H. "Die Entwicklung und Reform des deutschen Knappschaftswesens." Inaugural-dissertation, Universität Jena, 1907.

Katznelson, Ira. *City Trenches: Urban Politics and the Patterning of Class in the United States.* New York: Pantheon Books, 1981.

———. "Considerations on Social Democracy in the United States." *Comparative Politics* 11, no. 1 (October 1978).

———, and Aristide R. Zolberg, eds. *Working-Class Formation: Nineteenth-Century Patterns in Western Europe and the United States.* Princeton, N.J.: Princeton University Press, 1986.

Kaufhold, Karl Heinrich. "Handwerk und Industrie, 1800–1850." In Hermann Aubin and Wolfgang Zorn, eds., *Handbuch der deutschen Wirtschafts- und Sozialgeschichte.* Vol. 2. Stuttgart: Klett-Cotta, 1976.

Kelber, H., and C. Schlesinger. *Union Printers and Controlled Automation.* New York: Free Press, 1967.

Kerr, Clark, John Dunlop, Frederick Harbison, and Charles Myers. *Industrialism and Industrial Man.* Cambridge, Mass.: Harvard University Press, 1960.

Kerr, Clark, and Abraham Siegel. "The Inter-Industry Propensity to Strike." In A. Kornhauser, R. Dubin, and A. Ross, eds., *Industrial Conflict.* New York: McGraw-Hill, 1954.

Kipnis, Ira. *The American Socialist Movement, 1897–1912.* New York: Columbia University Press, 1952.

Klein, Fritz. *Deutschland von 1897/98 bis 1917.* Berlin: Pahl-Rugenstein, 1977.

Klessmann, Christoph. *Polnische Bergarbeiter im Ruhrgebiet, 1870–1945.* Göttingen: Vandenhöck und Ruprecht, 1978.

Kloth, Emil. "Graphische Gewerbe." In F. Thinne and K. Legien, eds., *Die Arbeiterschaft im Neuen Deutschland.* Leipzig: S. Hirzel, 1915.

Knowles, K. G. *A Study in Industrial Conflict.* Oxford: B. Blackwell, 1932.

Koch, Max Jürgen. *Die Bergarbeiterbewegung im Ruhrgebiet zur Zeit Wilhelm II, 1889–1914.* Düsseldorf: Drost-Verlag, 1954.

Kocka, Jürgen. "Problems of Working-Class Formation in Germany: The Early Years, 1800–1875." In Ira Katznelson and Aristide R. Zolberg, eds., *Working-Class Formation: Nineteenth-Century Patterns in Western Europe and the United States.* Princeton, N.J.: Princeton University Press, 1986.

Köllmann, Wolfgang. "Vom Knappen zum Bergarbeiter: Die Entstehung der Bergarbeiterschaft an der Ruhr." In W. Först, *Ruhrgebiet und neues Land.* Köln: Grote, 1968.

Kornhauser, William. *The Politics of Mass Society.* New York: Free Press, 1959.

Krahl, Willi. *Der Verband der Deutschen Buchdrucker.* Vol. 1. Berlin, 1916.

————, and Klaus Hemholz. *Der Verband der Deutschen Buchdrucker, 1866–1924.* Leipzig: Verband der Deutschen Buchdrucker, 1924.

Krampe, Hans-Dieter. *Der Staatseinfluss auf den Ruhrkohlenbergbau in der Zeit von 1800 bis 1865.* Köln: Rheinish-westfalisches Wirtschaftsarchiv, 1961.

Kuczynski, Jürgen. "Einleitung: Die wirtschaftlichen und sozialen Voraussetzungen der Revolution 1848/49." In Elisabeth Todt and Hans Radant, *Zur Frühgeschichte der Deutschen Gewerkschaftsbewegung, 1800–1849.* Berlin/DDR: Die Freie Gewerkschaft, 1950.

————. *Die Geschichte der Lage der Arbeiter unter dem Kapitalismus.* Vols. 1–5. Berlin/DDR: Akademie-Verlag, 1961.

————. *Zur Frühgeschichte des deutschen Monopolkapitals und des staatsmonopolistischen Kapitalismus.* Berlin/DDR: Akademie-Verlag, 1962.

Kynaston, David. *King Labor: The British Working Class, 1850–1914.* London: Allen & Unwin, 1976.

Lane, A. T. "American Trade Unions, Mass Immigration and the Literacy Test: 1900–1917." *Labor History* 25, no. 1 (Winter 1984).

Lange, Peter, George Ross, and Maurizio Vannicelli. *Unions, Change and Crisis.* London: George Allen & Unwin, 1982.

Langerhans, H. "Richtungsgewerkschaft and gewerkschaftliche Autonomie, 1890–1914." *International Review of Social History* 2 (1957).

Laslett, John H. M. *Labor and the Left.* New York: Basic Books, 1970.

————, and Seymour Martin Lipset, eds. *Failure of a Dream? Essays in the History of American Socialism.* New York: Anchor Press, 1974.

Leckebusch, Rudolf. *Entstehung und Wandlungen der Zielsetzungen, der Struktur und der Wirkungen von Arbeitgeberverbänden.* Berlin: Duncker und Humbolt, 1966.

Lederer, Emil. *Die Wirtschaftliche Organization.* Leipzig: B.G. Teubner, 1913.

Lenin, V. I. *On Britain.* Moscow: Foreign Languages Publishing House, V.I., n.d.

———. *Werke.* 5th ed. Vol. 35. Moskow: Marx-Lenin Institute, 1969.

———. *What Is To Be Done?* Peking: Foreign Languages Press, 1973.

Lidtke, Vernon L. *The Alternative Culture: Socialist Labor in Imperial Germany.* New York: Oxford University Press, 1985.

———. *The Outlawed Party: Social Democracy in Germany, 1878–1890.* Princeton, N.J.: Princeton University Press, 1966.

Liebman, Robert. "Repressive Strategies and Working-Class Protest." *Social Science History* 4, no. 1 (February 1980).

Lignau, J. *Das System sozialer Hilfeleistungen.* Köln, 1965.

Lijphart, Arendt. "Comparative Politics and the Comparative Method." *American Political Science Review* 65, no. 3 (1971).

Lipset, Seymour Martin. *The First New Nation.* New York: Basic Books, 1963.

———. "Radicalism or Reformism: The Sources of Working-Class Politics." *American Political Science Review* 77, no. 1 (March 1983).

———. "Socialism in America." In Paul Kurtz, ed., *Sidney Hook: Philosopher of Democracy and Humanism.* Buffalo, N.Y.: Prometheus Books, 1983.

———. "Why No Socialism in the United States?" In Seweryn Bialer and Sophia Sluzar, eds., *Sources of Contemporary Radicalism.* Boulder, Colo.: Westview Press, 1977.

———, Martin A. Trow, and James S. Coleman. *Union Democracy: The Internal Politics of the International Typographical Union.* New York: Anchor Books, 1956.

Livesay, Harold C. *Samuel Gompers and Organized Labor in America.* Boston: Little, Brown, 1978.

Loft, Jacob. *The Printing Trades.* New York: Ferrar & Rinehart, 1944.

Long, Clarence D. *Wages and Earnings in the United States, 1860–1890.* Princeton, N.J.: Princeton University Press, 1960.

Lorwin, Lewis L. *The American Federation of Labor: History, Policies, and Prospects.* Washington, D.C.: The Brookings Institution, 1933.

Lösche, Peter. "Stages in the Evolution of the German Labor Movement." In A. Sturmthal and J. G. Scoville, eds., *The International Labor Movement in Transition: Essays on Asia, Europe, and South America,* p. 109. Urbana, Ill.: University of Illinois Press, 1973.

Lovell, John. *British Trade Unions, 1875–1933.* London: Macmillan, 1977.

Lovell, John, and B. C. Roberts. *A Short History of the T.U.C.* London: Macmillan, 1968.

Lowe, R. "The Erosion of State Intervention in Britain, 1917–1924." *Economic History Review*, 2d. series, vol. 31, no. 2 (1978).

Lowi, Theodore J. "Why Is There No Socialism in the United States?" *Social Science and Modern Society* 22, no. 2 (January/February 1985).

Lüdtke, Alf. "The Role of State Violence in the Period of Transition to Industrial Capitalism: The Example of Prussia from 1815 to 1848." *Social History* 4 (May 1979).

Lynch, James M. *Epochal History of the International Typographical Union.* Indianapolis: ITU, 1924.

McCarthy, W.E.J. *The Closed Shop in Britain.* Berkeley: University of California Press, 1964.

McCormick, B. J. *Industrial Relations in the Coal Industry.* London: Macmillan, 1979.

Macdonald, D. E. *The State and the Trade Unions.* London: Macmillan, 1976.

McKibbin, Ross. *The Evolution of the Labour Party.* Oxford: Oxford University Press, 1974.

Maehl, William H., Jr. "The Northeastern Miners' Struggle for the Franchise, 1872–74." *International Review of Social History* 20 (1975).

Marks, Gary. "Neocorporatism and Incomes Policy in Western Europe and North America, 1950–1980." *Comparative Politics* 17 (April 1986).

Martin, Ross M. *T.U.C.: The Growth of a Pressure Group, 1868–1976.* Oxford: Clarendon Press, 1980.

Marwick, Arthur. *Britain in the Century of Total War.* Boston: Little, Brown, 1968.

Marx, Karl, and Friedrich Engels. *Letters to Americans.* New York: International Publishers, 1953.

Mather, F. C. *Public Order in the Age of the Chartists.* Manchester: Manchester University Press, 1959.

May, Timothy. *Trade Unions and Pressure Group Politics.* London: Westmead, 1975.

Mehring, Franz. *Geschichte der deutschen Sozialdemokratie.* Vol. 2. Berlin/DDR: Dietz Verlag, 1976.

Meyer, Evelies. *Theorien zum Funktionswandel der Gewerkschaften.* Frankfurt am Main: Europäische Verlaganstalt, 1973.

Michels, Robert. "Die deutsche Sozialdemokratie." *Archiv für Sozialwissenschaft und Sozialpolitik* 23 (1906).

Middlemas, Keith. *Politics in Industrial Society.* London: Andre Deutsch, 1969.

Miliband, Ralph. *Parliamentary Socialism.* London: Merlin Press, 1973.

———. *Politics in Industrial Society.* London: Andre Deutsch, 1979.

Milward, A. S. *The Economic Effects of the Two World Wars on Britain.* London: Macmillan, 1970.

Mink, Gwendolyn. *Old Labor and New Immigrants in American Political Development.* Ithaca: Cornell University Press, 1986.

Mitchell, B. R., and P. Deane. *Abstract of British Historical Statistics.* Cambridge: Cambridge University Press, 1971.

Mitchell, John. *Organized Labor.* Philadelphia: American Book and Bible House, 1903.

Mommsen, Hans. "The Free Trade Unions and Social Democracy in Imperial Germany." In Wolfgang J. Mommsen and Hans-Gerhard Husung, eds., *The Development of Trade Unionism in Great Britain and Germany, 1880–1914.* London: George Allen & Unwin, 1985.

———, and Ulrich Borsdorf, eds. *Glück auf, Kameraden! Die Bergarbeiter und ihre Organisationen in Deutschland.* Köln: Bund-Verlag, 1979.

Mommsen, Wolfgang J., and Hans-Gerhard Husung, eds. *The Development of Trade Unionism in Great Britain and Germany, 1880–1914.* London: George Allen & Unwin, 1985.

Montgomery, David. *Beyond Equality: Labor and the Radical Republicans, 1862–1872.* New York: Knopf, 1967.

———. *Workers' Control in America.* Cambridge: Cambridge University Press, 1979.

Moore, Barrington, Jr. *Injustice: The Social Bases of Obedience and Revolt.* New York: M. E. Sharpe, 1978.

Moore, R. Laurence. *European Socialists and the American Promised Land.* New York: Oxford University Press, 1970.

Moore, Robert S. *Pit-Men, Preachers and Politics.* Cambridge: Cambridge University Press, 1974.

Morris, R. J. *Class and Class Consciousness in the Industrial Revolution, 1780–1850.* London: Macmillan, 1979.

Mottek, Hans, Walter Becker, and Alfred Schröter. *Wirtschaftsgeschichte Deutschlands.* Berlin, DDR: Deutsche Verlag der Wissenschaft, 1974.

Moxon, J. *Mechanick Exercises*. Vol. 2. London, 1683.

Müller, H. *Geschichte der deutschen Gewerkschaften bis zum Jahre 1878*. Berlin: Verlag der Buchhandlung Vorwarts, P. Singer, 1918.

Murphy, Richard C. "The Polish Trade Union in the Ruhr Coal Field: Labor Organization and Ethnicity in Wilhelmian Germany." *Central European History* 2, no. 4 (1978).

Musson, A. E. *British Trade Unions 1800–1875*. London: Macmillan, 1972.

————. *The Congress of 1868: The Origins and Establishment of the Trades Union Congress*. London: Trades Union Congress, 1955.

————. *The Typographical Association: Origins and History Up to 1949*. London: Oxford University Press, 1954.

Nash, Michael H. "Conflict and Accommodation: Some Aspects of the Political Behavior of America's Coal Miners and Steel Workers, 1890–1920." Ph.D. dissertation, State University of New York at Binghamton, 1975.

Nestriepke, Siegfried. *Die Gewerkschaftsbewegung*. Vol. 1. Stuttgart: E.H. Moritz, 1922.

Nolan, Mary. "Economic Crisis, State Policy, and Working-Class Formation in Germany, 1870–1900." In Ira Katznelson and Aristide R. Zolberg, eds., *Working-Class Formation: Nineteenth-Century Patterns in Western Europe and the United States*. Princeton, N.J.: Princeton University Press, 1986.

————. *Social Democracy and Society: Working-Class Radicalism in Düsseldorf, 1890–1920*. Cambridge: Cambridge University Press, 1981.

Noyes, P. H. *Organization and Revolution: Working-Class Associations in the German Revolutions of 1848–1849*. Princeton. N.J.: Princeton University Press, 1966.

Oliver, W. H. "The Consolidated Trades' Union of 1834." *Economic History Review*, 2d series, vol. 19 (1964/1965).

Olson, Mancur, Jr. *The Logic of Collective Action*. Cambridge, Mass.: Harvard University Press, 1965.

Örtzen, Peter von. *Betriebsräte in der Novemberrevolution*. Berlin: J.H.W. Dietz, 1976.

Otto, Bernd. *Gewerkschaftsbewegung in Deutschland*. Kiel: Bund-Verlag, 1975.

Pelling, Henry. *America and the British Left*. London: Adam and Charles Black, 1956.

————. *A History of British Trade Unionism*. London: Penguin, 1976.

————. *The Origins of the Labour Party, 1880–1900.* Oxford: Clarendon Press, 1965.

————. *Popular Politics and Society in Late Victorian Britain.* London: Macmillan, 1968.

————. "Trade Unions, Workers and the Law." In Henry Pelling, *Popular Politics and Society in Late Victorian Britain.* London: Macmillan, 1968.

Perlman, Selig. *History of Trade Unionism in the United States.* New York: Macmillan, 1922.

————. *A Theory of the Labor Movement.* New York: Augustus M. Kelley, 1928.

Peterson, Larry. "One Big Union in International Perspective: Revolutionary Industrial Unionism, 1900–1925." In James E. Cronin and Carmen Sirianni, eds., *Work, Community and Power: The Experience of Labor in Europe and America, 1900–1925.* Philadelphia: Temple University Press, 1983.

Phelps Brown, E. H. *The Growth of British Industrial Relations.* London: Macmillan, 1959.

————. "New Wine in Old Bottles: Reflections of the Changed Working of Collective Bargaining in Great Britain." In Brian Barrett et al., eds., *Industrial Relations and the Wider Society.* London: Collier Macmillan, Open University Press, 1975.

————. *The Origins of Trade Union Power.* Oxford: Clarendon Press, 1983.

Pohl, Kurt, and Frauke Werther. "Die Freien Gewerkschaften im Ersten Weltkrieg." In Frank Deppe et al., eds. *Geschichte der deutschen Gewerkschaftsbewegung*, pp. 99–100. Köln: Pahl Rugenstein, 1977.

Polanyi, Karl. *The Great Transformation.* Boston: Farrar & Rinehart, 1944.

Pollard, Michael. *The Hardest Work under Heaven: The Life and Death of the British Coal Miner.* London: Hutchinson, 1984.

Powell, Leona Margaret. *The History of the United Typothetae of America.* Chicago: University of Chicago Press, 1926.

Präger, Max. "Grenzen der Gewerkschaftsbewegung." *Archiv für Sozialwissenschaft und Sozialpolitik* 20 (1905).

Price, Richard. *Masters, Unions and Men.* Cambridge: Cambridge University Press, 1980.

————. "The New Unionism and the Labour Process." In Wolfgang J. Mommsen and Hans-Gerhard Husung, eds., *The Development of Trade Unionism in Great Britain and Germany, 1880–1914.* London: George Allen & Unwin, 1985.

Prothero, Iowerth. *Artisans and Politics in Nineteenth-Century London.* London: Methuen, 1979.

———. "Chartism in London." *Past and Present* 42–45 (1969).

———. "London Chartism and the Trades." *Economic History Review*, 2d series, vol. 24 (1971).

Rayback, John G. *A History of American Labor.* New York: Macmillan, 1959.

Rees, Albert. *Real Wages in Manufacturing.* Princeton, N.J.: Princeton University Press, 1961.

Reid, Alastair. "The Division of Labour and Politics in Britain, 1880–1920." In Wolfgang J. Mommsen and Hans-Gerhard Husung, *The Development of Trade Unionism in Great Britain and Germany, 1880–1914.* London: George Allen & Unwin, 1985.

Rexhäuser, Ludwig. *Zur Geschichte des Verbandes der deutschen Buchdrucker.* Berlin: Verband der deutschen Buchdrucker, 1900.

Rimlinger, Gaston V. "Labor Protest in British, American and German Coal Mining Prior to 1914." Ph.D. dissertation, University of California, Berkeley, 1956.

———. "The Legitimation of Protest: A Comparative Study in Labor History." *Comparative Studies in Society and History* 2, no. 3 (April 1960).

———. *Welfare Policy and Industrialization in Europe, America, and Russia.* New York: John Wiley and Sons, 1971.

Ritter, Gerhard A. *Die Arbeiterbewegung im Wilhelminischen Reich.* Berlin-Dahlem: Colloquium Verlag, 1959.

———, and Klaus Tenfelde. "Der Durchbruch der Freien Gewerkshaften Deutschlands zur Massenbewegung im letzten Viertel des 19.Jahrhunderts." In Hans O. Vetter, ed., *Vom Sozialistengesetz zur Mitbestimmung.* Köln: Bund Verlag, 1975.

Roberts, Peter. *Anthracite Coal Communities.* New York: Macmillan, 1901.

Rogin, Michael. "Radicalism and the Agrarian Tradition: Comment." In John Laslett and Seymour Martin Lipset, eds., *Failure of a Dream? Essays in the History of American Socialism*, p. 149. New York: Anchor Press, 1974.

———. "Voluntarism: The Political Functions of an Antipolitical Doctrine." *Industrial and Labor Relations Review* 15 (1961/1962).

Rosenberg, Hans. *Grosse Depression und Bismarckreich.* Berlin: W. de Gruyter, 1967.

Ross, Howard N. "Economic Growth and Change in the United States under Laissez-Faire: 1870–1929." In Frederic C. Jaher, ed., *The Age of Industrialism in America*. New York: Free Press, 1978.

Rossiter, Clinton. *Conservatism in America*. New York: Knopf, 1962.

Rowe, D. J. "Chartism and the Spitalfields Silk-Weavers." *Economic History Review*, 2d ser., vol. 20 (1967).

Rudé, George. *The Crowd in History, 1730–1848*. New York: John Wiley, 1964.

Saalfeld, Diedrich. "Methodische Darlegungen zur Einkommensentwicklung und Sozialstruktur 1760–1860 am Beispiel einiger deutscher Städte." In H. Winker, ed., *Vom Kleingewerbe zur Grossindustrie*. Berlin: Duncker und Humbolt, 1975.

Sabel, Charles F. *Work and Politics*. Cambridge: Cambridge University Press, 1982.

Sadler, Philip. "Sociological Aspects of Skill." *British Journal of Industrial Relations* 8, no. 1 (March 1970).

Saloutos, Theodore. "Radicalism and the Agrarian Tradition." In John Laslett and Seymour Martin Lipset, eds., *Failure of a Dream? Essays in the History of American Socialism*. New York: Anchor Press, 1974.

Salvatore, Nick. *Eugene V. Debs: Citizen and Socialist*. Urbana Ill.: University of Illinois Press, 1982.

Saul, Klaus. *Staat, Industrie, Arbeiterbewegung im Kaiserreich*. Düsseldorf: Bertelsman Universitäts-Verlag, 1974.

Scheinberg, S. J. "Theodore Roosevelt and the A.F. of L.'s Entry in Politics, 1906–1908." *Labor History* 3–4 (1962–1963).

Schmidt, Jutta, and Wolfgang Seichter. "Die deutsche Gewerkschaftsbewegung von der Mitte der neunziger Jahre des 19.Jahrhunderts bis zum Ersten Weltkrieg." In Frank Deppe et al., eds., *Geschichte der deutschen Gewerkschaftsbewegung*. Köln: Pahl-Rugenstein, 1977.

Schmitter, Philippe. "Modes of Interest Intermediation and Models of Societal Change in Western Europe." in Philippe Schmitter and Gerhard Lehmbruch, eds., *Trends toward Corporatist Intermediation*. Beverly Hills, Calif.: Sage, 1979.

———, and Gerhard Lehmbruch, eds. *Trends toward Corporatist Intermediation*. Beverly Hills, Calif.: Sage, 1979.

Schmoller, Gustav. *Zur Geschichte der deutschen Kleingewerbe im 19.Jahrhundert, Statistische und Nationalökonomische Untersuchungen*. Halle: Buchhandlung des Waisenhauses, 1870.

Schorske, Carl. *German Social Democracy, 1905–1917: The Development of the Great Schism.* Cambridge, Mass.: Harvard University Press, 1955.

Schröder, Wolfgang. "Das Berliner Polizeipräsidium und die Gewerkschaftsbewegung 1878 bis 1886." In H. Bartel et al., eds., *Evolution and Revolution.* Berlin/DDR: Akademie-Verlag, 1976.

———. *Partie und Gewerkschaften.* Berlin/DDR: Verlag Tribune, 1975.

Shannon, David A. *The Socialist Party of America.* New York: Macmillan, 1955.

Shapiro, Stanley. "The Great War and Reform: Liberals and Labor, 1917–1919." *Labor History* 11 (1971): 326.

Simon, W. *Macht und Herrschaft der Unternehmerverbände BDI, BDA, and DIHT.* Köln: Pahl-Rugenstein, 1976.

Smith, John S. "Organized Labor and Government in the Wilson Era, 1913–1921: Some Conclusions." *Labor History* 3–4 (1962–1963).

Sombart, Werner. *Die deutsche Volkswirtschaft im neunzehnten Jahrhundert.* Berlin: G. Bondi, 1921.

———. *Der moderne Kapitalismus.* Vol. 1. München: Dunker, 1921.

Spencer, Elaine Glovka. "Employer Response to Unionism: Ruhr Coal Industrialists before 1914." *Journal of Modern History* 48, no. 3 (September 1976).

Steigerwalt, A. K. *The National Association of Manufacturers, 1895–1914.* Ann Arbor: Bureau of Business Research, Graduate School of Business Administration, University of Michigan, 1964.

Steinberg, Hans-Josef. "Die Entwicklung des Verhältnisses von Gewerkschaften und Sozialdemokratie bis zum Ausbruch des Ersten Weltkriegs." In Hans O. Vetter, *Vom Sozialistengesetz zur Mitbestimmung.* Köln: Bund Verlag, 1975.

Stephens, George A. *New York Typographical Union No. 6.* New York: New York State Department of Labor, 1912.

Stewart, Ethelbert. *A Documentary History of the Early Organizations of Printers.* Bulletin of the Bureau of Labor, no. 61 (1905).

Sturmthal, Adolph, and James G. Scoville. *The International Labor Movement in Transition: Essays on Asia, Europe, and South America.* Urbana, Ill.: University of Illinois Press, 1973.

Sturt, George. *The Wheelwright's Shop.* Cambridge: Cambridge University Press, 1923.

Suffern, Arthur E. *Conciliation and Arbitration in the Coal Industry of America.* Boston: Houghton Mifflin Company, 1915.

————. *The Coal Miner's Struggle for Industrial Status.* New York: The Macmillan Company, 1926.

Sutcliffe, John T. *History of Trade Unionism in Australia.* Melbourne: Macmillan & Company, Ltd., 1921.

Sykes, A.J.M. "The Cohesion of a Trade Union Workshop Organization." *Sociology* 1, no. 2 (May 1967).

————. "Trade-Union Workshop Organization in the Printing Industry—The Chapel." *Human Relations* 13, no. 1 (1960).

————. "Unity and Restrictive Practices in the British Printing Industry." *The Sociological Review*, n.s., vol. 8, no. 2 (1968).

Sykes, Robert. "Early Chartism and Trade Unionism in South-East Lancashire." In James Epstein and Dorothy Thompson, eds., *The Chartist Experience: Studies in Working-Class Radicalism and Culture, 1830–1860.* London: Macmillan, 1982.

Taft, Philip. *The A.F. of L. in the Time of Gompers.* New York: Harper, 1957.

————. *Organized Labor in American History.* New York: Harper & Row, 1964.

Tannenbaum, Frank. *A Philosophy of Labor.* New York: Knopf, 1951.

Tarbell, Ida M. *The Nationalizing of Business, 1878–1898.* New York: The Macmillan Company, 1936.

Tarrow, Sidney. *Struggling to Reform: Social Movements and Policy Change during Cycles of Protest.* Ithaca, N.Y.: Center for European Studies, n.d.

Tawney, R. H. "The Abolition of Economic Controls, 1918–1921." *Economic History Review* 13 (1943).

Taylor, Arthur J. *Laissez-Faire and State Intervention in Nineteenth-Century Britain.* London: Macmillan, 1972.

————. "The Miners' Association of Great Britain and Ireland, 1842–48: A Study in the Problem of Integration." *Economica* 22 (1955).

Tenfelde, Klaus. "Gewalt und Konfliktregelung in den Arbeitskämpfen der Ruhrbergleute bis 1918." In Friedrich Engel-Janosi et al., eds., *Gewalt und Gewaltlosigkeit.* München: Oldenbourg, 1977.

————. *Sozialgeschichte der Bergarbeiterschaft an der Ruhr im 19.Jahrhundert.* Bonn-Bad Godesberg: Neue Gesellschaft, 1978.

Thomis, Malcolm I. *The Town Labourer and the Industrial Revolution.* London: Batsford, 1974.

Thompson, Dorothy. *The Chartists.* New York: Pantheon Books, 1984.

Thompson, E. P. *The Making of the English Working Class.* London: Penguin Books, 1968.

———. "The Peculiarities of the English." In R. Miliband and J. Saville, eds., *The Socialist Register, 1965.* London: Merlin, 1965.

Tilly, Charles. *From Mobilization to Revolution.* Reading, Mass.: Addison-Wesley, 1978.

———, Louise Tilly, and Richard Tilly. *Rebellious Century.* Cambridge, Mass.: Harvard University Press, 1975.

Todt, Elisabeth. *Die Gewerkschaftliche Betätigung in Deutschland von 1850 bis 1859.* Berlin/DDR: Die Freie Gewerkschaft, 1950.

———, and Hans Radandt. *Zur Frühgeschichte der deutschen Gewerkschaftsbewegung, 1800–1849.* Berlin/DDR: Die Freie Gewerkschaft, 1950.

Tomlins, Christopher L. *The State and the Unions: Labor Relations, Law, and the Organized Labor Movement in America, 1880–1960.* Cambridge: Cambridge University Press, 1985.

Tracy, George. *History of the Typographical Union.* Indianapolis: ITU, 1913.

Treue, Wilhelm. "Wirtschafts und Sozialgeschichte Deutschlands im 19. Jahrhundert." In B. Gebhardt, *Handbuch der deutschen Geschichte.* Vol. 3. Stuttgart: Union Verlag, 1960.

Trist, E. L. *Organizational Choice: Capabilities of Groups at the Coal Face under Changing Technologies.* London: Tavistock Publications, 1963.

Turner, H. A. *Trade Union Growth, Structure and Policy.* London: Allen & Unwin, 1962.

Ullman, Hans-Peter. *Tarifverträge und Tarifpolitik in Deutschland bis 1914.* Frankfurt am Main: Lang, 1977.

Ulman, Lloyd. *The Rise of the National Trade Union.* Cambridge, Mass.: Harvard University Press, 1955.

Umbreit, Paul. *Die Deutsche Gewerkschaften im Weltkrieg.* Berlin: Verlag fur Sozialwissenschaft, 1917.

———. *25 Jahre Deutsche Gewerkschaftsbewegung, 1890–1918.* Berlin: General Kommission der Gewerkschaften Deutschlands, 1915.

Vale, Vivian. *Labour in American Politics.* New York: Barnes & Noble, 1971.

Varain, Heinz Josef. *Freie Gewerkschaften, Sozialdemokratie und Staat: Die Politik der Generalkommission unter der Führung Carl Legiens, 1890–1920*. Düsseldorf: Droste-Verlag, 1956.

Volkmann, Heinrich. "Modernisierung des Arbeitkampfes." In Harmut Kaelble et al., eds., *Probleme der Modernisierung in Deutschland*. Opladen: Westdeutscher Verlag, 1978.

Von der Vring, Thomas. "Der Verband der Deutschen Buchdrucker im Ersten Weltkrieg, in der Revolution und in der Inflationszeit, 1914–1924." Ph.D. dissertation, Frankfurt am Main, 1964.

Wallas, Graham. *The Life of Francis Place*. London: Allen & Unwin, 1951.

Waller, Robert J. *The Dukeries Transformed: The Social and Political Development of a Twentieth-Century Coalfield*. Oxford: Clarendon Press, 1983.

Walsh, W. J. "The United Mine Workers of America as an Economic and Social Force in the Anthracite Territory." Ph.D. dissertation, Catholic University of America, 1931.

Ware, Norman J. *The Labor Movement in the United States, 1860–1895*. New York and London: D. Appleton and Company, 1929.

Webb, Sidney, and Beatrice Webb. *The History of Trade Unionism*. 2d ed. London: Longmans, Green, 1920.

———. *Industrial Democracy*. 2d ed. 2 vols. London: Longmans, Green, 1920.

Weber, Adolf. *Der Kampf zwischen Kapital und Arbeit*. 5th ed. Tübingen: J.C.B. Mohr, 1930.

Wehler, Hans-Ulrich. *Bismarck und der Imperialismus*. München: Deutscher Taschenbuch, 1976.

———. *Das deutsche Kaiserreich, 1871–1918*. Göttingen: Vandenhock & Ruprecht, 1973.

Weinstein, James. "Big Business and the Origins of Workmen's Compensation. *Labor History* 7–8 (1966–1967).

———. *The Corporate Ideal in the Liberal State, 1900–1918*. Boston: Beacon, 1969.

Weitz, Eric D. "Class Formation and Labor Protest in the Mining Communities of Southern Illinois and the Ruhr, 1890–1925." *Labor History* 27, no. 1 (Winter 1985–1986).

Wieck, Edward A. *The American Miners' Association*. New York: Russell Sage Foundation, 1940.

Wigham, Eric. *Strikes and the Government, 1893–1974.* London: Macmillan, 1975.

Wilson, James Q. *Political Organizations.* New York: Basic Books, 1973.

Wilson, John. *History of the Durham Miners.* London: J.H. Veitch, 1907.

Winter, Jay M. *Socialism and the Challenge of War.* London: Routledge & Kegan Paul, 1979.

Witte, Edwin E. *The Government in Labor Disputes.* New York: McGraw-Hill Book Company, 1932.

Wolman, Leo. *Ebb and Flow in Trade Unionism.* New York: National Bureau of Economic Research, 1936.

———. *The Growth of American Trade Unions, 1880–1923.* New York: National Bureau of Economic Research, 1924.

Wright, C. W. *Economic History of the United States.* New York: McGraw-Hill Book Company, 1949.

Wright, Thomas. *The Great Unwashed.* London: Frank Cass, 1868.

Wrigley, Chris. "The Government and Industrial Relations." In Wrigley, ed., *A History of British Industrial Relations, 1875–1914.* Amherst: University of Massachusetts Press, 1982.

Wyman, Mark. *Hard Rock Epic: Western Miners and the Industrial Revolution, 1860–1910.* Berkeley: University of California Press, 1979.

Yearley, C. K. *Britons in American Labor.* Baltimore: The Johns Hopkins University Press, 1957.

Yellowitz, Irwin. *Labor and the Progressive Movement in New York State, 1897–1916.* Ithaca, N.Y.: Cornell University Press, 1965.

Zeitlin, Jonathan. "Craft Regulation and the Division of Labour: Engineers and Compositors in Britain, 1890–1914." Ph.D. dissertation, University of Warwick, 1981.

———. "The Labour Strategies of British Engineering Employers, 1890–1922." In Howard F. Gospel and Craig R. Littler, eds., *Managerial Strategies and Industrial Relations: Historical and Comparative Perspectives.* London: Heinemann Books, 1983.

Zorn, Wolfgang. "Typen und Entwicklungskräfte deutschen Unternehmertums." In Karl E. Born, ed., *Moderne Deutsche Wirtschaftsgeschichte,* Köln: Kiepenheuer und Witsch, 1966.

INDEX